MW01702238

Rav Asher Weiss on *Mo'adim*

Pesach to Shavuos

MOSAICA PRESS

Rav Asher Weiss on Mo'adim

Pesach to Shavuos

Copyright © 2021 by Mosaica Press

ISBN: 978-1-952370-39-7

All rights reserved. No part of this book may be used or reproduced or transmitted in any form or by any means, electronic or mechanical, including photocopying, recording, or by any information storage and retrieval system, without written permission from the publisher.

Published by Mosaica Press, Inc.
www.mosaicapress.com
info@mosaicapress.com

With profound gratitude to

HaRav Asher Weiss שליט"א

for guiding us with his leadership and fortifying us with Torah during the very difficult year of 2020.
And with tremendous appreciation for his insights on these *mo'adim* that will undoubtedly enhance the *Yamim Tovim* and the Sefiras Ha'omer period of our family and of Klal Yisrael.
May he merit to continue spreading his wisdom for many more years to come, עמו"ש.

NICOLE AND RAANAN AGUS
GABI, ALEX, AND ELAN
New York and Jerusalem

Table of Contents

Nissan

Shabbos Hagadol

Pesach

Shabbos Chol Hamoed

Shevi'i Shel Pesach

Sefiras Ha'omer

Pesach Sheini

Sheloshes Yemei Hagbalah

Shavuos

Yom Tov

Nissan

ONE

A New Beginning

Rabbi Yehudah said: "One who goes out in the month of Nissan and sees trees in blossom, should say, 'Blessed is He Who did not omit anything from His world, and created in it pleasant things and beautiful trees in which people may take delight.'"[1]

New blossoms! We open the month of Nissan not by rushing to bake matzah or to eradicate chametz, but rather by stepping outside and observing nature as it renews itself.

Indeed, two conditions prompt recitation of this special blessing, *Birkas Ha'ilanos*: the month of Nissan and the presence of a blossoming tree. We have separately discussed which criterion is the primary one and whether one may say the blessing as soon as the first blossoms of the season appear, regardless of the month.[2]

Here, we will take Rabbi Yehudah's statement at face value and address the unique relationship between the month of Nissan and *Birkas Ha'ilanos*, this special, once-in-a-season blessing.

1 *Berachos* 43b.

2 *She'eilos U'Teshuvos Minchas Asher* 3:14.

Anything to do with Nissan must include, on some level, an allusion to redemption, past and future. Chazal taught that "in Nissan we were redeemed and in Nissan we are destined to be redeemed." Just as our ancestors were taken from Egypt in the month of Nissan, so too will our final salvation occur during Nissan. Nissan is a time for redemption.

Chazal further taught, in the name of Rav: "The culmination [of the exile] has arrived; now all depends on *teshuvah* and good deeds." Shortly thereafter, the Gemara cites Rabbi Abba: "There is no more obvious culmination than this, as it says: 'And you, hills of Yisrael, your branches shall give forth and your fruit you shall bear for My people Yisrael.'"[3]

Trees in blossom, their fruits about to ripen, are a harbinger of a new dawn: "There is no more obvious culmination than this."

Spring's first blossoms, following a dark, cold winter that left trees bare of fruit or flower, reinvigorates hope for the future. Behold, the tiny blossoming flower! A fruit is on its way; the tree will soon be in full bloom, rich and bountiful as before.

Our redemption likewise unfolds slowly. During the final, difficult days of *galus* (exile), when neither fruit nor flower are apparent and all hope seems lost, new blossoms will eventually peek through on the hills of Yisrael, bearing fruit for His people.

> *Even though he tarries, nevertheless I will wait for him each day, that he shall arrive.*

---

3 *Sanhedrin* 97b–98a, citing *Yechezkel* 36:8.

TWO

From Redemption to Redemption

If the Megillah had been read in the first Adar, and then another month was added, it must be again read in the second Adar...[and it was taught in a] Beraisa: If they have read the Megillah in the first Adar, and a month was added, it must be read again in the second Adar, because all mitzvos that are obligatory in the second Adar are so also in the first Adar, except the reading of Megillah. Rabbi Eliezer bar Rabbi Yossi said: It must not be read in the second Adar, because all mitzvos obligatory in the second [Adar] are so also in the first. Rabban Shimon ben Gamliel says in the name of Rabbi Yossi: They must read it again during the second Adar, as all mitzvos that are practiced during the second Adar are not practiced during the first Adar...Rabbi Eliezer bar Rabbi Yossi's view is understood—so as not to pass over the opportunity for a mitzvah—but what is

Rabban Shimon ben Gamliel's reason? Rabbi Tavi answered: Rabban Shimon ben Gamliel's reasoning is that one redemption should be near to another redemption.[1]

According to halachah, when our calendar includes an extra month, we observe Purim in the second Adar because it is closer to Pesach. Doing so allows us to celebrate the salvation from Haman as close as possible to our commemoration of *yetzias Mitzrayim* (the Exodus from Egypt). Rather than rush to observe Purim immediately in the first Adar, we wait for the second Adar because it is closer to Nissan. What is so important about celebrating one redemption shortly before commemorating another, even at the expense of an existing principle that one should seize the first opportunity to do a mitzvah?

The Ramban in *Parashas Bo* famously discusses the two distinct types of miracles we know of—the hidden miracles and those that are obvious:

> *[By seeing] the great public miracles, one comes to acknowledge the implicit miracles that are the foundation of Torah. For one has no portion in the Torah of Moshe Rabbeinu until believing that every single event is a miracle—nothing is natural or automatic.*

Accordingly, the very purpose of a revealed miracle is to alert us to the existence of those implicit, hidden miracles. Acceptance of the latter forms the very foundation of our belief in Hashem and His Torah.

Such has been the prevailing challenge of our lengthy exile, during periods of *hester panim* (concealment of the Divine Presence), when we do not see His presence manifest. Even absent obvious and wondrous

1 *Megillah* 6b.

miracles, we must recognize that His care and kindness surround us at all times.

Yet, this principle is reciprocal. True, as the Ramban tells us, the grand, public miracles direct us to the minute wonders of daily existence. But only if we maintain faith throughout the hard moments of *galus* and sustain our belief in the hidden miracles, can we expect to witness the wondrous revelations at the end of days. As the *Yalkut Shimoni* teaches: "[T]he exiles only end in the merit of faith."[2]

To reinforce this message, Chazal deemed it appropriate to connect Purim and Pesach. Pesach commemorates the great and tumultuous wonders of *yetzias Mitzrayim* and *k'rias Yam Suf* (the splitting of the Yam Suf), while Purim demonstrates Hashem's involvement behind the scenes, in seemingly mundane, everyday events.[3]

Chazal wanted us to internalize the dual nature of our belief in Hashem's miracles. On Purim, we strengthen our belief in His small miracles, while also looking ahead to Pesach and the realization of Michah's great prophecy: "As in the days of your exit from Egypt I will show you great wonders."[4]

---

2 *Beshalach* 240.

3 This distinction also helps explain why we do not recite the usual *Hallel* on Purim, relying instead on the "hidden" *Hallel* of the *Megillah* reading.

4 *Michah* 7:15.

Shabbos Hagadol

THREE

What Happened on Shabbos Hagadol?

As codified in the *Shulchan Aruch*, the Shabbos immediately preceding Pesach is called Shabbos Hagadol, on account of the miracle that occurred on that day.[1]

Numerous suggestions have been offered to explain why this Shabbos merits a special name, though not all point to a miracle as the reason. Let us explore some of these approaches:

I. Miracles Occurred on This Day

Tosafos writes:

> *[It is] called Shabbos Hagadol because a great miracle happened on that day. We learn in the midrash that when B'nei Yisrael in Egypt selected their lambs for the korban Pesach on that day, the firstborn gentiles gathered and asked why B'nei Yisrael were doing so. The latter replied that these were to be the offering to Hashem on Pesach, during which He would kill all firstborns of Egypt. They in turn went to their parents and to Pharaoh and demanded that B'nei Yisrael be sent out of Egypt. When Pharaoh and his ministers refused, the firstborns*

1 *Shulchan Aruch, Orach Chaim* 430:1.

> *waged war and killed many of them. For this reason, we say, "To He Who struck Egypt with their firstborns."*[2]

A similar event is described elsewhere:

> *When the Egyptians saw B'nei Yisrael taking their Pesach offerings, they gathered to attack them, as these animals were Egyptian deities, and the Holy One, blessed be He, saved them miraculously. This day is called Shabbos Hagadol to commemorate that miracle."*[3]

II. Bar Mitzvah—Becoming a "Gadol"

The *Chizkuni* writes that the tenth day of Nissan, the day on which B'nei Yisrael took their lambs for the *korban Pesach*, "was Shabbos, and since this was the day on which the B'nei Yisrael did their first mitzvah, taking the *Pesach* on the tenth of Nissan, it was called Shabbos Hagadol."[4]

The *Abudraham*, citing *Machzor Vitri*, likewise notes that the day is celebrated as our people's entry into fulfillment of Hashem's commandments.[5] Just as we celebrate a child who becomes bar or bas mitzvah, entering the world of mandatory inclusion in the Torah's commandments, we likewise celebrate the Jewish People's introduction to mitzvos.[6]

III. The "Great" Sermon

Several Rishonim point to the lengthy sermon traditionally delivered by a community's rabbi on this Shabbos. Restless participants, normally unaccustomed to such drawn-out services, began calling this day Shabbos Hagadol, the "big" or "long" Shabbos. Alternatively, the Shabbos was named "*ha'gadol*" as a reflection of it being an annual event focused on the rabbi, the *gadol ha'ir*, the "prominent man of the

---

2 *Tosafos, Shabbos* 87b, citing *Shemos Rabbah, Parashas Bo*.

3 *Daas Zekeinim M'Baalei HaTosafos, Shemos* 12:3.

4 *Chizkuni, Shemos* 12:3.

5 *Abudraham*, p. 77a.

6 *Olelos Ephraim*, ch. 31.

town." Finally, along similar lines, *ha'gadol* is a reference to the large communities (*kehillos gedolos*) that would gather to hear exposition of important laws (*halachos gedolos*) pertaining to the upcoming holiday.[7]

IV. Haftarah—"Hashem's Great Day"

Others associate the day's name with its haftarah.[8] We read in the final *pasuk* of the special haftarah for the Shabbos before Pesach: "Behold I will send you Eliyah the Prophet before the arrival of Hashem's great (*ha'gadol*) and awesome day."[9] While the wording of the *pasuk* serves to reconcile our use of "*ha'gadol*," per the *pasuk*'s formulation, rather than simply "*gadol*," this explanation leaves us wondering why we would name the Shabbos for a word at the very conclusion of the haftarah and not instead refer to its opening line, "*v'arvah*."[10]

V. An Extended Shabbos

At some point during the period of their enslavement, Moshe interceded on behalf of B'nei Yisrael and begged Pharaoh to grant them a day of rest, a reprieve from their backbreaking labor. Moshe's request was granted, and Shabbos was selected as a day off. As each Shabbos drew to a close, the slaves were forced from their rest back to the harsh conditions of their work. At the conclusion of this Shabbos, however, their final Shabbos in Egypt, everything was different. This week, rather than returning to their work, they would continue enjoying a prolonged—"great"—Shabbos, one that would continue into the week and see their salvation from Egypt.[11]

VI. Not to Be Confused with Pesach

Finally, we find the suggestion that the Shabbos preceding Pesach is named "*Hagadol*" to differentiate it from Pesach, which is also referred to by the Torah as Shabbos:

---

7 See *Sefer HaPardes*, p. 343; *Shibolei Haleket* 205; *Tanya Rabasi* 42.

8 *Mateh Moshe* 542, citing *Maharshal*, who ultimately rejects the explanation on account of the question it raises.

9 *Malachi* 3:23.

10 Ibid., 3:4.

11 *Tzafnas Paneach* (Rabbi Yosef Mi'Trani), p. 67.

> *[O]ur authentic tradition teaches that when the Torah says, "And you shall count from the day after the Shabbos," it refers to the first day of Pesach, not Shabbos. This counters those who erred during the time of the Second Beis Hamikdash and claimed that Shabbos in the pasuk must be the weekly Shabbos...for this reason, I think that it was established that the Shabbos before Pesach should be known as Shabbos Hagadol. Doing so alludes that there will be a day later this very week that is also known as Shabbos, but, as a Yom Tov on which certain activities are permitted, its observance is not as stringent as that of the weekly—"greater"—Shabbos.*[12]

I would like to add that this Shabbos reinforces an essential message in our *emunah*, our unwavering belief in the Almighty.

Belief in Hashem is the very first of the Rambam's thirteen principles of faith. In the *Ani Maamin* ("I believe") formulation of this principle, we state, "I believe with complete faith that the Creator, blessed be His Name, created and guides all of creation." Two critical components are included in this affirmation. One, that Hashem is the one and only Creator of all beings, and moreover, that He continues to guide and direct the existence and activity of all creatures even after they are created.

In reciting this article of faith, we declare further that, "He alone did, does, and will continue to do everything that occurs." Not only did He create everything, but it is He Who animates all action, past, present, and future.

Shabbos is the foundation of our belief, bearing testimony to Hashem's creation of the world, as we cite the *pasuk*, "That in six days, Hashem made heaven and earth, and on the seventh day, He stopped and rested."[13] Yet, while Shabbos might attest that He created heaven and earth and their inhabitants, how does it serve to remind us that He

---

12 *Shu"t Shemen Hamor, Yoreh Deah* 15, in the name of *Sefer Orim Gedolim*; also cited in *B'nei Yisasschar, Nissan, maamar* 3, sect. 2.

13 *Shemos* 31:17.

is also the living pulse Who continues to guide and activate everything that happens?

Yetzias Mitzrayim changed this forever. When Hashem intervened in the natural course of history, striking Egypt with plagues, splitting the sea, and taking out His people with a mighty Hand, the entire world witnessed that He does in fact control and direct every moment of existence. Pesach and Shabbos, together, synthesize to teach us these fundamental aspects of belief in Hashem.

Moreover, Shabbos itself was transformed by *yetzias Mitzrayim*. Ever since then, we refer to Shabbos not only as a "reminder of Creation," but also as "the first of holy assemblies, a commemoration of the Exodus from Egypt." Following the wonders of the Exodus, Shabbos takes on richer meaning and import. Shabbos can now indeed affirm that Hashem both created the world in its entirety and continues to animate it at each moment and in every detail.

Through *yetzias Mitzrayim*, Shabbos became greater. In acknowledgment of the new, more profound meaning Shabbos assumes this week, we named the Shabbos preceding Pesach "Shabbos Hagadol."

FOUR

Why Shabbos?

One reason we refer to the Shabbos before Pesach as Shabbos Hagadol is to mark a miracle that occurred on that day. On the tenth of Nissan, which, during the year of *yetzias Mitzrayim* occurred on Shabbos, each family acquired a lamb to be used for their *korban Pesach*. Seeing this, their lamb-worshipping Egyptian neighbors inquired why B'nei Yisrael were purchasing lambs and tying them to their bedposts. Upon hearing of their plans to bring the lambs as an offering, the incensed Egyptians attempted to harm B'nei Yisrael but were unsuccessful. On account of this miracle, we name the day Shabbos Hagadol.

This reasoning is surprising. Every commemoration we observe, holiday or hardship, is marked by its date on the Jewish calendar, not by day of the week, which is considered incidental. Why then is this particular miracle any different? If the event is worthy of celebration, its date, the tenth of Nissan, should be so noted on the Jewish calendar, not the Shabbos before Pesach.

A novel approach to this difficulty suggests that the miracle's occurrence on Shabbos indeed made this event more significant. The soon-to-be Jewish nation, seeing that their Egyptian oppressors could not harm them, decided to take their rebellion a step further and refused to do any more work that day. For the first time since the beginning of their enslavement, the people were able to observe Shabbos, as had their ancestors going back to Avraham Avinu.

Thus, while Avraham, Yitzchak, and Yaakov, and their families after them, all kept Shabbos voluntarily, their descendants were ultimately forced to abandon Shabbos under Egypt's subjugation and imposed labor.[1] On Shabbos Hagadol, for the first time in centuries, so many generations later, they threw off the yoke of their enslavement and did not work on Shabbos. Powerless to harm them, the Egyptians could not force B'nei Yisrael to resume their labor. In honor of the unique association the miracle had with Shabbos, this day is commemorated as a day of the week rather than a calendar date.

True, this idea is not consistent with our above citation that Shabbos Hagadol was an elongated version of a Shabbos they were otherwise already observing.[2] Chazal, however, received conflicting traditions as to whether B'nei Yisrael observed Shabbos while in Egypt. As we know, Torah has "seventy faces" and all approaches are valid and true, each teaching us an important lesson.

The *Tur*, explaining the words of the Shabbos morning prayers, "Moshe will rejoice," cites the midrash we mentioned earlier and describes Moshe's intercession with Pharaoh on behalf of his brethren to beg for a day of rest.[3] An earlier halachic source, *Shibolei Haleket*, elaborates on this theme:

> *I found in the midrash a different reason: Moshe became respected by Pharaoh to the point that Pharaoh said, "Moshe, Moshe, what gift would you like me to give you?" He replied, "Give me one day of the week that B'nei Yisrael may rest from your service." Pharaoh granted this wish and Moshe chose the seventh day of the week as the day they would not work. Shabbos had not yet been commanded. Thus, when Hashem later forbade work on Shabbos, Moshe rejoiced that he had chosen Shabbos. We therefore say, "Moshe will rejoice in his portion."*[4]

---

1 See *Minchas Asher, Bereishis*, ch. 11.

2 See above, chapter 3, part V.

3 *Tur, Orach Chaim* 281.

4 *Shibolei Haleket, Inyan Shabbos* 76.

On the other hand, a teaching in the Gemara suggests that Shabbos was indeed new to B'nei Yisrael when they left Egypt:

> *Rabbi Yehudah taught in the name of Rav: If B'nei Yisrael had but kept the first Shabbos, no nation would ever have been able to harm them. As it says [in the pasuk]: "And it was, on the seventh day some of the people went out to gather [mann]," and immediately thereafter, "And Amalek approached."*[5]

---

5 *Shabbos* 118a. See also *Ritva* ad loc.

FIVE

Finding a Neighbor

But if the household is too small for a lamb,
let him share one with a neighbor who dwells
nearby, in proportion to the number of persons:
you shall contribute for the lamb according
to what each household will eat.[1]

Korban Pesach was the first mitzvah we received as a nation, even prior to leaving Egypt. While it shares certain characteristics common to other offerings, *korban Pesach* bears the added requirement that it must be shared by a group of people. True, according to some views, the *korban Pesach* can be brought by an individual, but all agree that ideally it should be offered by a group.[2]

Chazal also ruled that once an individual has joined a group and the *korban* has been slaughtered, he may not move to a different group.[3]

Most striking however, is Chazal's teaching that for the first *korban Pesach*, offered by B'nei Yisrael on the cusp of their deliverance from Egypt, they were required, explicitly, to form groups with those in

1 *Shemos* 12:4.

2 See *Pesachim* 95a and *Rambam, Mishneh Torah*, Laws of Korban Pesach 2:5.

3 *Pesachim* 85b.

closest physical proximity, i.e., "a neighbor who dwells nearby." Each person was obligated to join with those nearby, "so that no person should leave his neighbor and perform his *Pesach* with his friend."[4]

Such unique requirements should give us pause, inviting us to question their purpose and deeper meaning. In this case, I believe we can explain this special one-time mitzvah in light of a penetrating insight cited in the name of the *Sefas Emes*.

When the Torah tells us that "the Egyptians harmed us," it does not say "*va'yare'u lanu*," as we might expect it to, but rather "*va'yare'u osanu*."[5] This formulation suggests that not only were they bad *to* us, but that the Egyptians also *made us* bad. We see this approach reflected in the words of the *Shem MiShmuel*:

> *Given that B'nei Yisrael were so subsumed within Egypt—like a fetus in its mother's womb who is sustained by the same nutrients as its mother—B'nei Yisrael were affected by the bad character of the Egyptians.*[6]

Far earlier than these great rabbis, we find this idea in the *Shelah*:

> *"Va'yare'u osanu—And they harmed us." One might ask, the pasuk should say "lanu." Rather, the correct way to read it is that they made us wicked and bad.*[7]

Our Egyptian oppressors' cruel treatment brought us to such depths of deprivation and degradation that we began to lose our own humanity. Such has been our experience over the course of many exiles and the terrible suffering they wrought. Only select individuals, the most elevated souls among us, were able to maintain their humanity, even nobility, under the most horrifying of conditions. Sadly, many people, unable to withstand the challenge, saw their most base survival instincts overpower all sense of human dignity.

---

4 *Tosefta, Pesachim* 8:7.

5 *Devarim* 26:6.

6 *Shem MiShmuel, Parashas Bo*. See also *Tiferes Shlomo, Parashas Bamidbar*.

7 *Shelah Hakadosh, Pesachim, Matzah Shemurah* 189.

Tragically, we are all too familiar with this. We hear so much about those individuals who rose to great heights during the Holocaust, exemplifying the loftiest of characters. But so many others found themselves falling to unimaginable depths, their spirit and humanity shattered. Among the former, of course, was my great teacher, the Klausenberger Rebbe, *zt"l*, whose unwavering devotion even during those horrible years became legendary.

To take this a step further, the midrash states that our ancestors' subjugation under the tyranny of Egypt was caused by this very loss of humanity, characterized by internal enmity, incessant quarreling, and *lashon hara* (evil speech):

> *"And he said: Indeed, the matter has been revealed."*[8] *Rabbi Yehudah bar Rabbi Shalom in the name of Rabbi Chanina Hagadol and our teachers in the name of Rabbi Alexandri taught: Moshe used to question what sin caused the Jewish nation to be singled out for slavery. When he heard these words, he understood—they spoke lashon hara about each other. How could they merit redemption? Thus, he declared, "Indeed the matter is revealed"—now I understand what is causing their suffering.*[9]

Perhaps this is the very reason we must partake of the *korban Pesach* in a group, and, furthermore, that a participant may not switch from one group to another. Doing so promotes brotherhood and closeness between individuals and tames our instincts by requiring that each person makes sure the other has a portion. Thus, even if a new group is suddenly more appealing, one may not abandon those he initially joined with.

At that moment in Egypt, those same individuals who had suffered through so many years of slavery were commanded to form alliances specifically with their nearby neighbors. Even the most noble of

---

8 *Shemos* 2:14.

9 *Shemos Rabbah* 1:30.

reasons—such as to find a more devout group—would not be sufficient justification to go elsewhere.

How appropriate it is that this lesson is emphasized in relation to the *korban Pesach*. At our Seder, we teach that the Torah communicated to, and about, four different sons. Each one is beloved by Hashem, and to each we are instructed to recount the story of *yetzias Mitzrayim*.

We have much to learn from this important mitzvah. Different as we may appear, we are all brothers—"neighbors who dwell nearby." We must look beyond the externalities and afford each other the love and dignity we all so deserve.

Pesach

SIX

Withdraw from Your Idolatry

And Moshe called to the elders of Israel and said to them: Draw forth (mishchu) and acquire for yourselves lambs for your families and slaughter the Pesach.[1]

Chazal were intrigued by the strange and seemingly unnecessary insertion of the word "*mishchu*" in the above *pasuk*. Identifying a deeper intent in the extra verb, they read it homiletically and vastly extended its meaning. In their words, the commandment was to "withdraw (*mishchu*) your hands from idolatry."[2]

We are all familiar with the custom to hide ten crumbs of chametz, which are then to be "found" in fulfillment of the requirement to search for chametz. How can this activity be viewed as *bedikas chametz*—a true search for the soon-to-be-forbidden bread? What is the point of the whole charade?

1 *Shemos* 12:21.

2 *Shemos Rabbah*, ibid.

To understand this properly, we must consider how Chazal framed the unique requirement to eradicate all chametz from our midst before Pesach. To them, removal of physical chametz—wheat and barley—is but a part of the mitzvah. Well beyond our bread, and far harder to reach, lies a metaphysical chametz, which we likewise must hunt down and destroy.

What is this spiritual leaven? A sampling of this idea can be found in the words of the *Radbaz*:

> *You asked that I share my opinion as to why chametz is unique among all prohibitions in the Torah, such that we must search for it in every crack and crevice and then destroy it, and we must remove it all entirely from our possession. One who maintains any amount in his property violates a special mitzvah, and even a trace amount of it cannot be nullified in a larger mixture.*

Following a lengthy halachic review of the questions, the *Radbaz* concludes:

> *I lean toward what Chazal taught in the midrash, that chametz on Pesach is a metaphor for the yetzer hara, the corrosive force within the person. For this reason, we destroy and completely remove it from ourselves, searching deep in the recesses of our minds for even a trace amount...*[3]

Already in the *Zohar* we find allusions to chametz as a representation of evil. Drawing on the parallel words, "leaven shall not be seen *for you*," and "gods with an image you shall not make *for you*," the *Zohar* points to commonality between chametz, referenced in the former *pasuk*, and idolatry mentioned in the latter.[4] Accordingly, unique rules govern these two items. Both must be completely destroyed, and neither are

---

3 *Shu"t Radbaz*, vol. 3, 546 (977 in some versions).

4 *Zohar*, vol. 2, 40:2 and 182:1. See also, at length, in *Haggadah Shel Pesach Bris HaLevi*, by Rabbi Shlomo Alkabetz, chs. 11–12.

allowed in a mixture, even at trace quantities that would otherwise be considered null.

Part and parcel, then, of our ancestors' departure from Egypt was the need for them to eradicate their internal chametz, any relationship with idolatry, however slight. And this same requirement devolves upon us every year since.

Holy work this is indeed! We are called upon to uproot from our souls any attitudes that do not belong, traits we should not have acquired. Cleansing ourselves of our personal "chametz," we should seize the growth opportunity inherent in these auspicious days, a week during which we are granted special closeness to Hashem. *Yamim Tovim*, our holy days, are special not merely as days commemorating events that occurred in the past, but rather each is a sacred moment laden with unique spiritual content. Those historical events, the great miracles themselves, were made possible by the spiritual energy and momentous opportunity of the day; forces that continue to animate these days each time they reappear in our calendars.[5]

Our forefathers in Egypt were saved though they were unworthy and undeserving of special treatment, their spiritual state captured in the celestial angels' well-known argument that B'nei Yisrael standing on the banks of the Yam Suf (Red Sea) were just as idolatrous as their Egyptian pursuers. Why should Hashem favor one pagan group over the other? Yet, Hashem, in His great kindness and in fulfillment of his promise to Avraham Avinu, that he would "carry them forth on the eagles' wings," split the sea and saved His nation. Each year, we too are afforded an opportunity to transcend our natural limitations and reach for spiritual heights that are otherwise beyond our reach.

The Ropshitzer Rebbe would read the phrase we use in Kiddush, "*Techilah l'mikra'ei kodesh, zecher l'yetzias Mitzrayim*—It is the first of consecrated days, a remembrance of the Exodus," as follows: One's initial call to holiness—"*techilah l'mikra'ei kodesh*"—is contingent upon remembering the Exodus; how our ancestors, undeservedly, were able

---

5 See *Ramchal, Derech Hashem*, vol. 4, ch. 7 (6), and *Kedushas Levi, Sivan, Shavuos*.

to suddenly reach lofty spiritual heights.[6] Drawing inspiration from our ancestors, we should become energized to answer our individual "call to holiness" and pursue such growth ourselves.

We are told that one who is meticulous in removing every trace of chametz from his possession before Pesach is guaranteed to be free of sin the entire year. Flowing from the concept of chametz as a representation of the *yetzer hara*, by burning the chametz we symbolically destroy the *yetzer hara*. If the base impulses and harmful tendencies are rooted out from our souls, sin and its damage disappear.[7]

My heart tells me that our custom of hiding bread to "find" during *bedikas chametz* developed as a reminder that our *yetzer hara* was also granted place in our souls by us. Our mistakes gave it room to grow and our spiritual failures further fueled it. The *yetzer hara* thrived under our watch and it falls upon us to uproot and destroy it.

Rabbi Pinchas of Koritz, the Baal Shem Tov's great and innovative student, took this idea even further:

> *Destroying chametz is primarily destroying idolatry. This is why the prophet relates that in the time of Yoshiyahu HaMelech, who eradicated idolatry, the people fulfilled Pesach as they hadn't in a very long time. Thus, the pesukim in the Torah juxtapose observance of Pesach with the prohibition against idols, telling us that if all of B'nei Yisrael would burn their chametz with the intention of destroying idolatry, we would ease the burden of our exile.*[8]

Let us indeed follow in the footsteps of our ancestors, examine our souls for that which must be removed, and begin lightening our burden in advance of the final redemption, may it be speedily in our days.

---

6 See *Haggadah Shel Pesach Divrei Chaim* of the Tzanzer Rebbe.

7 See *Be'er Heitev* to *Shulchan Aruch, Orach Chaim* 447:1, drawing upon the *Zohar*, vol. 3, 282b. See also *Imrei Pinchas* 172, who struggles with the notion of such a guarantee!

8 *Imrei Pinchas, Erev Pesach* 167. See also *Sefer Rokeach, Hilchos Pesach* 271, for a similar idea.

SEVEN

A Time of Freedom

Each holiday's unique spiritual content gives the day its special character. And while the three major holidays, Pesach, Sukkos, and Shavuos, are all associated in some way with our departure from Egypt, they are not identical. We describe each holiday's "soul" in the day's prayers: Sukkos is "our time of joy," Shavuos is "the time our Torah was given," and Pesach is "our time of freedom."

But what is freedom?

Chazal tell us that a free person is one who devotes himself to Torah.[1] At first glance this seems implausible. Typically, servitude presupposes complete dependence on the desires of one's master, at whose pleasure the servant works, eats, and sleeps. It is the master who is free. A life committed to Torah appears far closer to that of the servant—who must consider his master's wishes before every action, word, and thought!

To properly answer this question, we must better define freedom and servitude. Servitude deserves its name only when it is involuntary, a forced state of being. One's *choice* to fully commit to something or someone is not servitude, but *service*. Such is what Hashem requests, calling upon us to "choose life."[2] Thus, we are indeed free, at liberty to choose life over death, blessing over curse, good over bad. Our

1 *Avos* 6:2.

2 *Devarim* 30:19.

judgment, however, can be clouded by the governing impulses of our natural state, leading us to poor choices.

Learning Torah provides an antidote for any such confusion, clarifying what is truly good and desirable and giving us a taste of closeness to Hashem. Only then is one truly free to "choose life."

Indeed, freedom means something very different to a Jew. We are told in the Torah that we were taken out of Egypt not to be free, but to serve the Almighty, "for B'nei Yisrael are servants to Me; they are My servants that I took out from Egypt."[3] Our release from physical subjugation to an earthly master was merely a prerequisite to our service of Hashem. But we are not truly free in the common sense of the word. As devoted servants of the Almighty, our very existence is one of all-consuming commitment.

The Rambam's words capture this idea perfectly and succinctly:

> *Those who separate from the ways of the community, who throw off the yoke of the mitzvos and do not count themselves among the people of Israel by doing the mitzvos and occupying the synagogue and study hall, instead they are* ***free to themselves like the other nations****...regarding them it is stated, "Behold those who hate You, Hashem, I shall hate."*

Other nations are "free to themselves"; our liberty is of a different sort. In securing our freedom from an earthly power, we do not become "free to ourselves," but free to serve Hashem. We voluntarily and lovingly choose to be in His service and follow His Torah.

---

3 *Vayikra* 25:55.

EIGHT

Four Sons—at the Seder and Beyond

A key component of the Seder is engaging our children, in order to listen to them, stimulate their curiosity, and respond appropriately. Each child is unique, his questions special, and our answers must address the individual child at his or her own place in that moment. As the Mishnah describes: "In accordance with the child's mindset, his father teaches him."[1]

Who are these sons and what are they struggling with? Which challenges are we trying to address?

We are joined at the Seder by the four children mentioned in the Torah: the wise, the wicked, the simple, and the one who does not know to question. Each one belongs at our table, and each has a claim to our attention. In introducing them to us and providing a framework for each one's response, the Torah urges us to address all their questions.

Enjoyably immersed in deep Torah conversation with the wise son, delving into the laws and lessons of Pesach, a father must still turn to the simple son and answer his modest inquiries. Nor may we ignore the son who does not know to ask. He may be content with his toys, but it

1 *Pesachim* 116a.

falls upon the parent to arouse the child's interest in the proceedings and inspire his imagination about the subject.

Likewise, we must listen to the wicked son, the one whose questions may be discomfiting. His challenges, difficult as they may be to hear, must land on receptive and empathetic ears. "What is the point of all this effort," he argues, frustrated by the holiday's rigorous—and, to him, unmeaningful—demands.[2]

Doubtless, we would much prefer not to hear such blasphemy, but the Torah does not allow us to turn away. If the Torah chose to mention him, we may not ignore him nor despair of ever getting through to him.

"If he would have been there, he would not have been saved." But he is not there, in Egypt. He is here, with us, at the Seder, and he too receives exposure to the tremendous opportunity of the Seder. In Egypt, when Hashem descended to redeem His people and forge a new nation, He left behind those whose attitudes and actions served to distance them from the community. That was then, in Egypt. After the Exodus, when those who merited were taken out by Hashem Himself, we are all part of the nation, and the Seder is for all of us. Each person at the Seder belongs with us.

Rav Tzadok HaKohen articulates this idea:

> *The response to the wicked son's question is—had he been there he would not have been redeemed. But after Hashem redeemed us and made from us the nation of Israel, since he too was born of a Jewish mother and circumcised at eight days, no wickedness in the world can cause him to be excluded from the people of Israel. Even if he sins and does terrible things, he is a Jew and can still repair his actions.*[3]

Our wicked son also belongs at the table. We will not like his questions, nor will he appreciate the Haggadah's harsh response. But he must be present, and we may not ignore him or his needs.

---

2 See also *Yerushalmi, Pesachim* 70b.

3 *Pri Tzadik, Pesach,* ch. 8.

Chassidim quote the following homily from Rabbi Levi Yitzchak of Berditchev: "Until their students came and told them, 'Our masters, the time has come to recite the morning (*Shacharis*) *Shema*.'" *Shacharis* (שחרית) should be read as an acrostic for the four sons: ***She****'eino yode'a* (שאינו יודע), ***Ch****acham* (חכם), ***R****asha* (רשע), ***T****am* (תם). We cannot stop relating the story of *yetzias Mitzrayim* until all four sons are ready to "recite the *Shema*" with the clarity of daylight.

NINE

Pathway to Faith

Portions of this section appear in Rav Asher Weiss on Emunah and Bitachon (Mosaica Press, 2019), ch. 7.

The Ramban's comments below introduce us to an entirely new perspective on the miracles performed by Hashem when He saved us from Egypt.

I. Emunah through Miracles

> *Many mitzvos are meant to remind us of the Exodus, all to attest to these great wonders for all generations so they are not forgotten...from the great public miracles one comes to acknowledge the implicit miracles that are the foundation of Torah. For one has no portion in the Torah of Moshe Rabbeinu until he believes that every single event is a miracle—nothing is natural or automatic.*[1]

Those wondrous events were not intended only for the local, immediate task of creating and freeing the Jewish nation. Illuminating our path far into the future, Hashem's actions served a grander purpose: to demonstrate, for all time and beyond a shadow of doubt, that everything that happens in the world, even nature's seemingly insignificant events, is indeed guided by His will. Our ancestors witnessed miracles

1 *Ramban*, end of *Parashas Bo*.

so they could pause and thank Him, not only for the great salvations, but, as Chazal instruct us, for "each and every breath."[2]

If we look at the Torah's word for miracle, *neis*, we see that the Ramban's idea is built into the terminology itself. Typically, we associate the word *neis* with "miracle," but the Torah, so precise with its language, assigns a different word to connote the wondrous or supernatural—"*pele*." *Neis*, on the other hand, is also used to refer to a "banner," flying aloft and calling to action.[3] It is used this way in many *pesukim* in Tanach, and we employ it in our daily prayer when we say in the *Amidah*, "And raise a banner to gather our exiles."

Surely, these are not two different translations of the same word. Rather, they communicate a single meaning, conveying to us that the supernatural miracles serve as banners, attesting to Hashem's intimate involvement even in that which appears to be "nature." Just as a flag declares sovereignty over a city or country, so does Hashem's "flag"—a miracle—proclaim to all that He is Master of the universe and everything within it.

Chazal taught us not to pray for miracles, warning us that to request that an unborn child be a male is a "wasted prayer."[4] And yet, the Rama rules in the *Shulchan Aruch* that one who forgets to recite *Al Hanissim* in its proper place in *Birkas Hamazon* should instead add, "May the Merciful One perform for us miracles and wonders, just as He did for our fathers."[5] How do we reconcile the Rama's ruling with the idea that one does not ask for miracles?

I believe that the distinction hinges upon our understanding of miracles. It is certainly appropriate to pray for the sort of miracles that will have the desired effect of fully revealing Hashem's presence in and control over the world. Just as the miracles of the Exodus brought widespread recognition of Hashem, so too should we wish and pray for events that might demonstrate full expression of His will in this

---

2 *Bereishis Rabbah* 14, 9.
3 See *Yeshayahu* 18:3 and *Yirmiyahu* 51:12.
4 See *Berachos* 54a and *Yeshuos Yaakov* ad loc.
5 *Orach Chaim* 682:1.

world. But a miracle that will not result in greater glory to His name is a wasted miracle; praying for the same is a vacuous prayer. Asking that one's unseen child be male is an entirely meaningless prayer, for even the one who prayed himself can never know if a miracle indeed occurred or if the child was a male all along. Such a miracle—one that can never result in a greater sanctification of His name—serves no purpose and thus should not be requested.

Chazal related the following:

> *It happened once that a man's wife died, leaving behind a nursing child, but [the father] did not have money to hire a wet nurse. A miracle occurred and he developed breasts like that of a woman and he nursed his child. Rav Yosef said, "Look how great this man is that such a miracle occurred to him." To which Abaye replied, "On the contrary, how unfortunate is this man that the order of Creation was disrupted on his behalf."*[6]

According to the midrash, a similar miracle was done for Mordechai HaTzaddik, and the child he nursed was Esther. In light of this, we may ask, how could Abaye comment negatively about this sort of miracle if it also happened to Mordechai and Esther?[7] However, based on our discussion, we can see that the two cases were not exactly the same. The miracle that happened to Mordechai was indeed of the sort that would result in greater manifestation of Hashem's presence in the world. Perhaps it was a private matter at the time, but ultimately, Esther's was the pivotal role in our salvation from Haman's scheme; her survival as a child proved to be of tremendous import. Such a miracle falls well within the parameters of a "desirable" miracle; one that points to Hashem's direct involvement in everything that happens in the world.

Sometimes, Hashem's true greatness as the Master of Creation can be more intensely felt when natural processes are overridden.

---

6 *Shabbos* 53b.

7 See *Tosafos Yeshanim, Shabbos* ibid.

A child, upon hearing the wonders of the splitting of the sea, once asked his father, "What is so remarkable about the splitting of the sea? After all, Hashem, Who created the sea, can also split it!" In response, his father offered the following parable.

> *A great sculptor once crafted a life-sized horse entirely of marble, its likeness perfectly matching that of a real animal, and left his masterpiece in the town square for all to marvel at. Lo and behold, passersby came and went, immersed in their business, and not a single one gave the stone horse a second glance, much less stopped to appreciate its striking beauty or its maker's superior craftsmanship. Devastated, the artist returned home, despondent at his apparent failure to gain recognition for his skill. Attempting to comfort him, his family members suggested that perhaps the sculpture was too perfect, its likeness to a horse too precise for anyone to notice—after all, who pays heed to a horse loitering in the street? Taken aback, the sculptor objected that a creation any less perfect would not do justice to his abilities. Should he so harm his reputation and livelihood? No, advised his relatives. Rather, take that very same horse and cut it in half, and leave the two sides in the same public place for all to see. Surely, everyone will notice such a hitherto unseen sight—a live horse cut down the middle yet standing upright! Upon further examination, observers will realize that this is not a real horse, but rather a specimen of masterful craftsmanship, formed by an exceptionally talented artist.*

So it is, continued the father, with the splitting of the sea. True, if we were all gifted with a pure heart and mind, predisposed to seek out Godliness in the world, there would have been no need to split the sea to reveal His grandeur. A normally functioning sea would itself attest to its Maker's greatness; a great mountain's majesty would engender in us awe of our shared Creator. In fact, the Rambam suggests just such contemplation as a strategy for developing love and fear of Hashem:

> *How should one approach loving and fearing Him? When one reflects upon His actions and great, wondrous creations, seeing in them His infinite wisdom, immediately he will love and praise and passionately desire to know His great Name...*

Unfortunately, though, familiarity dulls our senses, clouding our awareness of Hashem's wonders even as they envelope us on all sides. A split sea, its placid movements suddenly changed to violent convulsion and the laws of physics normally governing it suspended, jolts us from complacency. It calls attention, not only to the event itself, but to its subject, the sea, and to nature in its entirety. At that moment, no longer can anything be taken for granted; nature has no rules. It is only Hashem's will that directs water to the sea and away from dry land, and it is Him that we should praise for each and every breath.

Nor should we seek such inspiration only in natural phenomena. Every event in an individual's life should encourage him or her to see Hashem's Hand and close involvement each step of the way. Rather than seeking Him out only at moments of distress or in the face of major decisions, we should heed Chazal's call to praise Hashem for every breath. As Rabbeinu Yonah lamented centuries ago:

> *"Know Him in all your ways"—in every action that you pursue, remember Hashem, hope that He will bring you success, and rely on Him. Remind yourself that the outcome is not in your hand. This phrase adds to the earlier statement, "Trust in Hashem with all your heart." One might trust in Hashem more generally, believing that everything is in His hand, and not up to the efforts of Man. But he might not have fully internalized this trust with respect to every detail. Thus, the pasuk says, "in all your ways"—in each action you should remember Him...*
>
> *Know that there are those whose eyes are lifted to Hashem when it comes to major issues, such as embarking on a dangerous journey or the like, but do not remember Him in their daily activities. Therefore, the pasuk states, "in all your ways"—in*

> *matters large and small. Since all outcomes depend on His will and kindness, one must remember Him in each action.*[8]

Rabbeinu Yonah elsewhere uses this idea to explain Chazal's promise that one who begins his prayer immediately after mentioning Hashem's redemption of the Jewish People is guaranteed a place in the World to Come. To justify such a sweeping reward for what appears to be a relatively minor observance, Rabbeinu Yonah offers:

> *When one mentions the Exodus and prays immediately thereafter, he demonstrates his belief in Hashem by praying to Him for his needs. One who does not trust does not pray. So we see in the midrash that when B'nei Yisrael saw the miracles He was doing for them they trusted in Him, as it says in the pasuk: "And Israel saw the Great Hand that Hashem used against Egypt, and they believed in Him, etc." When one mentions the very redemption that caused our ancestors to believe in Him, and then immediately proceeds to pray, he shows his faith that he will be answered just as our forefathers were answered then... Trust is the core of awe and faith—achieving this assures one a place in the World to Come.*[9]

My belief in Hashem is expressed through my prayer: if I trust that He can provide my needs, I will ask them of Him. Perfecting this state of mind is a lifelong process, as developing complete trust in Him alone is no easy feat. But relying on anything other than Hashem betrays a lack of faith,[10] and we must work to remain aware of our complete dependency on Him. The Rambam asserted that belief in Hashem is innate to the soul of a Jew,[11] but we must do our part to strengthen our belief and live accordingly.

---

8 *Rabbeinu Yonah, Mishlei* 3:6.

9 *Rabbeinu Yonah, Berachos* 7b.

10 *Yirmiyahu* 17:5–6: "Cursed is the man who trusts in a man... Blessed is the man who trusts in Hashem."

11 *Rambam, Igeres Teiman.*

By contemplating the miracles our ancestors experienced, one's belief and trust in Hashem is reinforced. A deeper sense of awe and love for Hashem ensues, and the reflective person is inspired to rededicate himself to a meaningful relationship with Hashem. Ultimately, this was the very purpose of *yetzias Mitzrayim*—that we should accept His rule for all time, as Hashem Himself declared, "For they are My servants, that I took out from the land of Egypt."

Invoking the Exodus—"He Who redeemed Israel"—right before prayer actively demonstrates this correlation: I have internalized the message and purpose of *yetzias Mitzrayim*—to bring mankind to belief in Hashem—and I actualize my recognition by immediately turning to Him with my requests, confident that He can provide my needs. Chazal commented that prayer is service of the heart.[12] I serve Hashem not only through acts of devotion, but my very confidence that He alone is worthy of my trust is also an act of service. Thus, transitioning from acknowledgment of His historic miracles (redemption) to request for His ongoing grace (prayer) reflects the humble service of Hashem that earns one a place in the World to Come.

We might also use this idea to explain the Rambam's position that one should remember *yetzias Mitzrayim* every day and night, although he does not list such a requirement in his count of the Torah's mitzvos.[13] The Rambam understands the mitzvah to remember the Exodus not as an independent, stand-alone obligation, but rather a component of the mitzvah to recite *Shema* each day. While *Shema* is technically the acceptance of the yoke of Heaven and mitzvos, remembering *yetzias Mitzrayim* is a critically important pathway to awakening this very commitment to Hashem and His mitzvos. Upon thinking about *yetzias Mitzrayim*, one can be sufficiently moved to consider himself a servant of Hashem and do His bidding—the Torah and mitzvos.

---

12 *Taanis* 2a.

13 See *Rambam*, Laws of *K'rias Shema* 1:3 and the comments in *Ohr Sameach*, as well as *Tzlach*, *Berachos* 12b.

II. Emunah through Torah

In addition to arriving at faith in Hashem by contemplating His creation, the Rambam also tells us that learning Torah is another pathway to this goal:

> *[H]e commanded us to love Him, which happens when we think about and contemplate His mitzvos and statements and actions, to the point that we understand Him. We will then reach tremendous joy in understanding Him—this is the love we are obligated in.*[14]

The Rambam offers two distinct paths that lead to love of Hashem. More than simply two methods for achieving a single end, these paths represent two different modalities of love. The Rambam's words, just cited above, point to a love that is born of deep intellectual appreciation. Elsewhere, however, the Rambam describes a different kind of love: a deep, all-consuming, emotional connection modeled on the love between a man and a woman.[15] The Rambam describes such burning passion as "lovesick," borrowing the term from *Shir Hashirim*, which is, in its entirety, a metaphor for the relationship between the human soul and its Divine Source.

I suggest that the two pathways to love of Hashem—Torah study and contemplating His world—represent, in fact, these two distinct types of love. Intellectual connection is realized by delving into His Torah and understanding Him through His wisdom, while appreciating the wonder of Creation generates the overwhelming passionate desire of the beloved.

Let us note, however, that when describing the mitzvah to love Hashem through Torah, the Rambam concludes: "This is the love in which we are obligated." Torah study, and the resulting connection through wisdom, is an absolute obligation, and the Rambam therefore lists it as one of the 613 mitzvos. Loving Hashem in the passionate model of *Shir Hashirim* is described by the Rambam as the "appropriate

---

14 *Rambam, Sefer Hamitzvos*, mitzvah 3.

15 *Rambam*, Laws of Teshuvah 10:3.

love," implying perhaps that while desirable and praiseworthy, such a lofty level exceeds the minimum obligation of the mitzvah. This love is thus described in the Rambam's discussion of character development, rather than in a section dealing with absolute obligations.

Our understanding of the two ways in which one might love Hashem can also provide insight into the first *pasuk* of *Shema*. We all know that *Shema* is a declaration of our belief in One God and acceptance of His Kingship. But the commentators do not all agree as to its primary emphasis. In *Sefer Hachinuch* we learn that one acknowledges Hashem's kingship by affirming belief in His Oneness: "The meaning of *Shema* is to proclaim, 'Accept this, know it, and believe that Hashem, Who is the Almighty, is One'...which is acknowledgment of Oneness and belief [in Him]." Accordingly, "Hashem is *One*" is the essential statement of *Shema*.[16]

On the other hand, the *Abudraham*, citing earlier Rishonim, writes that affirming Hashem's Unity alone is not sufficient to fulfill the mitzvah of *Shema*. To accept the yoke of Heaven, one must also focus on the earlier phrase, "Hashem is *our* God," connoting our direct relationship with—and obligation toward—Him.[17]

I believe that these approaches exist side by side. Rather than competing, mutually exclusive interpretations, they represent two complementary, equally fundamental aspects of belief and acceptance of the yoke of Heaven. "Hashem is our God" reflects a direct, personal relationship with Hashem and acceptance of our obligations toward Him, while "Hashem is One" describes recognition of His absolute Unity.

These, in turn, align with the two avenues to loving Hashem that the Rambam described. One can only truly sense a personal relationship with Hashem—"our God"—through Torah study, a gift granted exclusively to His people. Contemplating the wonders of the natural world can bring one to love Hashem and appreciate His Oneness, affirming

---

16 See *Sefer Hachinuch*, mitzvah 417.

17 See *Sefer Abudraham, Seder Shacharis Shel Chol*, and *Rabbeinu Yonah* in *Shaarei Teshuvah, Shaar Ha'avodah*, pp. 23–24.

that "Hashem is One," but to draw near to the Divine, one must engage directly with His Wisdom, His Torah, the very blueprint for all Creation.

Moreover, perhaps we can associate the *Shema*'s two introductory blessings with these two principles. In the first blessing, we praise Hashem for the wonders of nature, and specifically for forming the wondrous luminaries, the sun and the moon. This blessing, of course, corresponds to "Hashem is One" of the *Shema*. As we draw closer to the *Shema*, we recite a blessing replete with references to the Torah and Hashem's love for His people. In fact, this blessing can serve, under certain circumstances, as the required blessing before learning Torah.[18]

Thus, the blessings introducing *Shema* represent two modes of understanding Hashem, which reflect the two pathways to loving Hashem, which correspond to the two affirmations of *Shema*: our personal relationship with Him (our God) as well as acknowledgment of His perfect unity (Hashem is One).

Indeed, while there are two available pathways, one who is fortunate enough to be fully immersed in Torah can achieve full appreciation of Hashem's greatness through learning. Such an individual does not need to contemplate nature to arrive at his own "Hashem is One" recognition. In fact, Chazal went so far as to say that any attempt to do so could be disastrous: "One who is traveling and stops his learning to say, 'How beautiful is this tree' is considered to have forfeited his soul." Someone who is deeply engaged in Torah study does not need the beauty of nature to inspire awe and love of Hashem. Everything is in Torah.[19]

In a chapter of *Tehillim* that we include in the Shabbos *Pesukei D'Zimrah*, we read: "The heavens proclaim the glory of God; the work of His hands is told by the sky..." Later in the chapter, we seemingly change topics, suddenly saying, "Hashem's Torah is perfect, restorative to the soul...the commandment of Hashem is clear, illuminating the eyes..." For all the grandeur of Creation and the majesty of nature, it is only His Torah that is perfect, energizes the soul, and illuminates reality.

---

18 See *Berachos* 9b.

19 *Avos* 3:7 with *Bartenura*.

III. Natural and Supernatural

Not only is nature itself nothing more than Hashem's hidden way of guiding the world, but, at its inception, Creation was meant to continue to function through Hashem's miraculous, supernatural mode of interacting with His world. Prior to Adam's sin in partaking of the Tree of Knowledge, the world was governed by ethical rules of right and wrong, not by natural law. Creation, and everything in and about it, was subordinate to Man's needs, so that he in turn could properly serve his Maker. Chazal captured this utopia in a description of angels roasting meat and decanting wine for Adam, while the earth produced only those trees that would benefit him.[20] Only after the Sin, whereby Man failed to meet his initial calling, did Creation likewise retreat from its original destiny to serve Man. Thus, each person is referred to as a miniature world, for with Man resides potential to dictate the very mode of Creation.[21]

Opportunity for Man to change the way his world functions did not end with Adam. Man, pinnacle and purpose of Creation, can affect nature itself. If "the world was only created for Torah and Yisrael," then Man indeed holds tremendous power over its functioning.

The Ramban writes:

> *When mitzvos are kept, the Land of Israel will be as the world was originally, prior to Adam's sin—no animal could kill a man.*[22]
>
> *When B'nei Yisrael are perfect, their affairs will not be governed by nature at all, neither their physical bodies, nor their land, on both the individual and societal levels. Hashem will bless their bread and water and remove illness from their midst, to the point that they will not need doctors or any medical interventions, for "I am Hashem your Healer."*[23]

---

20 *Sanhedrin* 59b.

21 See *Akeidas Yitzchak, Parashas Noach, shaar* 12, *Niggun Ha'olam.*

22 *Vayikra* 26:6.

23 Ibid., 26:11.

This idea is articulated already in the Mishnah:

> *Rabbi Shimon ben Elazar said: Have you ever seen a beast or a bird that has a trade? And yet they earn their livelihood without anguish. If these were created only to serve me, and I was created to serve the One Who formed me, is it not right that I should earn my livelihood without anguish? But I have committed evil actions and have lost my livelihood.*[24]

Accordingly, had Man not failed, he would earn his livelihood without effort or anguish, just as the animals do.

Such is his power, that Man's actions have impact far beyond his own efforts to provide for himself. Everything about the world and its functioning is influenced by Man:

> *Why was the world created with ten utterances? To grant reward to the righteous who sustain the world that was created with ten utterances, and to exact punishment from the wicked who destroy the world that was created with ten utterances.*[25]

Man's choice in this world makes all the difference, determining whether the world will be sustained or lost. On the individual level as well, a person who has elevated himself to the highest levels of character perfection can indeed dominate the natural world and bend it to his will. After all, the "natural" world was intended, from Creation, to serve a Man who is dedicated to serving his Creator.

With this, we can better frame Abaye's comment regarding the man who was miraculously able to nurse his child: "How unfortunate is this man that the order of Creation was disrupted on his behalf." After all, one might object, we have certainly seen many great people who were able to bring about miracles and facilitate the seemingly impossible! But those apparent wonders, when effected by holy people who have reached the loftiest heights of purity and greatness, are not aberrations

---

24 *Kiddushin* 82a.

25 *Avos* 5:1.

at all. Creation was always meant to be subordinate to the will of Man—when Man lives up to his calling. A man who has achieved that stature can dictate to the natural world how it should function. Nature is then merely returning to its original character as a tool of Man.

For this reason, Chazal emphasized the idea that *yetzias Mitzrayim* was carried out by Hashem Himself, not by an angel or messenger. Since B'nei Yisrael, still at their lowly spiritual state, were not worthy of miracles, their salvation took the form of circumventing nature. Such can only be done by Hashem Himself. Had they been worthy, it would have been assumed that nature would be subservient to their will. In the event, however, they were not, and only Hashem's direct kindness would recreate nature for His people.

IV. "Seeing the Sounds"

Hashem's miracles can also profoundly impact an individual's perception of the world, refining his attitudes toward events surrounding him. Commenting on the *pasuk*, "And the entire nation saw the sounds,"[26] Chazal taught that when Hashem revealed Himself to His people at Sinai, they were able to "see that which is normally heard, and hear that which is normally seen."[27]

Typically, of Man's five senses, the one he is most likely to trust unquestionably is his sight. That which I can see with my own eyes I am most likely to accept as factual; inputs into the other four senses can be questioned or doubted. Is that noise my imagination? Is that smell what I think it is? But I can be confident in the reality of an event I observe directly. Chazal summarized this idea in a halachic setting, arguing that a court's "hearing should not be more reliable than seeing" events directly.[28]

Yet, a Jew's awareness must transcend his physical nature. We know that our vision is limited and cannot grasp all of reality. Our belief in One Creator, Who created the universe and everything inhabiting

---

26 *Shemos* 20:15.

27 *Mechilta, Yisro.*

28 *Rosh Hashanah* 25b.

it, while He cannot be seen Himself, demands that we recognize the boundaries of physical existence. Our eyes of flesh and blood do not always apprehend reality across its many dimensions. Only Man's soul, breathed by Hashem directly into Man but which cannot itself be seen, can truly appreciate existence for what it is.[29]

We develop this sensitivity through "hearing"—the lessons of our parents and teachers. Children cannot see the angels they learn about, but they come to take the unseen for granted. They learn to understand that reality extends far beyond their field of physical vision.[30] "Hearing" thus has significant advantage over "seeing," serving to stimulate one's imagination and broaden his horizons.

Our ancestors reached this level at Sinai. When they "saw that which is heard," they heard Hashem's message to them with the same clarity one usually experiences when seeing something. At the same time, so elevated were they that their physical surrounding became less real—they "heard that which is normally seen"—the immediacy of vision became dulled in the face of Hashem's overwhelming presence.[31]

Perhaps we can use this lesson to understand the following passage in the Gemara:

> *Rabbi Yochanan sat and taught: In the future, the Holy One, blessed be He, will bring precious stones and pearls that are thirty cubits by thirty cubits, and He will hollow out in them ten by twenty and set them in the gates of Jerusalem. A certain student sneered at him, "Now we do not find precious stones even of the size of an egg of a dove, and yet all of this we will find?" After some time that student's ship went to sea, where he saw ministering angels sitting and sawing precious stones and pearls that were thirty by thirty and hollowed out in them ten by twenty. He said to them, "For whom are these?" They said to him that in the future, the Holy One, blessed be He, will*

29 See *Nefesh Hachaim, shaar* 3, ch. 11, and *Bnei Yissaschar, Chodesh Sivan, maamar* 5.

30 See *Ramban, Devarim* 4:9, and *Sefer Hachinuch*, introduction.

31 See also *Meshech Chochmah, Parashas Chukas*, and *Meor Einayim, Parashas Beshalach*.

> *place them in the gates of Jerusalem. He came before Rabbi Yochanan and said to him, "Continue to interpret, my teacher, it is fitting for you to interpret, as I saw just as you said!" Rabbi Yochanan said to him, "Empty one! If you had not seen, you would not have believed; you are mocking the statement of the Sages." He set his eyes upon him, and he was turned into a pile of bones.*[32]

Rabbi Yochanan's unnamed student was not punished when he scoffed at the original teaching. Yet, when he returned and attempted to validate his teacher's words he was struck down. Why would this be?

Returning to Rabbi Yochanan and offering his eyewitness experience as evidence that his teacher was correct demonstrated that the student gave greater credence to his own vision than he did to the lessons of his master. Only the student's personal experience justified accepting Rabbi Yochanan's words. It was to this critical error that Rabbi Yochanan reacted so harshly, calling his student an "empty man." Thus, the student, an individual of sufficient stature to converse with angels, was turned into a pile of bones. A man of his level should have internalized the need to "see that which one hears" from the traditions of our parents and teachers.

Nor was the mode of the student's punishment incidental. Rather, his fate directly attested to his failing. A human is indeed but a pile of bones—it is only the soul he receives directly from Hashem that keeps a man upright, living, breathing, and acting. This student, who overemphasized the power of physical sight, failed to appreciate the reality of that which might elude our vision. Rabbi Yochanan thus called him "empty," questioning him: "Are you indeed empty? Are you not aware of the soul that inhabits your body yet cannot be seen?"

Elsewhere, we find Rabbi Yochanan reinforcing to his students the importance of seeing reality through the truth of Torah rather than through the lens of physical sight: "...Our patriarch Yaakov did not die...'And was it for naught that the eulogizers eulogized and the

---

32 *Bava Basra* 75a.

embalmers embalmed and the buriers buried?' He replied, 'I am interpreting a *pasuk*'..."[33] Rashi there explains that indeed Yaakov only appeared to die, and those around him, constrained by their physical vision, thought he had died.

Similarly, the Gemara stresses this message in another episode:

> *Rav Sheshes was blind. Everyone was going to greet the king and Rav Sheshes stood up and went along with them. A heretic found him and said to him, "Intact jugs go to the river, why do the broken shards go?" Rav Sheshes said to him, "Come see that I know more than you." The first troop passed; when the noise grew louder, this heretic said to him, "The king is coming." Rav Sheshes said to him, "He is not coming." A second troop passed; when the noise grew louder, this heretic said to him, "Now the king is coming." Rav Sheshes said to him, "The king is not coming." A third passed, and when there was silence, Rav Sheshes said to him, "Certainly now the king is coming." This heretic said to him, "How do you know this?" He said to him, "Royalty on earth is like royalty in the heavens, as it is written: 'And He said: Go forth, and stand upon the mount before Hashem. And, behold, Hashem passed by, and a great and strong wind rent the mountains, and broke in pieces the rocks before Hashem; but Hashem was not in the wind; and after the wind an earthquake; but Hashem was not in the earthquake; and after the earthquake a fire; but Hashem was not in the fire; and after the fire a still small voice.'" When the king came, Rav Sheshes began to bless him. The heretic said to him, "Do you bless someone you do not see?" And what ultimately happened to this heretic? Some say that his friends gouged out his eyes, and some say that Rav Sheshes fixed his gaze upon him, and he became a pile of bones.*

---

33 *Taanis* 5b.

Here too, a profound message prevails. Not all knowledge can be discerned by one's sight. In fact, Rav Sheshes, relying only on his hearing, knew better than the heretic, even regarding worldly events happening in their presence. When the heretic failed to understand this lesson and continued to mock Rav Sheshes by asking him why he would bless the king he cannot see, he too was punished. Both versions of the heretic's punishment allude to our idea: either his eyes were gouged out, pointing to the overemphasis on physical sight, or he, like Rabbi Yochanan's unfortunate student, became a pile of bones, representing his failure to acknowledge that which cannot be seen.

In Gan Eden, Adam replied to Hashem's calls by saying, "I heard your voice in the Garden, and I was fearful because I am naked."[34] Adam, aware that he should be on the level of "seeing" Hashem, became frightened when he was only able to "hear" Hashem's voice.

At the time of our future redemption, we will likewise achieve the clarity of vision through hearing, when we will all "see, each with his eye, that Hashem has spoken."[35] We express this idea in *Mussaf* each Shabbos: "And He will again in His mercy make us hear, in the presence of all life, saying..." At that time, we will be fortunate enough to, once again, "see the sounds" of Hashem's revelation.

Perhaps this is why the Torah commands us specifically to remember what we *saw* at Sinai,[36] not demanding the same regarding any other wondrous event we experienced. Internalizing what is heard with a clarity typically associated with sight was a critical aspect of our ancestors' experience at Sinai, one that is meant to remain with us for all future generations.[37]

V. Everything the Merciful One Does Is for the Good

Miracles communicate to us an additional message. Hashem's actions at the time of the Exodus, the great wonders of the Ten Plagues and splitting the sea, were powerful expressions of His immense kindness

---

34 *Bereishis* 3:10.

35 *Yeshayahu* 52:8.

36 *Devarim* 4:9.

37 See below in our discussions about Shavuos.

toward His people. In disrupting every facet of nature and upending the very structure of Creation, Hashem was bestowing good upon His beloved children. In this sense as well, miracles serve as banners. Thus, even events that seem harsh or destructive, products of His attributes of judgment, in fact are truly acts of kindness and mercy. And, whether or not we are able to see the good in these acts, we are meant to faithfully assert, "Everything the Merciful One does is for the good." Even when one experiences what seems to be Hashem's judgment, he must always attempt to identify the underlying good and to feel Hashem's love. According to Ibn Ezra, this is the meaning behind the *pasuk*, "You are Hashem's children; do not gash yourselves nor shave the front of your head because of a death." One is meant to be so cognizant of Hashem's love, which exceeds even that of a parent, that His care for us is simply assumed. Just as a child does not question a parent's actions, even when these seem inexplicable to the child, so are we to relate to Hashem's.[38]

> *A Jew famously once approached the Mezritcher Maggid, requesting that the Rebbe guide him in how to properly fulfill Chazal's command to "thank Hashem for the bad just as one does for the good."*[39] *Rather than respond directly, the Maggid instructed the Jew to go to the study hall and seek out an individual named Reb Zusha; he would be able to assist the Jew in his quest. Immediately upon locating Reb Zusha, it became obvious to the Jew that Reb Zusha—his clothes threadbare and his appearance attesting to manifold physical suffering—did not have an easy life. Upon hearing of the Jew's mission and the Maggid's instructions, Reb Zusha exclaimed, bewildered, "Surely you must have misheard the Rebbe! I wouldn't know anything about thanking Hashem for bad things. Nothing bad has ever happened to me—I am perfectly happy with all the kindness Hashem has shown me throughout my life!"*

---

38 See *Ibn Ezra* and *Ramban*, commentaries to *Devarim* 14:1.

39 *Berachos* 54a.

Indeed, the *Kedushas Levi* uses a similar approach to explain the following incident reported in the Gemara:

> *And another incident with Rabbi Chanina ben Dosa, who went to study Torah before Rabbi Yochanan ben Zakkai, and Rabbi Yochanan's son fell ill. He said to him, "Chanina, my son, pray for mercy on his behalf so that he will live." Rabbi Chanina ben Dosa placed his head between his knees and prayed for mercy on his behalf, and he lived. Rabbi Yochanan ben Zakkai said, "Had Ben Zakkai stuck his head between his knees the entire day, they would have paid him no attention." His wife said to him, "And is Chanina greater than you?" He replied to her, "No, but he is like a servant before the King; I am like a minister before the King."*[40]

A servant and a minister both attend to the king and do his bidding. However, the servant, unlike the minister, is uninvolved in statecraft and is ignorant of the policy-making and various interests of the kingdom. He serves the king simply. Rabbi Yochanan ben Zakkai was noting that he himself, having achieved such stature that he fully recognized Hashem's actions as always just and good, would not be able to properly plead that Hashem save his son. Only Rabbi Chanina, whose mission was to serve Hashem with simplicity, would be sufficiently moved by the plight of the sick child that his prayers could move the Heavens and change the decree.[41]

Another such "minister," Rabbi Akiva, taught us to say, "Whatever the Merciful One does is for the good."[42] Nor was this an abstract teaching—the Gemara recounts a series of misfortunes that Rabbi Akiva encountered, in all of which he saw only Hashem's abundant kindness. Even during his final moments on earth, as he was murdered by the Romans, he remained joyful.[43]

---

40 *Berachos* 34b.

41 *Kedushas Levi, Chukas.*

42 *Berachos* 60b.

43 See also *Yerushalmi, Berachos* 9:5, and *Sotah* 5:5.

Rabbi Akiva was able to see Hashem's mercy even in the suffering of his great teacher Rabbi Eliezer:

> *When Rabbi Eliezer fell ill, his students entered to visit him. He said to them, "There is intense wrath in the world." They began to cry, and Rabbi Akiva was laughing. They said to him, "Why are you laughing?" He said to them, "And why are you crying?" They said to him, "Is it possible that a Torah scroll is afflicted with pain and we will not cry?" He said to them, "It is for that reason that I am laughing. As long as I would see that my teacher's wine does not spoil, nor is his flax stricken, nor does his oil spoil, nor does his honey turn rancid, I would say that perhaps, Heaven forbid, my teacher already received his world. But now that I see my teacher with suffering, I am happy."*[44]

In a similar vein, the Gemara further relates that Rabbi Eliezer's four students once came to visit him when he was sick. In an apparent attempt to lift his spirits, the students praised their great teacher, with each student's comment reflecting a unique perspective. After his comrades variously compared their master to the sun, the rain, a father and mother, Rabbi Akiva submitted that Rabbi Eliezer is fortunate because "suffering is beneficial." Rabbi Akiva truly saw Hashem's kindness in everything around him—even his teacher's suffering was a blessing.

In fact, so advanced was Rabbi Akiva in this area that he was able to view the pain of exile and the destruction of the Beis Hamikdash through the lens of Hashem's mercy.

> *And it once was that Rabban Gamliel, Rabbi Elazar ben Azarya, Rabbi Yehoshua, and Rabbi Akiva were walking along the road and they heard the sound of the multitudes of Rome from Puteoli at a distance of one hundred and twenty mil. They began weeping and Rabbi Akiva was laughing. They said to him, "For what reason are you laughing?" He said to them,*

44 *Sanhedrin* 101a.

> *"And you, for what are you weeping?" They said to him, "These gentiles, who bow to false gods and burn incense to idols, dwell securely and tranquilly while our House, the footstool of our God, is burnt by fire, and shall we not weep?" He said to them, "That is why I am laughing. If for those who violate His will it is so, for those who perform His will, all the more so!" On another occasion they were ascending to Jerusalem. When they arrived at Mount Scopus they rent their garments. When they arrived at the Temple Mount, they saw a fox emerging from the Holy of Holies. They began weeping, and Rabbi Akiva was laughing. They said to him, "For what are you laughing?" He said to them, "For what are you weeping?" They said to him: "A place about which it is written: 'And the non-priest who approaches shall die'—foxes walk in it; and shall we not weep?" He said to them, "That is why I am laughing...now that the prophecy of Uriah was fulfilled, it is evident that the prophecy of Zechariah will be fulfilled as well."*[45]

Rabbi Akiva, indeed a "minister" before Hashem, saw a hint of light even at the darkest moments, and recognized redemption springing forth from the ruins of the Beis Hamikdash.

Chazal relate that when Moshe Rabbeinu, objecting to his selection as the intended savior of B'nei Yisrael, begged that Hashem "send please in the hands of someone else," he was referring to Rabbi Akiva.[46] Moshe, who was shown every generation and its leaders,[47] specifically identified Rabbi Akiva as the potential savior out of scores of other candidates—prophets, kings, warriors, and religious leaders. For all Rabbi

---

45 *Makkos* 24a–b. We should not mistakenly infer that Rabbi Akiva's sanguinity in the face of hardship was merely expression of an optimistic, cheerful personality; elsewhere we find Rabbi Akiva weeping when reading a *pasuk* in the Torah (*Kiddushin* 81b). We must not reduce Chazal to simplistic psychological evaluation. Their character traits reflect an understanding of their souls' individual paths to serving Hashem, and, in turn, their lifelong efforts to perfect those attributes.

46 Midrash, *Osios D'Rabi Akiva* 90.

47 *Bamidbar Rabbah* 23:5.

Akiva's greatness, why did Moshe Rabbeinu single him out among all others?

After the sin of the Golden Calf, B'nei Yisrael's first crisis as a nation, Moshe asked of Hashem, "Show me Your ways." Moshe was requesting insight into the great mysteries of Divine Justice—why do the righteous suffer while the wicked prosper?[48] This particular question, at this specific moment, seems discordant and out of place. But perhaps Moshe was asking Hashem what would be of His people, just born, who had already strayed and incurred punishment for their actions. Perhaps all was lost already! In response, Hashem showed Moshe the multitudes of generations that were to follow, their highs and lows, their sorrows and successes, and each generation's leaders. Seeing all this prompted Moshe to seek an answer to the suffering of the righteous.

In this vein, surveying the future of his people, Moshe Rabbeinu saw Rabbi Akiva, perceiving not only the latter's Torah, but also his outlook on the world. In Moshe's eyes, Rabbi Akiva, who could celebrate a fox roaming the site of the Beis Hamikdash and teach the world to recognize that "everything the Merciful One does is for the good," would be a perfect candidate to lead B'nei Yisrael out of slavery and toward Sinai.

In response, Hashem told Moshe, "You shall see My back, and My face shall not be seen," which, according to Chazal, was a reference to the knot of Hashem's tefillin, as it were. We know that the tefillin's knot incorporates the letters *shin*, *dalet*, and *yud*, forming the holy name *Sha-day*. This name is interpreted, variously, as representative of both Hashem's attributes of restraint or constriction,[49] as well as His expansive, ever-giving traits of kindness.[50] Indeed, Hashem's lesson to Moshe, in showing him the knot of the tefillin, was that the two modes are intertwined, and that even that which appears to be harsh and exacting is also an expression of Hashem's mercy.

The Radomsker Rebbe explained that the *pasuk*, "To tell in the morning of Your kindness and faith in You by evening," alludes to the

---

48 *Berachos* 7a.

49 "*Ani hu she'amarti l'olami dai*—I am the One Who told My world to stop." See *Chagigah* 12a.

50 *Bereishis Rabbah* 46:3.

idea that a true test of one's faith is at night, when he is submerged in darkness and feels that all hope is lost. During those moments when Hashem's presence appears hidden, we need to strengthen our faith in Him and our belief that there is light even in darkness. For this reason, the requirements to eat in the sukkah and to eat matzah—both of which are designed to remind us of *yetzias Mitzrayim* and fortify our faith—are primarily at night.[51]

During the events known as the *Asarah Harugei Malchus* (the Ten Martyrs), we find the ministering angels objecting before Hashem that such incongruous treatment of these great Sages is an affront to the Torah itself. Hashem silences them with a warning: "If you are not quiet, I shall restore the world to *tohu va'vohu*." *Tohu va'vohu*, according to the Ramban's interpretation, were the raw materials Hashem "used" to form Creation. If He intends to destroy the world upon any further objections, what need would Hashem have for the raw materials? If the world is to cease existing, there is no need for its constituent elements either!

I once heard a wonderful illustration to explain this:

> *A man once went to an expert tailor to order a new suit. The tailor carefully took the customer's measurements and instructed him exactly how much material to purchase for the suit. Having purchased the requisite quantity of material, the customer brought it to the tailor and waited for his garment. Upon receiving word that his suit was ready, the customer returned to the tailor, tape measure in hand. Carefully measuring the fine garment, he turns to the tailor and accuses the craftsman of theft. According to his measurements, the suit has less fabric than what was originally submitted! "Fool," replied the tailor. "You know nothing about the craft of suit-making nor can you understand where all the material is. But if you wish, I can demonstrate my innocence. I can take apart the beautiful garment, lay it out flat on the table and show you that every inch of the fabric you provided is here in the suit. But surely,*

51 *Tiferes Shlomo, Sukkos.*

> *you do not wish to destroy this fine suit; instead, you will have to trust both my knowledge and my integrity."*

Likewise, the Almighty reminded the angels that they know nothing about the workings of the universe. He was telling them: My ways are far beyond comprehension; even angels are unable to penetrate the secrets of Creation and understand its inner mechanics. Only if I were to dismantle the universe and break it down to its components would I be able to demonstrate how each and every event is perfectly synchronized and choreographed with infinite care and kindness.

For this reason, teach the Chassidic masters, we cover our eyes while reciting *Shema*—accepting upon ourselves His kingship.[52] When declaring "Hashem is One," we assert that Hashem's attributes of kindness and judgment are in fact one. He does not have competing wills or impulses. Thus, even when an event presents to our eyes as an expression of harshness or judgment, we must remain steadfast in our faith that, at its core, the challenge is really Hashem's abundant kindness. We therefore cover our eyes while saying *Shema*, acknowledging the limits of our vision and affirming that everything He does is good even if we are sometimes blind to it.

Rabbi Avraham Yehuda HaKohen Schwartz,[53] in the introduction to his *Kol Aryeh*, suggests using this idea to explain Hashem's promise to Yaakov, "...Fear not to go down to Egypt, for I will make you there into a great nation. I Myself will go down with you to Egypt, and I Myself will also bring you back; and Yosef shall place his hand over your eyes." Yaakov was deeply concerned about moving his family to Egypt, a spiritual wasteland. To assuage his fears somewhat, Hashem hinted to him that it will ultimately be of great benefit to his descendants. Just as Yosef's initial descent to Egypt appeared thoroughly tragic, yet eventually proved to be his brothers' source of salvation, so is Yaakov's move part of Hashem's master plan and a representation of His infinite kindness. Yosef will be the one to "place his hand" over Yaakov's eyes,

52 *Berachos* 13a and *Tur, Orach Chaim* 61.

53 An influential *rav* and *posek* in nineteenth-century Hungary.

just as one covers his eyes for *Shema* and thereby affirms his faith that Hashem's mercy encompasses even those things that appear difficult. Indeed, regarding this very promise to Yaakov, the *Zohar* comments, "This is the secret of *Shema*."[54]

When Hashem responded to Moshe Rabbeinu's request to gain insight into the secrets of Hashem's ways, He said, "You shall see My back, but My face shall not be seen." We have no ability to penetrate the inner workings of His actions and see His kindness in them directly. Only after the fact, with the passage of time, might we be able to discern how everything is an expression of His mercy. We cannot look His conduct in the face; only after it passes can we even attempt to review its effects in the world successfully.[55] Hashem told the ministering angels that the deaths of the Ten Martyrs "is part of the plan before Me," hinting that only much later, well after the events have occurred and certainly not in the throes of the decree, might we be fortunate enough to see more of the plan.

Eventually our eyes will open. In the future, when "the world is filled with knowledge of Hashem, like the sea is filled with water,"[56] we will see the full picture. We will rejoice at understanding how every exile and each challenge we experienced through our history were in fact all kindness and mercy, steps bringing us closer to Him and the final redemption. The relationship between exile and redemption is much like the experience of raising and harvesting grain. Hardship and the suffering of exile are akin to the toil and effort required to plant and care for crops, while the joy of redemption is the celebration of a successful harvest: "Those who plant in tears shall harvest in song."[57]

Even the *Kinnos*, the sorrowful reflections on our nation's travails, conclude with a comparison between the Jewish People's suffering and the pain of childbirth: "Mourn for Tzion and her cities, like a woman in childbirth." Just as the contractions and pain of childbirth yield to the

54 See responsa *Kol Aryeh, Pesach Tov*, no. 7.

55 Ibid., citing his teacher, the Chasam Sofer.

56 *Yeshayahu* 11:9.

57 *Tehillim* 126:6.

joy of new life, so too do the rays of redemption peek forth from the darkness of exile.

Another passage in Chazal demonstrates this idea:

> *"On that day, Hashem will be One and His name will be One." Is His name not One currently? Rav Acha bar Chanina said, "This world is not like the future world: in this world one says the blessing upon the good when hearing good news, and the blessing of righteous judgment upon bad news. In the future world, it will always be the blessing upon the good."*[58]

At first glance, Rav Acha's resolution is troubling. He seems to say that the mode of blessing will change in the future world, but not the underlying events. Good and bad will both still occur! Is the change of blessing, even of our outlook, indeed such a noteworthy change that it will bring unity to Hashem's name?

Yes, in the future reality, we will look back at those tragedies over which we already recited "*Dayan ha'emes*—[the blessing of] righteous judgment," and, with eyes newly opened, we will see that all those misfortunes were all expressions of His vast kindness. With a newly acquired view of the bigger picture, we will recite, "*Ha'tov v'ha'meitiv*—He is Good and bestows good."[59]

Our exiles evoked a double suffering—the difficulty of our circumstances under the conditions of the moment, as well as the pain of feeling that Hashem has turned away from us. Yosef HaTzaddik, who was fortunate enough to be transported on a wagon bearing pleasant fragrances, was reminded of Hashem's love for him even under such harrowing circumstances. We have not been so lucky—our exiles filled with days, months, and years during which we felt abandoned, left to suffer on our own. Yet, Chazal taught that just as we suffered this double punishment, so shall we be comforted with double comfort.[60] In our

---

58 *Pesachim* 50a.

59 See also a similar idea in *Tzlach*, *Pesachim* ad loc.

60 *Yalkut Shimoni*, *Yirmiyahu* commenting on the *pasuk*, "For she has been doubly struck by Hashem."

future redemption, when the clouds of exile disperse and the blinding tears dry, we will not only breathe a sigh of relief at our freedom, but we will also be comforted when we learn how each event was for our good; indeed, His kindness never wavered.

Accordingly, we might better understand Chazal's assertion that in the future, all our holidays will be eliminated, with the exception of Purim.[61] Surely, this is a curious teaching. Why would Purim, a later Rabbinic enactment, outlive the Torah-prescribed celebrations of Pesach or Sukkos?

All the other holidays are characterized by commemoration of great miracles, supernatural events that demonstrated with great fanfare Hashem's presence in the world. In the future, when His presence will be manifest and palpable to all creation, there will be no need for "proof" of miracles. A world that is "entirely good and lasts forever" does not need to celebrate miracles that occurred millennia earlier. Purim is different. On Purim we learned that lurking right behind the most difficult of challenges is actually Hashem's intimate involvement in His people's well-being. Each event in the saga that formed the Purim story was intricately designed to lead to our salvation.

Purim, uniquely, is named after a painful feature of the story it commemorates, the lots Haman cast when plotting against the Jewish People. This is unlike other holidays, whose names evoke positive associations—Pesach for our salvation from the plague, Sukkos for the clouds of protection, and Chanukah for rededication of the Beis Hamikdash. As the *Bnei Yisasschar* points out, this is because the lesson of Purim is that even challenging moments—even Haman's decree—are part of the redemption. Purim will be upheld even at that future time, so we might continue to contemplate all the hidden kindness He has done for us.

Chazal noted that Esther is hinted at in the Torah's promise, "*V'anochi haster astir panai*—And I shall surely hide My face." The hint is not merely in the similarity of the words. Esther's story is the story of

---

61 *Midrash Mishlei* 9:4, and in the *Yotzer* for *Shabbos Zachor*.

Hashem orchestrating His people's salvation, while remaining hidden from their view. On Purim, therefore, we do not recite *Hallel*. *Hallel* is reserved for days that commemorate Hashem's manifest and majestic revelation in the world. Instead, say Chazal, reading the *Megillah* is our fulfillment of *Hallel* on Purim.[62] The *Megillah*, relating the long sequence of events that ultimately led to a great outcome, reflects the lesson of Purim—Hashem sometimes, even often, operates in hidden and mysterious ways, but He is never less involved or any less powerful.

Finally, Chazal taught that Haman planned to hang Mordechai at the time for reciting *Shema*.[63] Here too, is a hint at the idea that all of Haman's scheming and plotting ultimately turned out for the good of Hashem's people, and, as we cited above, "This is the secret of *Shema*."

We learn in the Gemara:

> *It was taught in the name of Rabbi Meir, why was Torah given to Yisrael? Because they are bold. It was taught in the name of Rabbi Yishmael: "From His right, a code of fire [was given] to them."[64] Hashem said, "These are worthy of receiving a code of fire."[65]*

Rashi explains that the Torah was given to B'nei Yisrael as an antidote to their boldness. Torah, with its rigorous intellectual and physical demands, would subdue our untamed boldness. All this would suggest that Torah was meant to address a deficiency of B'nei Yisrael. Consistent with our theme, however, we would argue that, quite the contrary, B'nei Yisrael were chosen due to their ability to remain stubbornly faithful even at the darkest moments. Only a nation so bold and tenacious could withstand the suffering of destruction and exile, remaining committed to sanctifying His name even under the harshest of challenges. The Ramban adds that "from His right, a code of fire" is meant to refer to Hashem's "right hand," which is associated with

62 *Megillah* 14b.

63 *Midrash Talpiyos, Achashveirosh*.

64 *Devarim* 33:2.

65 *Beitzah* 25b.

His attribute of mercy. Only a spirited and bold Jewish nation can recognize that its myriad suffering, the heavy price of being chosen to receive Torah, a "code of fire," indeed comes from Hashem's "right," His infinite kindness.[66] As, Rabbi Tzvi Chajes writes regarding the Gemara just cited: "They are bold and worthy of receiving the Torah, for throughout all the decrees they experienced they did not abandon their inheritance from Sinai."[67]

Indeed, Chazal noted this idea in a midrash:

> *Rabbi Yakim taught: Three are bold—of the animals, the dog is most bold; among birds, the chicken; among the nations, Yisrael. Rabbi Yitzchak bar Redifa said in the name of Rav Ami, "You might think it is derogatory, but it is in fact praise..."*[68]

The commentators add that B'nei Yisrael, who continue to sanctify Hashem's name time and again, are the boldest of nations.[69]

Moshe Rabbeinu asked, "Please Hashem, walk among us, for the nation is stubborn." A nation's stubbornness hardly seems like a compelling argument in favor of Hashem's presence in its midst. To explain this, the *Kesav Sofer* explains that it is our stubbornness that has allowed us to persist in the face of constant persecution and torment. Despite all we have been subjected to, we continue to uphold the covenant Hashem sealed with us at Sinai. We are indeed stubborn—our fidelity to Hashem and His Torah remain strong come what may, and we are thus fully deserving of Hashem's presence.

VI. Faith and Trust in Difficult Times

Our faith has been our lifeline through the exiles and even at the darkest times. Time and again, our holy ancestors sanctified Hashem's name, placing in Him their fervent trust that salvation would soon arrive.

---

66 *Ramban, Devarim* 33:2.

67 *Chiddushei Mahara"tz Chajes* to *Beitzah* ad loc.

68 *Shemos Rabbah, Ki Sisa* 42.

69 See *Matnos Kehunah* and *Eitz Yosef* ad loc.

I believe we can thus address *Tosafos*'s question on the following Gemara:

> *They found Rabbi Chanina ben Teradiyon while he sat teaching Torah in public, with a Torah scroll in his arms. They seized him and wrapped him in the Torah scroll, surrounded him with twigs, and set them on fire. They brought sponges soaked in water and placed them on his heart to delay his death...his students asked him, "Our master, what do you see?" He said to them, "Pages burn, but the letters escape."*[70]

Tosafos are troubled by the students' assumption that Rabbi Chanina saw something. Rabbi Chanina made no comment or any other indication. What prompted them to ask, "What do you see?" I believe they were not asking whether he was seeing something physical with his eyes. Rather, they were asking what he perceived, in his heart and mind, for the future of the Jewish People. Suffering under the harsh Roman subjugation, his students saw a bleak future ahead. As their master was passing on to the next world, leaving them bereft of his leadership, they anxiously asked if Rabbi Chanina could offer any words of comfort and hope for their future.

Rabbi Chanina indeed reassured them. While it is true that "pages burn," and evil despots can issue decrees aimed at weakening Jewish bodies, the beating heart and soul of the Jewish People can never be destroyed—"the letters escape." Chazal taught that each Jew is a Torah scroll: "One who is present at the time of death is obligated to tear [his garment]. To what is this compared? To one who sees a Torah scroll being burned."[71] A Jew's body is like the parchment of a Torah, while his soul is compared to the letters of Torah.[72] Rabbi Chanina promised his students that while the letters must temporarily disperse, they will

---

70 *Avodah Zarah* 18a.

71 *Shabbos* 105b.

72 See *Meor Einayim, Parashas Va'eschanan*; *Kedushas Levi, Parashas Bamidbar*; *Nefesh Hachaim, shaar* 4, ch. 11; and *Pnei Yehoshua, Kiddushin* 30.

ultimately come back together again—public teaching of Torah will once again take place and Torah will never be forgotten.

Our steadfast commitment and dedication to Torah, even at times of great challenge and darkness, will serve to hasten our redemption. With this in mind, let us take a look at another set of statements in Chazal:

> *A miracle occurred to Nikanor's doors and they were mentioned with praise.*[73]

> *All the gates of the Beis Hamikdash were converted to gold, except the doors of Nikanor, because miracles occurred to them.*[74]

Miracles in the Beis Hamikdash were commonplace. In addition to the ten miracles enumerated in *Pirkei Avos*,[75] we find that the Beis Hamikdash, rather than needing sunlight, itself illuminated its surroundings;[76] the *Aron* did not occupy physical space;[77] and other recurring wonders.[78] What then was so special about the miracles associated with Nikanor's gates, such that they were never replaced, even when all the other doors were upgraded to gold?

Chazal tell us more about the miracle of Nikanor's doors:

> *When Nikanor went to bring doors from Alexandria in Egypt, on his return, a storm arose in the sea to drown him. They took one of the doors and cast it into the sea. And still the sea did not rest from its rage. They sought to cast the other and he stood and embraced it and said to them, "Cast me with it!" Immediately, the sea rested from its rage, and he was pained about the other door. When they arrived at the port of Akko it was poking out under the sides of the ship.*[79]

---

73 *Yoma* 37a.
74 Ibid., 38a.
75 *Avos* 5:5.
76 *Menachos* 86b.
77 *Megillah* 10b.
78 *Yoma* 21a.
79 Ibid., 38a.

Nikanor's actions appear, at first glance, to be reckless and suicidal. Surely, he did not expect to convince his fellow passengers to risk their lives to save his door. Moreover, rather than try to convince them to keep the door, he asked to be thrown in with the second door. Why? What benefit would there be in his drowning?

Nikanor was teaching us an important lesson. When a storm is raging, threatening to drown us and everything we hold dear, we are called upon to summon unnatural reserves of dedication and sacrifice. At those dark moments, when the harshest decrees threaten to drown us—our nation's physical and spiritual existence—and some might suggest that our only salvation is to lighten our ship's burden by tossing the doors overboard, we are to wrap ourselves around those doors and ask to be cast with them, just as Nikanor did. Nikanor's doors were never changed, to remind us of this message.

This obligation persists, especially during our times. Toward the end of our exile, when one door—our ability to serve Hashem in the Beis Hamikdash—has already been eliminated, we must cling to the second door—Torah study—with all our might. If we do so, demonstrating our love for Hashem and the joy of Torah, we will be fortunate enough to reach shore and see the other door poking out from under the side of the ship.

> *And Hashem's glory will be revealed, and all life will see, together, that the mouth of Hashem has spoken.*[80]

---

80 *Yeshayahu* 40:5.

TEN

Upon Our Salvation and the Redemption of Our Souls

I. A Call to Service

So unique and transformational is the mitzvah of remembering and recounting *yetzias Mitzrayim* that it has the power to elevate one to the greatest of heights at the Seder.

We cited above Rabbi Naftali of Ropshitz's teaching, that the phrase we use in Kiddush, "*Techilah l'mikra'ei kodesh, zecher l'yetzias Mitzrayim*—It is the first of consecrated days, a remembrance of the Exodus," can be read as "*Techilah l'mikra'ei kodesh*—One's initial call to holiness," is contingent on "*zecher l'yetzias Mitzrayim*—remembering the Exodus.[1] How does this work?

To be saved is to become indebted to one's savior. Rabbeinu Yonah uses this idea to explain the Gemara's pronouncement that "one who connects redemption [i.e. the blessing "*Ga'al Yisrael*—He Who redeemed Israel"] to his prayer is guaranteed a place in the World to Come."[2] In invoking Hashem's redemption of His people, one acknowledges the

1 See *Haggadah Shel Pesach Divrei Chaim* of the Tzanzer Rebbe.

2 *Berachos* 4b.

kindness He showed us when removing us from Egypt. By turning immediately to prayer, which is *avodah*, "service," we demonstrate our recognition that we are in His debt and must now serve Him loyally. A place in the World to Come is thus a natural result of one's full awareness—and actualization—of his obligation to the Almighty.

That we should serve Hashem was the very purpose of our salvation, expressed early on to Moshe, "When you take the nation from Egypt you shall serve Hashem on this mountain."[3] Service of Hashem—Who is infinite and has no needs that we can supply—is defined by Chazal repeatedly as prayer: "'And you shall serve Hashem'—this refers to reciting *Shema* and prayer,"[4] and "What is service of the heart? This can only be prayer."[5] By bringing to fruition Hashem's intention that we should serve Him, the individual secures for himself a place in the World to Come.

II. The Power of Trust

We previously mentioned Rabbeinu Yonah's second explanation for the great award promised to one who connects "redemption" and "prayer." By invoking the great kindness Hashem already delivered on our behalf, and then immediately praying for his material needs, one shows firm trust that Hashem will indeed provide for him, just as He did for our ancestors in Egypt. *Yetzias Mitzrayim* is the foundation of *emunah*, "belief"; while *bitachon*, "trust" is the testing ground for that belief.

What is the difference between *emunah* and *bitachon*, between faith in His existence and trust in Him? Some have proposed that the teachings of the great Chassidic masters conflict with the definitions set forth by the Chazon Ish in his famous work on the subject. I believe this to be an error. Let us review their respective comments:

Students of the Baal Shem Tov taught, in his name, that the *pasuk*, "And one who trusts in Hashem will be surrounded by kindness,"

---

3 *Shemos* 3:12.

4 *Bava Kama* 92b.

5 *Taanis* 2a.

promises that a person who fully trusts in Hashem is protected by His angels every step of his life and no harm can befall him.[6] So much so that the forces of destruction cannot reach him even if it was already decreed that he should be harmed.

According to the Chazon Ish, on the other hand, one who faces a hardship and, due to his or her trust in Hashem, simply expects that everything will work out favorably, is making a mistake. After all, if we believe in a Divinely ordained cause and effect, and subscribe to a world of rules and consequences, why should the individual assume that Hashem will help him? Rather, a person, when confronting a challenge, should be cognizant and fearful of Hashem's judgment and pray for mercy. In the Chazon Ish's view, *bitachon*—trust in Hashem, is the practical expression of one's *emunah*—faith. The abstract concept of "faith"—that there is a single Hashem Who controls everything at all times—must be accompanied by a corresponding conviction that indeed He can change any outcome, no matter how dire a situation. In the face of fully developed trust in Hashem, probability vanishes: Hashem can bring healing even to someone whose "chances of survival" have been deemed nonexistent by the medical profession. But one does not have any right to assume that indeed such will be his or her outcome if he or she is undeserving.[7]

I do not think these positions are necessarily inconsistent. Rather, trusting in Him, in the manner prescribed by the Chazon Ish, has the power to effect the outcomes promised by the Baal Shem Tov's teachings. Rav Chaim Volozhiner writes:

> *Truthfully, there is a great matter and a wondrous treasure that eliminates other judgments and forces, such that they cannot control him, nor have any effect at all. When a person fixes it in his heart that, after all, Hashem is the true Master and there is no other power in the universe nor in all the worlds at all, other than Him, and everything is filled only with His*

6 See *Toldos Yaakov Yosef*, *Parashas Miketz* and other works of the Baal Shem Tov's students.

7 *Emunah U'Bitachon*, ch. 2.

> *simple unity, and, in his heart he completely nullifies all others, and does not attend to any power or will in the universe, while affixing his thoughts purely on the One and Only Hashem, then He will in turn make it happen, that all powers and forces in the universe will be nullified from upon him and they will not be able to affect him in any way at all.*[8]

It seems reasonable that the Chazon Ish did not dissent from Rav Chaim Volozhiner's teaching, which most certainly represented the views of the latter's teacher, the Vilna Gaon. Indeed, the Chazon Ish himself adds that:

> *Bitachon has the power to bring upon the person who trusts in Him a holy spirit that accompanies him with the bold knowledge that Hashem will in fact help him. As David HaMelech said, "If you encamp an army against me, I shall not fear; if you wage war against me, in this I shall trust."*[9]

Thus, any disagreement between the views of the Chazon Ish and the Chassidic masters is far more nuanced. Certainly, one who trusts in Hashem will be enveloped in His kindness, but achieving such lofty confidence is the work of a lifetime and varies according to each individual's accomplishments. The promises of the Chassidic masters were directed at those who believe and trust in Hashem with every fiber of their being, whose lives are infused with a constant awareness of Hashem's presence, and who have reached the highest levels of self-perfection. According to the Chazon Ish, it is the greatness and holiness of the individual—on all fronts—that will determine whether the assurance applies to him, while the Chassidic teaching suggests that it depends solely on the strength of one's *bitachon*.

Indeed, many sources point to the idea that unwavering trust has the power to safeguard one from harm even when he is otherwise unworthy of such protection.

---

8 *Nefesh Hachaim, shaar* 3, ch. 12.

9 *Emunah U'Bitachon* 2:7.

Sefer Ha'ikarim explains the above *pasuk* this way:

> *"And one who trusts in Hashem will be surrounded by kindness"—which is to say, even if he is not deserving in his own right, it is the manner of bitachon to bring kindness upon those who trust in Him.*[10]

We find this idea already in Chazal:

> *"Many pains afflict the wicked, and one who trusts in Hashem will be surrounded by kindness." Rabbi Eliezer and Rabbi Tanchum taught in the name of Rabbi Yirmiyah: even a wicked person will be surrounded by kindness if he trusts in Hashem.*[11]

Each of us is prepared to profess complete faith in Hashem and in the miracles He did for His people when taking them out of Egypt. But the true test of these declarations comes only when one is faced with challenges in his or her own life, when he is willing to lean on Hashem and entrust to Him all concerns for ongoing and daily needs. Thus, Rabbeinu Yonah teaches, Chazal assured us that one who connects *geulah*, the recounting of *yetzias Mitzrayim*, which is our affirmation of belief, with *tefillah*, articulating absolute dependence on Hashem by expressing one's full trust that He will provide, is guaranteed a place in the World to Come. Such a person has achieved a lofty level of awareness of Hashem and His involvement in our lives.

III. Salvation of the Soul

Rabbeinu Yonah offered two explanations for Chazal's promise: either that connecting redemption and prayer demonstrates my subservience to Hashem or that turning to Him signifies my trust in His power to provide my needs. In both approaches, Rabbeinu Yonah stresses that to recall the Exodus from Egypt is not simply to commemorate a historic event, but to internalize a message. Daily, our recollection of *yetzias Mitzrayim* and acknowledgment of Hashem's role in our lives are to

10 *Sefer Ha'ikarim* IV, ch. 46.

11 *Yalkut Shimoni, Tehillim* 32:10.

thoroughly transform us—our mundane activities and life decisions. Indeed, Chazal taught that "in every generation, a person must see himself as having left Egypt,"[12] which the Rambam paraphrases as, "In every generation, a person must demonstrate that he himself left Egypt at this moment."[13] Remembering our nation's miraculous birth is only the start; the goal of doing so is to transform oneself into a new person.

Rabbi Yisrael of Ruzhin teaches that *bedikas chametz*, searching for the chametz, represents identifying our unhealthy characteristics, our internal chametz. This is done at night, alluding to the fact that in the darkness of our exile we cannot vanquish the forces of evil entirely. Only when the sun shines with the arrival of Mashiach will we be able to burn the chametz—eradicate evil completely.[14] Destroying the internal chametz is part and parcel of the Rambam's instruction that one must actively "demonstrate that he has left Egypt."

Chametz has a unique status. It is one of only two items we are commanded to destroy—no remnant may remain in our possession. Chametz and idolatry must both be completely eradicated. Idolatry represents the *yetzer hara*, reflected in one's desires to choose his own master rather than be answerable to One God. This is the very essence of our internal chametz, our personal barriers to greatness. Chametz and idolatry therefore share several attributes and requirements: both must be nullified, burned, and removed from one's possession. Rooting out the physical chametz is a Torah obligation before Pesach starts, and conquering one's personal chametz is an essential element of remembering *yetzias Mitzrayim* and the fundamental goal of the Seder.

As we welcome Shabbos each week, we sing in *Lechah Dodi* the phrase "*Karvah el nafshi ge'alah*—Draw near to my soul; redeem it." According to the Baal Shem Tov, these words, which originate in *Tehillim*,[15] teach of our individual power to hasten the final redemption. Each of us is submerged in a personal exile, enslaved to the natural impulses we were

12 Mishnah, *Pesachim* 10:5.

13 *Mishneh Torah*, Laws of Chametz and Matzah 7:6.

14 See *Knesses Yisrael* and *Oros Yisrael* on Pesach.

15 *Tehillim* 69:19.

created with. As we confront our weaknesses, tame our instincts, and refine our characters, we not only experience a private exodus, but we also bring the great redemption a little bit closer.[16]

Indeed, *yetzias Mitzrayim*, the archetypical redemption, itself included two stages—a physical exodus followed by spiritual elevation. The Ramban names *Sefer Bereishis*, "*Sefer Hayetzirah*—The Book of Creation," consistent with his approach that everything recorded about our forefathers and their actions is intended to serve as a roadmap for future generations.[17] The great deeds of Avraham, Yitzchak, and Yaakov created a spiritual infrastructure that continues to sustain their descendants for all time. Hence, the entirety of *Bereishis* describes things coming into being—beginning with the creation of the universe and closing as Yosef HaTzaddik closes his eyes for the last time. Similarly, *Sefer Shemos* is "*Sefer Ha'galus V'Ha'geulah*—The Book of Exile and Redemption," even though the Exodus is seemingly complete one third of the way through the book. To the Ramban, however, redemption has no meaning until B'nei Yisrael reclaim the stature of their ancestors. Only upon accepting the Torah and building a sanctuary in which the Divine Presence could dwell among them are they indeed a free people. Deliverance from slavery was only stage one of their redemption; stage two occurred when their spirits were fully imbued with Hashem and His Torah. Thus, all of *Shemos* describes redemption, culminating with the consecration of the *Mishkan* at its very end.

According to the *Sefas Emes*, these phases are reflected in the respective miracles of leaving Egypt proper and the splitting of the sea thereafter.[18] Their bodies were freed from physical subjugation when they marched out of Egypt, but it was the salvation at the sea that raised their souls and brought them close to Hashem. Chazal taught that our faith was still weak as we crossed the seabed. Famously, it wasn't until Nachshon ben Aminadav jumped in that the rest of the nation was

16 *Toldos Yaakov Yosef, Parashas Vayechi.*

17 See *Ramban, Bereishis*, end of *Vayechi*.

18 See *Sefas Emes al HaTorah, Beshalach* (5645).

willing to wade into the sea,[19] and even upon crossing, they worried that "just as we came up on the other side, so shall the Egyptians."[20] Only after seeing their miraculous salvation and corresponding destruction of Egypt was their faith secure, their souls elevated from spiritual slavery, to the extent that "a maidservant at the sea saw that which Yechezkel ben Buzi did not see."[21] Whether the spiritual redemption occurred at the sea, or extended until the *Mishkan* stood (as per the Ramban), our understanding and remembrance of *yetzias Mitzrayim* must also reflect the personal transformation inherent to *geulah*—redemption.

IV. The Journey of Redemption

Each of the holidays commemorates a phase of *yetzias Mitzrayim*; indeed, in both the prayers and Kiddush for every holiday we include the statement "a remembrance of *yetzias Mitzrayim*." Pesach begins with relating our physical exit from Egypt; the seventh day of Pesach is the anniversary of the splitting of the sea; Shavuos commemorates the covenant at Sinai; and Sukkos represents an interim stage—the mode in which Hashem protected us while we traveled from Egypt toward Sinai.

Personal growth likewise involves three stages. First, one must leave Egypt—abandon bad habits and improper behavior. Lofty heights cannot be reached when one is stuck in the mud at the bottom of the ladder:

> *The Dubno Maggid would illustrate this idea by way of a rural farmer who was envious of his city-dwelling friends and relatives. While he wore a bulky coat that enveloped his body like a blanket, they were adorned with finely tailored, well-fitting clothes. Eventually, having saved up enough money to purchase a fine coat, he traveled to the city, and, entering the tailor's shop, asked to try on a suit. Attempting unsuccessfully to put on the fine garment he was proffered, he accosted the salesman for having given him the wrong size. Immediately seeing the farmer's mistake, the salesman pointed out that the farmer was*

---

19 *Pirkei D'Rabi Eliezer*, ch. 42.

20 *Pesachim* 118b.

21 *Mechilta, Beshalach* 15:2.

still wearing his own heavy coat. Unless he removed the bulky, ill-fitting garment, he should not expect to don a fine suit. Likewise, until one cleanses himself of his bad habits, a burden accumulated over repeated poor choices, he should not expect to be able to properly elevate himself with Torah and mitzvos.

But before he reaches that stage whereby his body and soul are infused with holiness, rejoicing at every opportunity to connect with the Divine, there is an interim phase, that of preparation. To meaningfully perform a mitzvah and realize its full opportunity, one must take time to contemplate it, understand its purpose, and anticipate its fulfillment. As the author of the *Chayei Adam* comments: "I tested this myself—when I did a mitzvah without due preparation, I did not fulfill it properly."[22]

Throughout the teachings of *Chassidus*, we find tremendous emphasis on the importance of *hachanah*—preparation and anticipation before prayer or a mitzvah. Some even suggest that, in certain ways, preparation is greater than the mitzvah itself. Chazal refer to the first day of Sukkos as "the first day of counting sins," because the days between Yom Kippur, when we are cleansed of all prior sin, and Sukkos, when we take the lulav and sit in the Sukkah for the first time, are consumed with preparation for the mitzvos of the holiday. So imbued with holiness are these days of anticipation that there is no possibility of sin.[23]

According to the Ritva, the importance of preparation is one of the reasons we are required to say the blessing upon a mitzvah specifically *in advance* of the prescribed act. As mental preparation, the blessing must precede the physical fulfillment. A mitzvah done without preparation is indeed a different action.

Chazal relate that Rabbi Akiva was apprehended and sentenced to death by Roman authorities for teaching Torah unlawfully:

At the time that Rabbi Akiva was led out to his death it was time to recite the Shema. While they were combing his flesh

22 *Chayei Adam, klal* 28:25.

23 *Sefas Emes, Parashas Haazinu* (5634).

> *with steel combs, he was accepting upon himself the yoke of Heaven. His students asked him, "Our teacher, to such an extent?" He said to them, "My whole life I struggled with the words 'with all your soul'—even if He takes your soul. I wondered when I might have an opportunity to fulfill it. Now that it has arrived, should I not fulfill it?"*[24]

What was so surprising to Rabbi Akiva's students about their master's devotion? Surely, they must have learned with him Chazal's interpretation of the *pasuk* "with all your heart and all your soul" and knew that its words were a call for *mesirus nefesh*—self-sacrifice to sanctify Hashem's name. Indeed, I believe their question to Rabbi Akiva was not why he was reciting the *Shema*, but rather how: how was it possible for Rabbi Akiva to attain such unfathomable stature and greatness of character, that even in the face of unspeakable torture he lovingly accepted Hashem's absolute Kingship? In fact, according to some views, Rabbi Akiva was laughing at this time as well, further fueling their astonishment.[25] Rabbi Akiva replied that his intense focus was no momentary outpouring of devotion—rather, his entire life's work was being put to the test. One does not achieve such greatness in one moment! "My whole life I struggled with these words—I have spent a lifetime preparing for this opportunity." Preparation is what enabled Rabbi Akiva to enthusiastically sanctify Hashem's name when the time came, and preparation is a true mark of one's personal efforts to give meaning to everything he or she does.

Each holiday bears a unique character and individual message. If Pesach represents the abandoning of evil by leaving Egypt, and Shavuos connotes our embracing of that which is good and right (the Torah), then Sukkos celebrates preparation—the stage that lays the groundwork for all spiritual accomplishment—by reminding us of our travel toward Sinai in anticipation of Hashem revealing Himself to His people.

---

24 *Berachos* 61b.

25 *Yerushalmi, Berachos* 9:5, and *Sotah* 5:5.

Even within the laws of Pesach itself, we might notice the significance attached to preparation. Matzos must be prepared and baked with explicit intent for the mitzvah one fulfills when eating them, and Chazal even forbade eating matzah before Pesach to ensure our anticipation and excitement will not be dulled in any way.

V. A Long Journey Indeed

Each year, Nissan approaches and we prepare to remember, discuss, and celebrate *yetzias Mitzrayim*. We are also prompted to marvel at the curiosity of commemorating events that occurred millennia ago. Not only have the wonders of the Exodus long since passed, but that exhilarating freedom we initially enjoyed is all but forgotten, leading the author of the *Bnei Yissaschar* to write, nearly two hundred years ago, that the current, final exile—*galus Edom*—is even worse than the slavery of Egypt.[26] In the intervening years since that comment was put to print, we have experienced the most horrendous of tragedies. So hidden was Hashem's presence that the most concerted attempt in history to eradicate the Jewish nation nearly succeeded.

And yet, even in the shadow of death and through all the blood and tears, we always remembered *yetzias Mitzrayim*, conducting barely recognizable *Sedarim* at which we sang and praised Hashem for His miracles and kindness. My father, *zt"l*, would often speak of the Pesach he spent during the Holocaust with the Klausenberger Rebbe, *zt"l*, when a handful of simple, devout Jews risked their lives to bake matzos for the Seder. How are we to understand our own commitment to this annual remembrance, irrespective of anything else—good or otherwise—that we may be experiencing?

In response to this question, Rabbi Yosef Shaul Natanzon offered the following illustration:

> *A poor Jew was once deeply distressed by his lot in life—but not due to his material deprivation or the difficulty of making ends meet. He was pained that he did not have time to learn Torah,*

26 *Bnei Yissaschar, Adar, maamar* 3, *drush* 4.

> *nor the wherewithal to properly educate and raise his children to study Torah. One day, Hashem answered his prayers, and he became a wealthy man. Indeed, he took advantage of his fortune in the manner he had previously aspired to, studying Torah day and night and ensuring his children were immersed in Torah and devotion. And every year, on the anniversary of the day he became rich, he invited his friends and family to a festive celebration, giving recognition and thanks to Hashem for his great privilege. However, as is so often the case, the wheels of fortune turned, and the Jew was once again reduced to poverty. His family members feared that the day previously reserved for celebration would this year be marked as a day of pain and mourning. To their surprise, on that day, the Jew once again invited his friends and family and they enjoyed a meager celebration together, exhibiting the same joy as ever. Eventually, his children found their voices and inquired about the celebration. "After all, the years of plenty are gone and you are now a poor man—what are you celebrating?"*
>
> *"True," their father answered, "my money is no more, but the Torah we learned, the home we established, these are everlasting—the wheel of fortune does not take them away with it."*

This, concludes Rabbi Nathanson, characterizes our celebration on Pesach. *Yetzias Mitzrayim* led us to Har Sinai, where we became a nation and received the Torah. Torah is ours forever, remaining with us wherever our travels and travails have led, through blood, tears, and the smoldering ruins of homes we were forced to abandon. Our relationship with Hashem and His Torah are constant; unshakeable and immutable for all time and in all places. This is the celebration of Pesach and the reason we rejoice, come what may.

ELEVEN

Pesach and Parah: Two Mysteries

"May I wholeheartedly follow Your statutes"— these are the laws of Pesach and of the Red Cow.[1]

Yearning for a purity of spirit that is apparently necessary to fulfill these two mitzvos, David HaMelech connects the laws of Pesach and those of the *parah adumah*, the "red heifer," whose ashes are used to purify those who are *tamei*, ritually unclean, due to contact with a dead person. How are these mitzvos similar and why do they, in particular and more than other obligations, call for wholehearted commitment?

I believe that it is not the similarity of, but rather the contrast between these mitzvos that prompted David HaMelech's prayer. Pesach and *parah* are remarkably different. At the Seder, we are commanded to ask questions, to probe the depths of its myriad obligations and to contemplate the meaning of the night. Even the most inarticulate and unaware of participants at the table must be encouraged to inquire about

1 *Shemos Rabbah* 19:2, commenting on *Tehillim* 119:80.

the goings-on, using whatever simple language he or she can muster. *Parah adumah* could not be more different. Shrouded in mystery, this mitzvah, which is called "the statue of the Torah," is impenetrable even to individuals who have otherwise mastered the secrets of Torah and of all creation. Shlomo HaMelech, the wisest of men, wished to understand *parah adumah* and found it beyond his reach.

Sometimes the Jew is required to ask questions, and at other times he may not. Pesach demands inquiry; *parah adumah* forbids it. A Jew's wholeness, the completeness of his relationship with Hashem, lies in his ability to resolve these contradictory themes, and perhaps even embrace the complexity of Hashem's world. Such was the essence of David HaMelech's desire to "wholeheartedly follow" these two contrasting mitzvos.

So, how are we to know? At which times is it appropriate to probe and challenge, and when are we called to silent obedience?

Avraham Avinu taught us the answer to this question. After stopping Avraham Avinu from carrying out His instruction to bring Yitzchak as an offering, Hashem stated: "For now I know that you are a God-fearing person."[2] According to Chazal, it was only at this point that Avraham Avinu began to question Hashem's initial instruction, challenging Him to reconcile the command to slaughter Yitzchak with the earlier assurance that Yitzchak would succeed Avraham and continue his legacy. Avraham Avinu did not raise these objections at the more obvious moment—when Hashem first instructed him to take Yitzchak to the mountain and sacrifice him. At that time, when Hashem's call to action was in force and immediate, there was no room for questioning. Now, when the command was reversed and Hashem had told him to stop in his tracks, Avraham could engage with Hashem and attempt to understand His intent.

Chazal teach that when B'nei Yisrael at Sinai "preceded '*Naaseh*—We will do' before '*Nishma*—We will listen,' six hundred thousand angels came and adorned each Jew with two crowns—one for 'we will do' and

---

2 *Bereishis* 22:12.

one for 'we will listen.'" As emphasized in Chazal's wording, the crowns were earned by virtue of the fact that one affirmation preceded its counterpart. Yet, that was a single act; there are two ways to sequence a pair of statements and they chose one. Even if their selection was the laudable one and deserving of recognition, why should they receive two crowns?

The answer is that B'nei Yisrael in fact made two separate commitments. Their choice of sequence carried a double statement—it was not merely about which clause is more important. Placing "doing" before "listening" represents the *parah adumah*, which we fulfill while knowing we cannot understand its meaning. At the same time, having "listening" *after* "doing" represents the mitzvos of Pesach, an entire event organized around our desire to question, to probe, and to understand more about Hashem, His miracles, and His Torah. Our ancestors' proclamation of "we will do and we will listen" was therefore glorious, not only in its promise of unquestioning adherence to the Torah, but also in their desire to come back after fulfilling the mitzvos, to learn and understand whatever secrets He wishes to reveal to His children. This double commitment earned B'nei Yisrael two crowns, for *naaseh*, "we will do," and for *nishma*, "we will listen."

Much of our time we engage in the laws of *parah*—we follow and fulfill without challenge or question. At the Seder we experience the laws of Pesach, taking full advantage of this transcendent evening to probe, to ask, to explore, and, ultimately, to gain insight.

TWELVE

"Ba'avur Zeh—For This!"

One passage from the Torah—not even a complete *pasuk*—appears and reappears as a continuous theme throughout the Seder. We repeat the words, "It is because of this that Hashem did for me when I went out of Egypt,"[1] four times in the Haggadah. In response to the *rasha,* the wicked son, we emphasize "for me" to suggest that he, having excluded himself from the community, would not have been saved. We then use this passage to prompt even the *tam,* the unaware son, the one who cannot articulate a question. It is this *pasuk* that teaches us to each year reexperience the Exodus ourselves, and the word "*zeh*—it" reflects the immediacy of the moment: we are to relate the story of *yetzias Mitzrayim* in the presence of matzah and *maror*, as we are about to fulfill the obligations to eat them. Clearly, its prevalence at the Seder suggests that this *pasuk* is central to the evening's mission.[2]

Indeed, we discussed above the desired progression from recalling the events of *yetzias Mitzrayim* to recognizing our resulting debt and

1 *Shemos* 13:8.

2 See *Haggadah Shel Pesach Minchas Asher*, where we discuss the disagreement among Rishonim as to the proper reading of "*Ba'avur zeh asah Hashem li b'tzeitsi MiMitzrayim.*" According to the Ramban and Rav Saadia Gaon, "*zeh*" refers to the matzah and *maror*, which are being eaten to commemorate the events of *yetzias Mitzrayim*. Hence, the *pasuk* reads, "This [matzah and *maror*] is on account of this that Hashem did for me when I left Egypt." Rashi however reads the *pasuk* without reference to matzah and *maror*, but rather the "*zeh*" simply describes our service of Hashem: "Hashem did for me when I left Egypt so that I will fulfill His commandments."

obligation to Hashem. The Torah expressly demands this association, "for B'nei Yisrael are servants to Me—they are My servants that I took out from Egypt,"[3] and Chazal drive the point home: "I took you out on this condition—that you accept My Kingship."[4] And, we know well that our daily obligation to remember *yetzias Mitzrayim*, the third paragraph of *Shema*, concludes with the affirmation that Hashem took us from Egypt "to be your God." If each of us is required to relive the Exodus year after year, then we are likewise each obligated to renew our acceptance of His kingship and our obligation to Him at the Seder every year.

Thus, four sons gather at the Seder table. They are all happy to be there, to enjoy the company and recount the miracles and wonders of *yetzias Mitzrayim*. But only the wise son understands the implications of these events. He immediately inquires after the consequent obligations: "What are the statutes and rules?" The wicked son, by contrast, objects to the onerous rituals that he is asked to repeat year after year.[5] We rebuke him, noting that, indeed, we left Egypt for the very purpose of fulfilling Hashem's commandments at all times; the person who, rather than embrace the opportunity to serve Hashem, sees the mitzvos as a burden would have remained a slave to Pharaoh.

And when we engage the son who cannot ask any questions, who barely understands what is happening around him, we approach him with the same message. Hashem took us from Egypt to keep His mitzvos. Even while the son cannot yet appreciate the events of *yetzias Mitzrayim* or their meaning, we nevertheless train him to observe the mitzvos and serve Hashem wholeheartedly.

---

3 *Vayikra* 25:55.

4 *Pesikta Zutrasa* (*Midrash Lekach Tov*), *Parashas Shelach* (*Bamidbar* 113a in Buber edition) and cited in *Rashi*.

5 See *Yerushalmi*, *Pesachim* 70b.

THIRTEEN

Accept My Decrees!

For B'nei Yisrael are servants to Me—they are My servants that I took out from Egypt.[1]

I am Hashem, your God, Who brought you out of the land of Egypt to be for you a God, I am Hashem your God.[2]

Rashi, citing Chazal: "On this condition I redeemed you—that you should accept My decrees."[3]

Each name of Hashem alludes to a mode in which He interacts with His creation. The name *Yud-Hei-Vav-Hei* represents conduct of kindness and mercy, while *Elokim* characterizes judgment. We must believe, as a fundamental tenet of our faith, that everything Hashem does is just and for our good. "*Ani Hashem Elokeichem*"—there is but One Hashem, Who is both just and merciful. As we learned above, this unshakeable faith and fortitude is

1 *Vayikra* 25:55.

2 *Bamidbar* 15:41.

3 *Rashi, Bamidbar* 15:41, citing *Pesikta Zutrasa*.

a hallmark of *tzaddikim* across time, from Rabbi Akiva, who proclaimed, "Everything Hashem does is for the good," to my holy teacher, the Klausenberger Rebbe, *zt"l*, who, despite losing his wife and eleven children in the Holocaust, told me that he never once questioned Hashem's will for a moment.

When a Jew is confronted with challenges, even of the most extreme nature, he is not to question Hashem's plan, but rather he should do whatever he can to immerse himself in Torah and mitzvos. Such devotion is displayed in a question that was posed to Rabbi Ephraim Oshry in the Kovno ghetto:

> *As Pesach 5702 (1942) approached, Reb Moshe Goldkorn sought to ensure that the Kovno community would be able to obtain some matzos for the Seder. As holder of a permit allowing him to go in and out of the ghetto periodically, he was able to secure a small amount of flour from a local Lithuanian outside the ghetto. On Erev Pesach however, a Nazi officer, discovering Reb Moshe's oven and makeshift matzah operation, struck Reb Moshe with merciless beatings. Blood dripping from his face, Reb Moshe stumbled to Rabbi Ephraim Oshry's door. Terrified at seeing Reb Moshe in such a state and having heard his story, Rabbi Oshry listened to Reb Moshe's question. But Reb Moshe did not ask the rav why Hashem was doing this to His people, or why his own efforts to fulfill the mitzvah had been thus thwarted. Instead, he asked what he should do about eating the matzah—would he be allowed to soak his matzah in water before eating it? As a Chassid, his family's custom was not to eat matzah that touched water on Pesach, but now that he had lost his teeth due to the Nazi's beating, he would be unable to chew the dry matzah!*[4]

We did not survive our trials and tribulations by having all the answers. We are still here today, having outlived so many of our tormentors,

---

4 *She'eilos U'Teshuvos Mimaamakim*, vol. 5, ch. 6.

because we ask questions like that of Reb Moshe Goldkorn. With unshakeable faith and unwavering focus, we accept that which is beyond our comprehension and pursue what is demanded of us.

FOURTEEN

Remember This Day

At the Seder, we are commanded to recount the events of *yetzias Mitzrayim*. But we are also obligated to remember the Exodus daily, morning and evening—which we fulfill when reciting the *Shema*. How do these two distinct requirements complement each other?[1]

Recalling the miracles of our salvation from Egypt and acknowledging their impact on us takes two forms. One consequence of remembering *yetzias Mitzrayim* is our acceptance of Hashem as our King and our Master. As we cited above, the Torah expressly states: "For B'nei Yisrael are servants to Me—they are My servants that I took out from Egypt,"[2] and Chazal comment that we were taken out of Egypt on condition that we are to accept His Kingship. Hashem saved us for a purpose, and it is incumbent upon us to understand and realize that mission.

Additionally, the events of *yetzias Mitzrayim* and the wonders Hashem did for us all demand that we rejoice and praise Him for His everlasting kindness. David HaMelech called for every person who experiences a personal salvation to "thank Hashem for His kindness and publicize it to people." How much more so, then, when we recollect Hashem's

1 See also *Minchas Asher*, *Pesachim*, ch. 82, where we addressed this well-known question through its halachic lens.

2 *Vayikra* 25:55.

intervention with nature to save an entire people and form them into a kingdom of priests and a holy nation!

Every day of the year, we remember *yetzias Mitzrayim* to help us accept Hashem's commandments and our obligation to Him. Indeed, Chazal appended the daily recollection of *yetzias Mitzrayim* to the two paragraphs of *Shema* for this very reason—the three sections correspond to and complement each other. We declare our belief in One God, articulate our obligation to Him for having taken us from slavery, and reaffirm our commitment to serve Him faithfully.[3]

At the Seder, however, we go further than acknowledging our submission to Hashem. On this evening, we sing the songs of *Hallel* and *Nirtzah*. Tonight, *yetzias Mitzrayim* inspires in us joy, celebration, and songs of praise and gratitude.

Indeed, the obligation of the Seder explicitly includes a requirement to talk about the miracles and wonders of *yetzias Mitzrayim*, not simply the fact of our exit from Egypt. The latter is fine for the daily remembrance, but at the Seder, when we are meant to sing to and praise Him for his kindness, we need to go further and recollect all the joy-inducing and uplifting details of the events.

---

3 Perhaps this is why the Rambam famously excluded the daily remembrance of *yetzias Mitzrayim* from his list of mitzvos. As a component of accepting *ol malchus Shamayim*, it was subsumed with the rest of *Shema* into a single mitzvah.

FIFTEEN

So That You Shall Remember

You shall not eat anything leavened with it; for seven days thereafter you shall eat unleavened bread, bread of affliction—for you departed from the land of Egypt hurriedly—so that you may remember the day of your departure from the land of Egypt as long as you live.[1]

Rashi: "So that you may remember—by eating the Pesach and matzah—the day of your departure."

Oddly, although this *pasuk* pertains to one's daily obligation to remember *yetzias Mitzrayim*, Rashi comments that eating the *Pesach* and matzah—which is only done once a year—will serve to remind us of *yetzias Mitzrayim*. So transcendent is the Seder, so laden with transformative opportunity, that eating matzah and *maror*

1 *Devarim* 16:3.

on this one night can supply the spiritual energy of *yetzias Mitzrayim* throughout the year. Thus, the Seder, with its unique mitzvos and captivating energy, offers a platform for infusing the message of *yetzias Mitzrayim* into our consciousness to such a level that later on, throughout the year, all one needs is the brief recollection of *yetzias Mitzrayim* to access that power of recognition achieved at the Seder. The Seder functions, in some sense, like the speed dial feature of a phone—by entering all the numbers in advance, one can later call the desired party with the press of a single button. Done properly, the Seder's lessons are readily summoned up later with the brief daily recitation of the third paragraph of *Shema*.

There is an ancient custom, cited by Acharonim, to preserve a piece of one's afikomen and hang it up on display in one's home.[2] Perhaps this custom developed to symbolize our idea—to demonstrate that after the Seder is complete, all one needs throughout the year is a small reminder of *yetzias Mitzrayim* to remain awake to its awesome implications.

To this end, it is not sufficient at the Seder to merely acknowledge the fact that we left Egypt. The requirements of the Seder include discussion of the events themselves and the miracles and wonders attendant to them. We are meant to be moved, inspired, and uplifted, and to experience the salvation ourselves. If we successfully reach that point, our daily remembrance of *yetzias Mitzrayim* will remain impactful throughout the year.

We have been emphasizing that a central purpose of remembering *yetzias Mitzrayim* is meant to be renewed acceptance of Hashem as our King and Master. This idea is alluded to in the *pesukim* "For B'nei Yisrael are servants to Me" and "I am Hashem your God," and spelled out by Chazal as a fundamental condition of *yetzias Mitzrayim*. A Chassidic teaching suggests that this is the message of the Haggadah's story about a group of Tanna'im who prolonged their Seder all night, stopping only when a group of students arrived and said to them, "Our masters, the time has come to read the morning *Shema*." The Tanna'im continued

2 See *Magen Avraham, Orach Chaim* 500:7, and *Shevus Yaakov* 3:52.

talking about the wonders of *yetzias Mitzrayim* until every last student heard the call to reaffirm Hashem's Kingship.

Two distinct pathways might lead one from relating stories of the Exodus to accepting the yoke of Heaven—modes of love and fear, respectively.

Chazal noted these different approaches. One midrash presents the relationship of coercion and fear:

> *Why is the Exodus from Egypt mentioned in connection with every mitzvah? An analogy: The son of a king's loved one was taken captive. When he [the king] redeems him, he redeems him not as a son, but as a servant, so that if he does not accept his decree, he can say to him, "You are my servant!" When they enter the province, he [the king] says to him, "Put on my sandals and carry my things before me to the bathhouse." The son begins to object, whereupon the king presents him with his writ of servitude and says to him, "You are my servant!" Thus, when the Holy One, blessed be He, redeemed the offspring of His loved one, He did not redeem them as sons, but as servants, so that if they reject His decree, He says to them, "You are My servants!" When they went to the desert, He began to decree upon them some light mitzvos and some formidable ones, such as Shabbos, illicit relations, tzitzis, and tefillin, and Israel began to object—whereupon He said to them, "You are My servants! On that condition I redeemed you; that I decree, and you fulfill!"*[3]

The servant dutifully fulfills the commands—after all, he is forever contractually bound to the king. He carries out the king's wishes in trembling and fear, meticulous to ensure he does not violate any condition of his freedom.

In parallel, Chazal offer a different paradigm:

> *Why were the ten commandments not stated at the beginning of the Torah? An analogy: A man enters a province and says*

3 *Sifri, Bamidbar* 115 (on the *pasuk* "I am Hashem your God Who took you out of Egypt…").

> *[to the inhabitants], "I will rule over you." They respond, "Did you do anything for us that you would rule over us?" Whereupon he builds the city wall for them, provides water for them, wages war for them, and then says, "I will rule over you," whereupon they respond, "Yes! Yes!" Thus, Hashem took Israel out of Egypt, split the sea for them, brought down manna for them, raised the well for them, brought in quail for them, waged war with Amalek for them, and then said to them, "I will rule over you," whereupon they responded, "Yes! Yes!"*[4]

In this model, B'nei Yisrael embrace their obligations to Hashem with love and joy, recognizing the tremendous kindness He has shown them.

Our daily mention of *yetzias Mitzrayim*, at the conclusion of *Shema*, represents the first avenue. "I am Hashem your God Who took you out of Egypt to be to you a God," describes a contract—we are obligated to Hashem as a condition of our salvation, just as the prince became his father's servant as a consequence of being saved. As Rashi comments on that very *pasuk*:

> *Why [are the words "I am Hashem your God"] stated again? In order that Israel should not say, "Why has Hashem said it? Is it not in order that we should perform the commandments and receive reward? We will not perform them, and we shall not receive any reward!" Therefore, it states again in general terms and without reference to the Exodus from Egypt, "I will be Hashem your God: in spite of yourselves I will be your King." In a similar sense it states, "Surely with a strong hand...will I reign over you."*[5]

Thus, there is no need, on a regular day or night, to recall the miracles and wonders of our departure from Egypt. These are entirely secondary to our central obligation to serve Hashem and obey His decrees.

---

4 *Mechilta, Parashas Yisro* (20:2).

5 *Rashi, Bamidbar* 15:41.

On the Seder night, however, we seek to attain the second pathway to our recognition of our commitment to Hashem—the relationship of loving subjects who willingly accept as their king the person who did so much for them. At the Seder we therefore recount every detail of His kindness, the miracles—small and big—He performed for us, and we call out "Yes! Yes!"—joyously singing His praises.

SIXTEEN

Remembering and Retelling

Our awareness of *yetzias Mitzrayim* and the obligations it places on us is informed by the two mitzvos we have been discussing. Daily remembrance of *yetzias Mitzrayim* and the annual event of relating its specific events and miracles at the Seder are woven together to promote a consciousness of our nation's formation and its relationship with Hashem.

Rabbi Isaac Sher, the great *baal mussar* and Rosh Yeshiva of Slabodka, once famously commented that we owe a debt of gratitude for those routine mitzvos—the daily obligations that we grow accustomed to fulfill every day without giving them much thought. True, the prophets warned us of the danger inherent to uninspired rote performance of mitzvos. But we should consider what our spiritual lives might look like if we were to actively serve Hashem only when moved to do so by deep inspiration and desire to draw near to Him. How often would we say *Shema* or put on tefillin if we were to wait for the "right" moment and perfect level of emotional engagement. Thus, we are indeed fortunate to have mitzvos that are part of our daily routine. With these mitzvos, opportunities to serve Hashem encounter us throughout our day—morning, afternoon, and evening.

And yet, while service of Hashem is surely meant to be infused with excitement and joy, human nature is such that daily activities do not elicit the same emotions as do those high points of one's calendar and life. Rather, serving Hashem properly and fully demands both elements, the routine and the special. Our daily lives need to be full of routine opportunities to serve Him, but we also need the rare mitzvos that can generate an emotive response and engage us more deeply.

Daily mitzvos inform our schedules and form our habits. A devout Jew acknowledges his Maker each morning in a dozen small ways before going about his affairs. Through the course of the day, pausing to pray and say blessings, he is constantly reminded that he is beholden to Hashem.

These daily efforts do not readily excite us. Activities that are repeated day after day, by their nature, do not create transformative or transcendent experiences. For that we need the special moments, the rare mitzvos we are privileged to fulfill only once a year. Such events we prepare for with great care, and, when the awaited moment arrives, we approach the mitzvah enthusiastically, embracing the opportunity to eat the matzah, discuss the events of *yetzias Mitzrayim*, and feel Hashem's love wash over us.

In this way, the obligations to remember *yetzias Mitzrayim* each day and to tell its story on Pesach complement each other. The former shapes our routines and our daily awareness, while the latter moves and inspires the Jew to greatness and to sense his personal relationship with Hashem and the history of the Jewish People.

SEVENTEEN

How I Made a Mockery of Egypt

In order that you may recount in the ears of your sons and of your sons' sons how I made a mockery of the Egyptians and how I displayed My signs among them—in order that you may know that I am Hashem.

Simply read, the *pasuk* teaches that we are meant to describe to our descendants how Hashem punished Egypt for enslaving and torturing His people.

However, I submit that this *pasuk* carries a deeper message as well. Let us begin with the Rambam's discussion of *teshuvah*:

> *And, it is possible that a man should commit either one grievous iniquity or a multitude of sins so that the Judge of Truth will decree against him that, whereas this sinner committed those sins of his own free will and consciously, repentance should be withheld from him altogether, and grant him no leave to repent, so that he might die and perish in the iniquity he committed...It is, therefore, written in the Torah: "And I will*

> *harden Pharaoh's heart," because at the beginning he sinned of his own free will, and meted out evil to Israel who sojourned in his land, even as it is said: "Come, let us deal wisely with them." Thus, justice demanded to withhold repentance from him, so that due punishment might be visited upon him. So, the Holy One, blessed be He, hardened his heart. If it is so, then* ***why did He delegate Moshe to him, charging him to let Israel go forth and turn to repentance?...To demonstrate to future generations that whenever the Holy One, blessed be He, withholds repentance from a sinner he cannot repent—rather he will die on account of the original evil he perpetrated of his own free will.***[1]

Elsewhere, the Rambam takes this even further. Not only will repentance be withheld, but opportunity for additional sin will be provided:

> *When it comes time to exact punishment from them and to repay their actions, they will be given opportunities to violate the Torah, in order that they should be deserving of punishment...*[2]

Accordingly, Hashem hardened Pharaoh's heart and prevented him from repenting, yet still sent Moshe to warn him of his coming destruction, to demonstrate that, in some instances, a person might stray so far that Hashem bars the sinner from making amends and correcting course.

Perhaps this is why the details of *yetzias Mitzrayim* we are required to relate at the Seder include not only the miracles Hashem did for His people, but also, explicitly, the plagues and other punishments He directed at Egypt. Mentioning these reinforces a powerful lesson in reward and punishment and how Hashem runs His world.

Seforno adds a fascinating angle to Hashem's warning to Pharaoh, further illuminating our obligation to discuss Egypt's downfall.

---

1 *Mishneh Torah*, Laws of Teshuvah 6:3.

2 *Peirush HaMishnah*, end of *Berachos*.

> *The purpose was to increase many miracles so that maybe some Egyptians would be moved to repent. And so that the Israelites in the future would be able to tell their children of Hashem's greatness and kindness. Thus, the warning to Pharaoh was needed even though Pharaoh would not listen.*[3]

So great is Hashem's mercy and compassion for His creation, even toward the wicked! Hashem hardened Pharaoh's heart and then struck him again and again, just so that some individual Egyptians might repent!

3 *Seforno, Shemos* 10:1.

EIGHTEEN

Tanna'im in B'nei Brak

It once happened that Rabbi Eliezer, Rabbi Yehoshua, Rabbi Elazar ben Azaryah, Rabbi Akiva, and Rabbi Tarfon were conducting the Seder in B'nei Brak. They were discussing yetzias Mitzrayim the entire night, until their students arrived and said to them, "Our masters, the time has come to recite the morning Shema."

Strangely, these Sages had all apparently convened for the Seder in B'nei Brak, the hometown of Rabbi Akiva, the most junior of the group. Rabbi Eliezer, Rabbi Yehoshua, and Rabbi Tarfon, all of whom were Rabbi Akiva's teachers and his seniors, lived elsewhere.[1] Why then did they all gather at Rabbi Akiva's home? Moreover, Rabbi Eliezer, who was known to object to those who left their homes and families on holidays,[2] does exactly that in our account.

---

1 See *Sanhedrin* 32b, for Rabbi Eliezer and Rabbi Yehoshua; *Chagigah* 18a and *Bava Metzia* 49b, for Rabbi Tarfon.

2 See *Sukkah* 27b.

To properly address these difficulties, let us reflect some more on the essence of the night's mitzvah—to recount the events of *yetzias Mitzrayim*.

We already discussed the relationship between two distinct mitzvos, the daily obligation to remember the Exodus, and the once-a-year requirement of the Seder, at which we must talk about the details and miracles of *yetzias Mitzrayim*. Simply understood, our daily obligation is to mention and remember the fact of our ancestors' deliverance from slavery, while on Pesach we are meant to experience it ourselves and be moved by its events as if we were participants in them.

Many Rishonim struggle to explain why we do not say a blessing before performing the mitzvah to relate the story of *yetzias Mitzrayim* on Pesach. Chazal instituted a blessing prior to nearly every active mitzvah—why should this one be any different? One approach suggests that the blessing "*ga'al Yisrael*," which concludes the *Maggid* portion of the Seder, effectively serves as the blessing on the mitzvah. An exception to a procedure that normally places the blessing in advance of the mitzvah, the order is changed at the Seder to reflect the evening's progression. When we open the Haggadah, we are at a lowly state, per Chazal's instruction to "begin with our degradation"[3]—we are not yet ready to recite this blessing. Only upon experiencing our own Exodus and elevating ourselves out of Egypt do we become worthy of saying a blessing.[4]

"In every generation, each person must feel as if he himself left Egypt" captures more than simply the experience of leaving slavery for freedom. Each person is required to internalize the entire redemption process, from worshipping Egyptian deities to declaring with prophetic clarity, "This is my God and I shall honor Him."

Perhaps this idea is reflected in the opinion that the first two of the evening's four cups are to be drunk while sitting upright, not while leaning. According to this view, only the final two cups are drunk while

---

3 *Pesachim* 116a.

4 See *Chasam Sofer, Derashos*, vol. II, Pesach 5580.

reclining (normative practice prescribes leaning for all four).[5] This paradigm sees the first two cups as part of the "slavery stage" of the evening. Only having progressed through our own Exodus are we able to demonstrate freedom by drinking in the manner of kings, leaning on our left side.

What then is the ultimate purpose of one "seeing himself as if he came out of Egypt," and indeed, what are we meant to gain from relating and discussing the events of *yetzias Mitzrayim*?

We have already considered various aspects of these obligations. Clearly, we are meant to acknowledge Hashem's relationship with us and His kingship, and to thank and praise Him for His everlasting kindness. But fundamentally, Pesach is the holiday that is meant to reinvigorate our belief and trust in Hashem. We read the Ramban's words above:

> *[By seeing] the great public miracles one comes to acknowledge the implicit miracles that are the foundation of Torah. For one has no potion in the Torah of Moshe Rabbeinu until he believes that every single event is a miracle—nothing is natural or automatic.*[6]

Belief alone is insufficient though. True faith must lead to trust, as we cited above from Rabbeinu Yonah:

> *When one mentions that very redemption that caused our ancestors to believe in Him, and then immediately proceeds to pray, he shows his faith that he will be answered just as our forefathers were answered then...Trust is the core of awe and faith—achieving this assures one a place in the World to Come.*[7]

Remembering *yetzias Mitzrayim* facilitates and strengthens one's belief, but to fully realize its impact one needs to develop his or her faith into a complete trust in Hashem.

---

5 *Pesachim* 108a.

6 *Ramban*, end of *Parashas Bo*.

7 *Rabbeinu Yonah, Berachos* 7b.

This is likely the implicit lesson of the prophet Chavakuk's summation that "a righteous person lives with his faith."[8] Abstract belief is not enough—it must manifest in an abiding, constant trust in Hashem across all areas of one's life. When acquired, it represents the singular accomplishment of the righteous individual.

Going further, the Vilna Gaon's comments evoke a similar approach:

> *Trust [in Hashem] is the root of everything—one who lacks trust cannot sustain his Torah knowledge.*[9]

> *For the root of everything is perfect trust; it is the principle of all mitzvos.*[10]

In what way is *bitachon*, trust in Hashem, the root of everything and the unifying principle of the entire Torah? To better appreciate this, let us read a passage from the *Maharal*:

> *One who believes commits himself fully to Hashem and trusts in Him. He does not waver from Hashem for any reason. This is true faith—complete attachment to Hashem. When a person believes in Hashem with all his heart, he clings to Him and does not leave Him. This represents complete perfection, for all mitzvos are meant to bring a person to cling to Hashem. This is why [Chavakuk] summarized them all into one principle.*[11]

Bitachon and *deveikus* (closeness to Hashem), are reciprocally intertwined. One who clings to Hashem entrusts himself to Him, and one who trusts in Him, at all times and in all situations, will also feel Hashem's intimate and constant presence. If the purpose of mitzvos is to bring us close to Hashem (*deveikus*), then indeed trust (*bitachon*) is the fundamental unifying factor of the Torah.

---

8 *Chavakuk* 2:4, described in *Makkos* 24a as a foundational summary of the Torah: "בא חבקוק והעמידן על אחת".

9 *Even Sheleimah*, ch. 3.

10 *Mishlei* 22:19.

11 *Nesivos Olam, Nesiv Ha'emunah*, ch. 2.

Accordingly, the Rambam's comment should hardly surprise us:

> *For to teach the fundamentals of faith is dearer to me than anything else I may teach.*[12]

The great Tanna'im were completely engrossed in the evening's requirements:

> *Until their students arrived and said, "Our masters—the time has come to recite the morning Shema."*

The words of *Shema*—*"Shema Yisrael, Hashem [Yud-Hei-Vav-Hei] Elokeinu, Hashem [Yud-Hei-Vav-Hei] Echad"*—affirm, succinctly yet powerfully, the essence of our belief in One God and our submission to His rule. Everything about Torah and the life of a Jew flows from this statement of faith.

My great teacher, the Klausenberger Rebbe, *zt"l*, explained why we cover our eyes when we say the first *pasuk* of *Shema*. Hashem's Name that is spelled י-ה-ו-ה (*Yud-Hei-Vav-Hei*), represents Hashem's kindness, while the Name *Elokeinu* connotes His judgment. On some occasions we may experience what feels like Hashem's harsh judgment, and at other times we may be beneficiaries of His kindness. But these are always our purely subjective interpretations of events, informed by our limited knowledge and understanding of how Hashem runs the world. Deep inside our minds and hearts, we must always know that He is One, and everything He does—regardless of whether it seems to us like kindness or judgment—is always only for the good. We cover our eyes when we affirm this belief, demonstrating that our vision is limited, but our faith is nevertheless unshakeable.

In the future, we are promised by the prophets, the scales will fall from our eyes and knowledge and wisdom will pervade our consciousness.[13] At that time, we will see through all the suffering and pain and recognize how it all was indeed for good. As Chazal taught:

---

12 Mishnah, end of *Berachos*.

13 *Yeshayahu* 11:9: "ומלאה הארץ דעה את ה' וכו'".

> *"And it will be on that day, Hashem will be One and His Name will be One."*[14] *Is He not One now? Rav Acha bar Chanina said, "This world is unlike the World to Come. In this world, we recite 'Baruch ha'tov v'ha'meitiv—Blessed is He Who is good and provides good to others' upon hearing good news, while we recite 'Baruch dayan ha'emes—Blessed is the true Judge' upon hearing bad news. In the World to Come, it will always be 'He Who is good and provides good to others.'"*[15]

After the final redemption, when our vision is corrected and we are granted access into all the intricacies of reality, we will be able to see each event—whether it seemed good or bad at the time—in its true light. Appreciating how it all was and is only for our good, we will be able to proclaim, "Everything Hashem did is for the good" and, retrospectively, recite, "He Who is good and provides good to others" on those same occurrences we previously said, "Blessed is the true Judge."

We eat *maror* on Pesach to remind us of the painful challenges of our slavery. This recollection serves a dual purpose, advancing in lockstep with the progression of the Seder.

First, we must properly celebrate freedom. But only one who has experienced the darkness of subjugation will fully appreciate his release to freedom and light. We eat the *maror* to help us reenact that sense of bitterness and despair, such that our *Hallel*, our songs of praise, can truly reflect the relief of freedom.

Secondly, as the Seder guides us to higher places—clarity of faith, firm trust, and closeness to Hashem—we are meant to reach a stage whereby we can ourselves begin to assert that "everything Hashem does is for the good," and all the bitterness of our past is seen through a post-redemption lens—as expressions of Hashem's infinite kindness.

Indeed, we eat *maror* twice—first on its own, and then, immediately thereafter, in the *korech* sandwich together with matzah. *Maror* on its own evokes the bitterness of slavery, needed for full appreciation

---

14 *Zechariah* 14:9.

15 *Pesachim* 3a.

of redemption. *Korech*, on the other hand, combines the freedom represented by matzah with the slavery embedded in the *maror*, signaling that *maror*, too, can be sweet when viewed in retrospect.

Many have commented on the intriguing sequence of the Seder. Although *maror* represents slavery and matzah represents freedom, we eat them in a counterintuitive order—first matzah, then *maror*.

One answer, suggested in the name of the Vilna Gaon, is that the subjugation and slavery in Egypt, which lasted two hundred and ten years, was actually shortened from the four hundred originally promised to Avraham. Thus, even while the slavery was still progressing, redemption was underway. The idea that the period of slavery was accelerated is hinted at in the reading notes (*trop*) on the words, "And they embittered their lives."[16] "*Kadma v'azla*," the names of the notes that accompany these words, can be literally translated as "and it arrived speedily."[17]

Simply, however, we delay the *maror* until after the matzah because our primary obligation at the Seder is to remember the redemption and freedom. While we are also called upon to experience the slavery by eating *maror*, it is a secondary requirement to be fulfilled after the matzah, which represents freedom.

Consistent with our theme, we might add that since the *korech* is meant to extract the sweetness of freedom from the bitter *maror*, we wait to eat the *maror* until after we have already tasted the freedom of matzah. In the same way, symbolically, we will be able to understand the meaning and purpose of our suffering after the future redemption.

Rabbi Akiva, host of the famous Seder we opened our discussion with, was the one who taught us the formula, "Everything Hashem does is for the good."[18] And Rabbi Akiva was the one who, as noted earlier, was able to see joy and light where his colleagues saw only ruin and

---

16 *Shemos* 1:14: "וימררו את חייהם".

17 See *Kol Eliyahu, Shemos* 48. I have also seen quoted in the name of Rabbi Shimshon of Ostropol that the numerical value of *kadma v'azla* (קדמא ואזלא) is the same as *ketz* (קץ), meaning "end," hinting that the end of slavery was hastened.

18 *Berachos* 60b.

misfortune.[19] For Rabbi Akiva, no suffering was dark enough that it could not be illuminated by Hashem's love and kindness.

Perhaps that Pesach, when Rabbi Akiva's great colleagues gathered in his home for the Seder, was shortly after the destruction of the Beis Hamikdash. Bar Kochva and his followers had led a rebellion against the Romans, fighting for the identity and values of the Jewish nation. Many, including Rabbi Akiva, believed that Bar Kochva would be Mashiach and they would rebuild the Beis Hamikdash. Alas, the rebellion was crushed, the stronghold at Beitar was conquered, and Bar Kochva himself was killed. Defeated in body and spirit, the remaining Jews, young and old, simple folks and great sages alike, were on the verge of losing hope.

Perhaps, as Pesach approached, their dejection intensified. Some still recalled the electrifying scene in the Beis Hamikdash as tens of thousands of Jews gathered from near and far to bring the *korban Pesach* and to pay their respects at the Beis Hamikdash. Now desolate, in its place was only a reminder of what they had lost.

Yet, some of the sages knew where to turn for inspiration. They knew who would be able to provide succor for their pain—who would be able to see light amidst the prevailing darkness. Gathering in Rabbi Akiva's home for the Seder, these Tanna'im spent the night delving into the secrets of exile and redemption and Hashem's master plan for His people and the world. Eventually, even their students were so inspired that they too exclaimed, "Our masters! It is time to recite the morning *Shema*"—we can now all say Hashem is One, and everything He does, even when it appears to be harsh, is indeed nothing but good and kindness.

---

19 *Makkos* 24a.

NINETEEN

Hallel at Night

As we conclude retelling the wondrous events surrounding *yetzias Mitzrayim*, we burst into song. Rather than compose a special song of praise for Pesach, Chazal directed us to sing *Hallel* at the Seder—the same *Hallel* we recite on each holiday and Rosh Chodesh. Yet, the Gemara rules quite explicitly that *Hallel* is generally not to be recited at night! The question is of course glaring; attempts to reconcile these seemingly inconsistent instructions date back to early Rishonim.[1]

One such answer suggests that although the words themselves are identical to *Hallel*, our recitation at the Seder falls into the category of *shirah*, "song," rather than *Hallel*, "praise."[2] To understand such a distinction, we must develop the concept and meaning of *shirah*.

Our prototypical *shirah* is the song our ancestors sang after crossing the Yam Suf, having been saved from the pursuing Egyptians. Their song is introduced with a curious structure: "Then, Moshe and B'nei Yisrael will sing,"[3] mixing past and future tense in a single phrase. In explanation, Rashi submits that the *pasuk* describes Moshe's intention to sing ("*alah b'libo she'yashir*"), rather than the act of singing itself. Accordingly, the *pasuk* would read, "Then, Moshe and B'nei Yisrael

1 See responsa *Chasam Sofer*, *Orach Chaim* 51.

2 See *Ran*, *Pesachim* 26b in *Rif*.

3 *Shemos* 15:1.

planned to sing." As a textual matter, this might resolve the difficulty, but it just leads to a follow-up question: every action one does is preceded by some intent or plan. What was unique about the song at the sea that calls for focus on their intent?

The Maharal rereads Rashi. "*Alah b'libo she'yashir*" is not to be translated as one typically would. While "*alah b'libo*" usually connotes thought or planning, here it is to be understood more literally—the song rose up in their hearts. True song represents the bubbling up of joy and ecstasy in one's heart, to the point that it must burst forth in the form of song.

This, then, is the distinction between *Hallel* and *shirah*. *Hallel*, though certainly recited with joy, is a calculated and prescribed formula for praising Hashem, while *shirah* is the expression of uncontrollable emotion.

> *Shortly before his death, the great tzaddik, Rebbe Uri of Strelisk, told his students that somewhere in the Ukraine there is a young, holy tzaddik. Upon their Rebbe's passing, the students understood that their master had left them instructions—to find this young, holy man and make him their new Rebbe.*
>
> *Traveling from village to village across the Ukrainian countryside, they finally met the holy Rebbe, Rebbe Yisrael of Ruzhin. Immediately taken by him, they approached Reb Yisrael and asked that he accept them as his chassidim.*
>
> *Rebbe Yisrael assured them that he would gladly accept them into his court, but he stipulated one condition. They were to agree to pray in accordance with the custom in Ruzhin, with silent intensity, unlike the practice of their late master, Rebbe Uri of Strelisk, who was known for his loud and ecstatic devotions. Eager to join their new Rebbe, the chassidim accepted Rebbe Yisrael's terms.*
>
> *Their first Shabbos with their new Rebbe was Shabbos Shirah. Indeed, at the beginning of the prayers they maintained their promise and prayed with silent decorum. When they reached*

the shirah however, they could no longer control themselves and burst out in ecstasy, clapping their hands and stomping their feet as they sang.

Upon the conclusion of Shabbos, they entered Rebbe Yisrael's room, eyes downcast and full of remorse for violating their new Rebbe's instruction. To their surprise, the Rebbe said, "True, you promised not to clap your hands, but regarding your hands clapping themselves—that we never discussed! One is forgiven for that which he does involuntarily."

Such is the definition of *shirah*. It is the song that bursts out of a heart overflowing with joy and gratitude that its song cannot be kept within.

Hallel can be contained, limited to daytime recitation; *shirah* defies such boundaries. One who invests enough effort to appreciate the sheer magnitude of *yetzias Mitzrayim* and succeeds in experiencing its miracles as if he himself were present at that time, cannot be expected to withhold his song. Joy, gratitude, and praise flow from his lips of their own accord—he cannot be silenced simply because it is nighttime.

True, *Hallel* cannot be said at night, but the Seder is no regular night. As Chazal note, this evening is illuminated just as is the daytime;[4] the clarity of daylight permeates the evening, dispelling the veil of darkness. Indeed, according to the *Ohr HaChaim*'s commentary, the Torah itself describes the Seder as a daytime event: "'And you shall tell your son on that day'...informing us that this night is called day, not night, which is alluded to in the *pasuk*, 'And night will be bright as day.'"[5]

Night represents the bitter darkness of exile, a time when we eagerly anticipate the arrival of morning: "My soul yearns for Hashem among the watchmen for the morning."[6] Times of good and closeness to Hashem

4 *Megillah* 20b. See also comments of Rashash on this Gemara, as well as the Vilna Gaon's commentary on *Mah Nishtanah*, elaborating further on the difference between the Seder night and other nights.

5 *Ohr HaChaim, Shemos* 13:8.

6 *Tehillim* 130:6.

are akin to daylight: "To tell of Your kindness in the morning."[7] While we are experiencing the light of Hashem's presence, we can surely be expected to sing His praise, but the true test of one's faith is at night, when the road is full of obstacles and we can scarcely find our way. *Hallel*, reflecting Hashem's great kindness, is thus reserved for daylight, a time when Hashem's love is manifest. It is inappropriate to say *Hallel* during such time as one is navigating through darkness and the challenges of Hashem's judgment.

But, as we point out at the onset of the Haggadah, the Seder night is different. A night whose very purpose is to bring us to sense Hashem's presence and everlasting love and kindness is more day than night—it is indeed a time for *Hallel*.

---

7 Ibid., 92:3.

TWENTY

Half on Me and Half on You: Breaking the Middle Matzah

Avraham, Yitzchak, and Yaakov are present at our Seder table. We are taught that the three matzos we place on our table correspond to our three forefathers.[1] This is fitting, as Chazal emphasize that we were saved only in the merit of Avraham, Yitzchak, and Yaakov.[2]

Why then do we break the middle matzah, the one associated specifically with Yitzchak?

Perhaps the following passage can help shed light on this matter:

> *In the future, the Holy One, blessed be He, will say to Avraham, "Your children have sinned against Me." Avraham will say before Him, "Master of the Universe, let them be eradicated to sanctify Your name." Hashem will say, "I will say it to Yaakov, who experienced the pain of raising children; he will ask for mercy on their behalf." He will say to Yaakov, "Your children have sinned." Yaakov will say before Him, "Master of*

1 *Maaseh Rokeach, Seder Leil Pesach* 56.

2 *Shemos Rabbah* 15:4.

> *the Universe, let them be eradicated to sanctify Your name." Hashem will say, "There is no reason in elders and no wisdom in youth." He will say to Yitzchak, "Your children have sinned against Me." Yitzchak will say before Him, "Master of the Universe, are they my children and not Your children? At Sinai, when they accorded precedence to 'We will do' over 'We will listen' before You, didn't You call them, 'My son, My firstborn son Israel'? Now they are my children and not Your children? And furthermore, how much did they actually sin? How long is a person's life? Seventy years. Subtract twenty during which one is not punished for sins committed then. Fifty years remain for them. Subtract twenty-five of nights, and twenty-five years remain for them. Subtract twelve and a half years during which one prays and eats and uses the bathroom, and twelve and a half years remain for them. If You can endure them all, excellent. And if not, half shall be upon me to bear and half upon You. And if You say that all of them shall be upon me, I sacrificed my soul before You!" They will say to Yitzchak, "You are our father!" Yitzchak will say to them, "Before you praise me, praise the Holy One, blessed be He." And Yitzchak will point to the Holy One, blessed be He, before their eyes. Immediately, they will lift their eyes to the heavens and say, "You, Lord, are our Father, our Redeemer, everlasting is Your name."*[3]

Yitzchak advocates for his descendants, willing to accept upon himself responsibility for half the sins of B'nei Yisrael. We allude to his fatherly compassion by breaking the matzah in half, representing his offer to relieve Hashem's children of half their burden. We eat only the smaller half initially, while the larger half is set aside. Surely, Yitzchak too would take on the larger half of our load and leave us with the lighter burden.

---

3 *Shabbos* 89b.

TWENTY-ONE

Why Do We Eat Maror?

Our Seder is incomplete if we recount only the miracles of redemption; we are meant to taste the slavery as well.

Just as a sweet taste can only be fully appreciated by someone who has experienced the sensation of a bitter taste, so is light only useful when it illuminates the darkness.[1] Tasting the bitterness of slavery affords a great appreciation for the subsequent freedom. As Chazal comment:

> *If I had not fallen, I would not rise up; When I sit in darkness, Hashem is my light—had I not sat in darkness I would not have light.*[2]

This sounds strange. True, Hashem's kindness is such that he helps those who fall rise up and illuminates the darkness for us. But we certainly prefer to never encounter those experiences to begin with!

In reality, however, light cutting through darkness is different than light unimpeded by adversity. When Hashem assists the person who falls, he can rise to heights previously unimaginable and inaccessible without stumbling. Chazal captured this in their observation that "fully

1 *Zohar*, vol. 3, 47b.

2 *Yalkut Shimoni*, *Tehillim*, *remez* 628.

righteous people (*tzaddikim gemurim*) do not reach the place of those who repent (*baalei teshuvah*)."[3]

We need to eat matzah on Pesach. But without the *maror*, the matzah does not have its full flavor. Freedom can only be tasted properly by a tongue familiar with the bitterness of slavery.

Beyond merely setting the stage for redemption, slavery also had its own inherent purpose. According to the *Zohar*, Hashem sent Yaakov's descendants into harsh exile, where they would be repudiated and distanced so they would remain forever apart from the other nations.[4] Thus, their suffering in Egypt formed them into a nation distinct and proudly separate from others, and it is this aspect of Hashem's kindness that we commemorate by eating *maror*.[5]

Rabbi Meir Simcha of Dvinsk famously describes how our people's ongoing persecution and seemingly endless suffering ensures that—despite individual Jews' attempts to "fit in"—we will always be reminded of our unique mission and character.[6] We need the *maror* to keep us intact and our collective heart beating with vitality.

After we eat the *maror* and internalize the purpose of slavery and darkness, we combine the *maror* with matzah. *Korech* takes us to the next step, where we can recognize and acknowledge that not only must we thank Hashem for what appears to have been bad, but it is in fact all only for the good.

---

3 *Berachos* 34b.

4 *Zohar*, vol. 3, 14b.

5 See also *Sefas Emes*, *Pesach* (5644).

6 See *Meshech Chochmah*, *Vayikra* 26:42.

TWENTY-TWO

Because the Egyptians Embittered the Lives of Our Ancestors

Sitting regally at our Seder table to celebrate their freedom, we nevertheless summon up memories of our ancestors' harsh slavery in Egypt. Eating *maror* at the Seder, alongside the matzah that connotes hasty redemption, reinforces the lesson that our field of vision is so narrow. What we might experience as bad, is in truth, an expression of Hashem's kindness, and everything He does is good.

Above, we cited the Ibn Ezra's comments on the *pasuk*, "You are Hashem's children; do not gash yourselves nor shave the front of your head because of a death." One is meant to be so cognizant of Hashem's abundant love that he trusts that whatever Hashem does must be for our good. Just as a child does not question a parent's actions, even when these seem inexplicable to the child, so are we to relate to Hashem's actions.[1]

Rabbi Akiva taught us to say, "Whatever the Merciful One does is for the good," but for him this was far more than a mantra. His entire worldview was suffused with steadfast assurance that Hashem's love is

---

1 See *Ibn Ezra* and *Ramban, Devarim* 14:1.

everlasting and omnipresent.[2] Rabbi Akiva was able to see Hashem's abundant kindness in tragedy and misfortune—whether these afflicted him personally or shook the entire nation—throughout his life and even at its end. During his final moments on earth, as he was murdered by the Romans, he remained joyful.[3]

We also mentioned the Klausenberger Rebbe's explanation of our practice to cover one's eyes when saying the first *pasuk* of *Shema*. Hashem's Name that is spelled *Yud-Hei-Vav-Hei*, represents Hashem's kindness, while the Name *Elokeinu* connotes His judgment. We may alternately experience what feels like Hashem's judgment at some times and His kindness on other occasions, but these are purely subjective interpretations of events. Our finite knowledge and meager understanding of how Hashem runs the world limit our perspective. Deep inside our minds and hearts, we must always know that He is One, and everything He does—regardless of whether it presents itself to us as kindness or judgment—is always only for the good. We cover our eyes when we affirm this belief, demonstrating that while our vision is limited, our faith is unshakeable.

Similarly, we noted that Rabbi Avraham Yehuda HaKohen Schwartz uses this idea to explain Hashem's promise to Yaakov, "Fear not to go down to Egypt, for I will make you there into a great nation. I Myself will go down with you to Egypt, and I Myself will also bring you back; and Yosef shall extend his hand over your eyes." To soothe Yaakov's concerns about moving his family to a spiritually compromised Egypt, Hashem alluded that it will ultimately be of great benefit to Yaakov's descendants. Just as Yosef's initial descent to Egypt appeared thoroughly tragic, yet eventually proved to be his brothers' source of salvation, so is Yaakov's move a part of Hashem's master plan and infinite kindness. Symbolically, Yosef will "extend his hand" over Yaakov's eyes, just as one covers his eyes for *Shema* and affirms thereby his faith that Hashem's mercy encompasses even those things that appear difficult.

---

2 *Berachos* 60b.

3 See also *Yerushalmi, Berachos* 9:5, and *Sotah* 5:5.

Indeed, regarding this very reference to Yosef's hand, the *Zohar* comments, "This is the secret of *Shema*."[4]

Even Moshe Rabbeinu was not granted full visibility into the world's inner machinations, instead being told by Hashem, "You shall see My back, but My face shall not be seen." Only with the passage of time may we be able to see how everything is an expression of His mercy. We cannot look His conduct in its face and attempt to understand His actions while they occur; after the fact we might hope to observe and perhaps interpret their effects in the world.[5] Hashem told the ministering angels that the deaths of the Ten Martyrs were "part of the plan in front of me," hinting that only much later, well after the events have passed and certainly not in the throes of the decree, might we be fortunate enough to see more of His plan.

Hashem made this point to Moshe in another dialogue we find in Chazal:

> *Rabbi Yehudah says in the name Rav: When Moshe ascended on High, he found the Holy One, blessed be He, sitting and tying crowns on the letters of the Torah. Moshe said before Hashem, "Master of the Universe, who is preventing You [from giving the Torah without crowns]?" Hashem said to him, "There is a man who is destined to live after several generations, and Akiva ben Yosef is his name; he is destined to derive from each and every point [of the crowns] mounds of halachos." Moshe said before Hashem, "Master of the Universe, show him to me." Hashem said to him, "Return behind you." He went and sat at the end of the eighth row [in Rabbi Akiva's study hall] and did not understand what they were saying. Moshe's strength waned. When Rabbi Akiva arrived at the discussion of one matter, his students said to him, "My teacher, how do you know this?" He said to them, "It is a halachah transmitted to Moshe from Sinai." When Moshe heard this, his mind was put at ease.*

---

4 See *Responsa Kol Aryeh, Pesach Tov*, no. 7.

5 Ibid, citing his teacher, the Chasam Sofer.

> *He returned and came before the Holy One, blessed be He, and said before Him, "Master of the Universe, You have a man such as this and yet You give the Torah through me. Why?" Hashem said to him, "Be silent; this intention arose before Me." Moshe said before Hashem, "Master of the Universe, You have shown me Rabbi Akiva's Torah, now show me his reward." Hashem said to him, "Return there." Moshe went back and saw that they were weighing Rabbi Akiva's flesh in a butcher shop. Moshe said before Him, "Master of the Universe, this is Torah and this is its reward?" Hashem said to him, "Be silent; this intention arose before Me."*[6]

In objecting to Rabbi Akiva's fate, Moshe was attempting to understand Hashem's reasoning and the sequence of spiritual cause and effect that could lead to such a horrific end. This, Hashem reminded Moshe, is precisely what he had been told that even he—Moshe, the prophet of all prophets—would be unable to approach.

Maror and matzah, ultimately, are one and the same, mixed together symbolically in the *korech* sandwich. What presents itself to us as tragedy is but Hashem's kindness, even if we are unable to understand how, for everything He does is for the good.

---

6 *Menachos* 29b.

TWENTY-THREE

Four Expressions of Redemption

Therefore, say to B'nei Yisrael, I am Hashem, and ***I will free you*** *from the burdens of Egypt, and* ***I will save you*** *from their service, and* ***I will redeem you*** *with an outstretched arm and great judgments. And* ***I will take you*** *to Me to be a nation, and I shall be your God...*[1]

According to several Rishonim, the four cups of wine we drink at the Seder correspond to these four descriptions of Hashem's salvation.[2] Many lessons and homilies can be ascribed to this association, one of which is the criticality of the fourth expression, "*V'lakachti*—I will take you." Chazal ruled that one is permitted to drink other wine between the first, second, and third cups, but between the third and fourth cups one may not drink (or eat) anything else. The first three expressions of redemption all

1 *Shemos* 6:6–7.

2 See *Rashi* and *Rashbam* on *Pesachim* 99b.

pertain to physical freedom—Hashem saved His people from harsh enslavement to Egypt—while the final term, "I will take you," captures the ultimate purpose of Hashem's intervention: to form us into a holy nation. Lest anyone err and suggest that physical salvation was the primary goal, and spiritual commitment merely an afterthought that can be neglected, Chazal commanded us to maintain continuity from the third description of physical freedom, "I will redeem," represented by the third cup, to the spiritual demand, "I will take you," alluded to by our fourth cup of wine. No other wine is allowed between the two cups—physical redemption devoid of spiritual purpose is not worthy of celebration. Salvation from Egypt was but the first step toward a life of walking with and being close to the Almighty.

Capturing Hashem's manifold kindness toward His people, the four expressions of salvation are not four distinct ideas, but represent a continuum of freedom from slavery to true freedom. Servitude can take many forms; these experiences are not identical. At its most extreme, slavery entails submission to a cruel master, who, in addition to imposing harsh labor on the unfortunate servant, also abuses the latter mercilessly and makes his life physically and emotionally unbearable. A slave subservient to a milder master may be treated better, yet still suffers under the demands of endless hard work. Another slave might be fortunate enough to avoid even a heavy workload, but at the end of the day he is still the property of another person, unable to influence his own destiny and determine his own path in life.

Under Pharaoh in Egypt, our ancestors' experience was that of the first slave—hard and endless labor, compounded by evil decrees designed to subjugate and dehumanize the people.

Thus, Hashem promised to save us and free us of any type of servitude—freedom from the murderous regime of Pharaoh (*v'hotzeisi*), salvation from the hard labor of enslavement (*v'hitzalti*), and complete redemption from the yoke of Egypt (*v'gaalti*). Each Jew would be free to pursue his or her own destiny.

Finally, "I will take you to Me to be a nation, and I shall be your God (*v'lakachti*)."

TWENTY-FOUR

Five Expressions of Salvation

Afterward, he washes his hands and recites Birkas Hamazon over a third cup and drinks it. And afterward, he pours a fourth cup and finishes the Hallel over it. Then he recites the Blessing over the Song, which is: "May all of Your creatures praise You, etc." He recites the blessing Borei Pri Hagefen and does not taste anything afterward the whole night except for water. He should then pour a fifth cup and say the Great Hallel upon it, from, "Give thanks to Hashem, for He is good,"[1] to "Upon the rivers of Babylon."[2] And this cup is not obligatory like the other four cups.[3]

---

1 *Tehillim* 136.

2 Ibid., 137.

3 *Rambam*, *Mishneh Torah*, Laws of Chametz and Matzah 7:10.

A fifth cup has now joined us. Unlike the four cups, which we drink upon reciting the prescribed blessing, the fifth cup is not drunk. Instead of a blessing, the Great *Hallel* is sung over this cup. The passage above, from the Rambam, is silent on whether or not one should drink the cup at all.

Other Rishonim introduced us to a fifth cup as well. Its function, according to some, is entirely discretionary. If an individual wishes to drink another cup after having completed the four cups, he may do so, provided that he recites the Great *Hallel* over it. Singing the Great *Hallel* with this cup signifies that it is distinct from the four mandatory cups.[4]

Another view suggests that a fifth cup is, in fact, desirable. Describing it as either "praiseworthy" or a "mitzvah," some Rishonim encouraged the consumption of a fifth cup in conjunction with the Great *Hallel*.[5] While perhaps not mandatory, it is more than a mere option allowed by Chazal, on condition that it is accompanied by the Great *Hallel*.

What is the Rambam's position? Would his comments above suggest that a fifth cup is desired, in accordance with the latter view, or simply a personal choice Chazal accommodated?

I believe the Rambam takes an entirely novel view, conforming to neither of the opinions mentioned. Using his ever-so-precise language, the Rambam instructs us to pour a fifth cup and recite the Great *Hallel* upon it. Wholly absent is any instruction—or permission—to drink the fifth cup, an omission made glaring by such an instruction's straightforward inclusion with respect to the other four cups. According to the Rambam, we are meant to pour a fifth cup and thereby elevate the *Hallel*, but we are not to drink this cup. Why would this be?

Simply understood, our fifth cup corresponds to the fifth expression of redemption: "I will bring you to the Land." This promise has yet to be fully realized. While we await a final redemption and a gathering of all Jews to the Land, we pour a fifth cup—acknowledging Hashem's manifold kindnesses—but we are not ready to drink it yet.

---

4 *Ramban, Milchamos Hashem, Pesachim* 26b.

5 *Raavad, Hasagos L'Baal Hamaor*, ibid.

As the Chasam Sofer points out, Chazal established four cups and not five to emphasize that the main goal of our salvation from Egypt was to realize the fourth promise, "I will take you." Receiving the Torah and becoming Hashem's chosen holy nation was, and remains, more central than entry to the Holy Land.

TWENTY-FIVE

I am Hashem Your God Who Took You Out from Egypt

Not only is the statement "I am Hashem your God Who took you out from Egypt" the first of the Ten Commandments, it is the foundational creed upon which rests the very concept of a binding commandment. Without belief in One God, there can be no absolute demand on one's conduct and actions.

Why, then, does Hashem introduce Himself with "I am...Who took you from Egypt" and not "Who created you" or even "Who created the heavens and earth?" How does the event of *yetzias Mitzrayim* attest to Hashem's Oneness even more so than Creation?

Explaining the underlying meaning in the mitzvah of *korban Pesach*, the Ramban writes:

> *The reason for this mitzvah is that the constellation of the lamb is at its strongest during the month of* Nissan*...therefore He commanded to slaughter a lamb and eat it, to demonstrate that not by will of the constellations did we leave Egypt, but through His decree. Moreover, according to Chazal, the*

> *Egyptians worshipped the lamb. Thus, surely this mitzvah demonstrates how Hashem destroyed their deity and power...*[1]

Korban Pesach fundamentally affirms Hashem's absolute dominion over His world; His people, the Jewish nation, operate outside the influence of astrological determinants. To further underscore this point, we were commanded to slaughter the very animal that serves as an Egyptian deity. No created being can manifest any power in the face of Hashem's will!

In the *Yehi Ratzon* prayer many recite before putting on tefillin each day, we describe one of the reasons for tefillin: "So that we may remember the miracles and wonders He did for us when we left Egypt, and that He alone has the power and dominion over that which is above and below, to do with them as He wishes." *Yetzias Mitzrayim* was indeed meant to teach us the very message of the first commandment—that Hashem alone controls everything.

Yetzias Mitzrayim, rather than Creation, is invoked in the first commandment for another reason. A central feature of the Exodus from Egypt was Hashem forcibly separating His people from the nations of the world. The Torah later describes this as Hashem coming "to take for Him a nation from the midst of another nation."[2]

On each of the holidays, we open the fourth blessing of the *Amidah* with "You chose us from all nations, You loved us and You desired us, and You elevated us from the other peoples and sanctified us with Your commandments." All this began with Hashem stepping in and dramatically removing us from our entrenchment in Egypt on the night of that first Pesach.

To properly internalize the meaning of the first commandment, we must believe not only in Hashem's Oneness as Creator of the world, but also that He is "our God," Who chose us as His people and in turn can make demands on us and our behavior.

---

1 *Ramban, Shemos* 12:3.

2 *Devarim* 4:34.

TWENTY-SIX

Eh-yeh Sent Me

Upon first hearing from Hashem of his mission to lead the Jewish nation out of Egypt, Moshe asked Hashem, "How shall I communicate Your name to the people—how will they know who is promising to secure their freedom after centuries of exile?" In response, Hashem seemingly instructs Moshe to use a Divine Name known to us only from this one exchange. Hashem tells Moshe, "This is what you should say to the people: *Eh-yeh* (I will be) sent me to you."

We know that Hashem has many names, each of which captures a particular attribute of His conduct. Above, we noted names that are used to characterize His mercy and judgment. Others allude to His might or to His presence in nature. But this name, "*Eh-yeh*," appears only in this one context and was never introduced or explained to us by Chazal.

In fact, Rishonim disagreed whether this name is even a proper name of Hashem, bearing the stringencies of other Names that cannot be erased and must be treated with sanctity, and, if it is, whether the holy formulation consists only of the one word "*Eh-yeh*" or it is comprised of the full phrase "*Eh-yeh asher Eh-yeh*—I will be Who I will be" as a single Name.[1]

Rashi explains that "*Eh-yeh asher Eh-yeh*—I will be Who I will be" was a promise by Hashem that "I am with them in this suffering just as I shall be with them in future exiles." The Ramban offers two interpretations,

1 See *Rambam, Mishneh Torah*, Laws of Foundations of the Torah 6:2, and *Kessef Mishneh* ad loc.

neither of which assume that "I will be" refers to a Divine Name. In the first, the Ramban explicitly states that Hashem rejected Moshe's request to invoke Hashem's name when speaking to the Jewish People: "...I will be with them in all their suffering—they should call out to Me and I will answer them." Even according to the Ramban's second explanation, it is not apparent that "I will be" alludes to a Divine Name: "...Just as you will be with Me, so I will be with you—If they open their hands in righteousness, so shall I open my Hand."

All three interpretations just cited suggest that Hashem is teaching the soon-to-be-freed nation an important lesson. But Moshe's request appears to go unfulfilled—"*Eh-yeh*" is a promise, not a Name. Moshe is not provided a Divine Name to invoke when telling the slave-nation about their impending freedom.

In an alternate approach suggesting that *Eh-yeh* may in fact be Hashem's Name, the Ramban cites:

> *Rav Saadia wrote that its meaning is "He Who has not passed and never will pass," for He is first and He is last...the Rambam stated in Moreh Nevuchim: "He Who is present," meaning He Who is true existence. They are saying that He is true existence, that is to say—Hashem Who was always present and always will be present.*

Likewise reading *Eh-yeh* contextually, as a Divine Name offered by Hashem in response to Moshe's plea, the *Rashbam* offers a novel interpretation. *Eh-yeh* is the same name as the one we are most familiar with but do not pronounce as written—*Yud-Hei-Vav-Hei*—albeit in a different formulation. Whereas created beings—we humans—use the third-person form suggested by the beginning *yud* of *Yud-Hei-Vav-Hei*, Hashem refers to Himself with the first person "I am" implied by the *alef* of *Eh-yeh—Alef-Hei-Yud-Hei*. The two names are one and the same; the usage of *Eh-yeh* is isolated to this one instance because nowhere else does Hashem openly introduce Himself to Man by name.

If *Alef-Hei-Yud-Hei* and *Yud-Hei-Vav-Hei* diverge only in form but in essence are the same, it follows that *Alef-Hei-Yud-Hei*, like the latter, reflects Hashem's attribute of mercy. And, indeed, in arming Moshe with the name *Eh-yeh*, Hashem is sending Moshe back to the nation with a message: it may seem overwhelmingly dark right now, but Hashem's mercy lies in wait and redemption is on hand. On account of His infinite mercy, He has shared with His people the pain of enslavement and of Pharaoh's murderous regime. Moshe's report struck a chord with exhausted slaves: "And the nation believed, and they heard that Hashem had remembered the Jewish People..."[2]

We carry our ancestors' firm belief with us, marching through exile after exile amidst ongoing persecution. Steadfast in our knowledge that Hashem is all-merciful and everything He does has meaning and significance, our eyes remain focused on the horizon and the redemption that surely waits just beyond it. "*Eh-yeh asher Eh-yeh*—I am Who I am"—unchanging, Hashem, Who saved us so many times, will continue to do so until we arrive at our final destination.

Rashi paraphrases the *pasuk*, "I will be with you in this exile, and I will be with you in other exiles." Promise of an imminent salvation is meant to elevate the nation and divert their focus from the miserable present to a hopeful future. As dark as the exile may seem at any particular moment, a bright morning awaits in short order.

Centuries earlier, a fledgling nation newly entrenched in Egypt was about to learn of their eventual exit from its clutches. Yaakov Avinu, intending to fortify his family for the difficult years ahead, called out to his sons, "Gather and I will tell you what shall occur to you at the end of days."[3] Hashem had other plans, however—Yaakov was unable to transmit his vision to the family and their hearts clouded with worry.

Rabbi Shimshon of Ostropol explained that, in fact, Yaakov knew what sin had caused his descendants' enslavement in Egypt, and consequently, how long their suffering would last. Recognizing that the exile was meant to cleanse the family of their sin in selling Yosef, Yaakov calculated that this sin specifically was an affront to the Divine

---

2 *Shemos* 4:31.

3 *Bereishis* 49:1.

Name "*Eh-yeh*," which carries the numerical value of 21. Exponentially increasing the sin's damage, the nine brothers who participated in the sale of Yosef each carry the burden of guilt. Nine brothers, multiplied by 21 (the numerical value being a proxy for Hashem's Name), equals 189. Yaakov, perceiving all this, wished to reveal to his sons when the punishment would end. Drawing on the numerical value of the word *keitz*, "end" (190 = קֵץ), Chazal tell us that he was about to inform them that their salvation would arrive in the 190th year—following 189 years of slavery-atonement.

Yaakov, however, did not know the full story. He was unaware, however, that in their pact of silence surrounding the events of Yosef's sale, the brothers had incorporated the support of the Divine Presence, increasing the responsible group to ten. Thus, 21 should be multiplied by 10, rather than 9, yielding a 210-year punishment. Accordingly, Chazal tell us that indeed "Yaakov wished to reveal to his sons what will come at the end, *but the Divine Presence eluded him*."[4]

Centuries later, Moshe, the future leader, likewise knew that the exile was necessary to atone for the crime committed so many years earlier when Yaakov's sons conspired against Yosef. But Moshe had the wrong Divine Name—and therefore an incorrect calculation. Moshe understood that *Yud-Hei-Vav-Hei*, with a numerical value of 26, was the name in need of rectification. Thus, Moshe's calculation led him to believe that his brothers would not be freed until 260 years of slavery were complete. "And Hashem saw that Moshe had turned (סר—*sar* = 260) to see." To correct Moshe's assumption, Hashem revealed that it was not the name of *Yud-Hei-Vav-Hei* that was impacted, but *Eh-yeh*, so redemption would arrive sooner than Moshe had expected. Hashem rushed him to tell his brethren that salvation was around the corner: "Tell the children of Israel, *Eh-yeh* has sent me to you..."

Twice Hashem invoked His relationship with our forefathers Avraham, Yitzchak, and Yaakov when commissioning Moshe to assure the Jewish People that redemption was nigh:

---

4 See *Rashi* ad loc.

And Hashem said further to Moshe, "Thus shall you speak to the Israelites: Yud-Hei-Vav-Hei, the God of your fathers, the God of Avraham, the God of Yitzchak, and the God of Yaakov, has sent me to you: This shall be My name forever, this is My mention for all eternity.[5]

In this passage, Hashem's relationship with each of the forefathers is singled out and mentioned discretely—"God of Avraham, God of Yitzchak, God of Yaakov." Immediately thereafter, however, they are grouped into a single unit:

Go and assemble the elders of Israel and say to them, "Yud-Hei-Vav-Hei, the God of your fathers, the Hashem of Avraham, Yitzchak, and Yaakov, has appeared to me and said, 'I have taken note of you and of what is being done to you in Egypt.'"[6]

Why the change from a separate mention of Hashem's name in association with each forefather to a single grouping?

To explain this matter, I often cite Chazal's remarkable account:

Eliyahu was often found in the academy of Rebbi. One day there was a new moon, and he was delayed and did not come. Rebbi said to Eliyahu, "What is the reason the master was delayed?" He said to him, "I had to wake up Avraham, wash his hands for him to pray, and then lay him down. And similarly, for Yitzchak, and similarly for Yaakov. He said, "Let the master wake them all together!" Eliyahu responded, "I maintain that they would then generate such powerful prayers and bring Mashiach prematurely."[7]

When Avraham, Yitzchak, and Yaakov join together in prayer, they can effect any outcome, even hastening the coming of Mashiach.

---

5 *Shemos* 3:15.
6 Ibid., 3:16.
7 *Bava Metzia* 85b.

Addressing Moshe and calling upon him to inform the Jewish People that Hashem had remembered them, Hashem invokes their ancestors' unique standing in His eyes. In the first reference however, Hashem was referencing not the immediate salvation from Egypt, but rather the future—final—redemption. As Eliyahu told Rebbi, Avraham, Yitzchak, and Yaakov had not yet interceded together to hasten the future salvation. Thus, each is introduced using his own individual relationship with Hashem.

The second *pasuk*, on the other hand, pertains to the concern at hand—the plight of Hashem's nation enslaved in Egypt. Grouping the three names and assigning to them a shared pact with Him, Hashem tells Moshe that Avraham, Yitzchak, and Yaakov have successfully joined in prayer to speed up the redemption: "Go and assemble the elders of Israel and say to them...I have taken note of you and what is being done to you."

As we conclude exploring the Torah of *galus* and *geulah,* Exile and Redemption, we lift our eyes in prayer. May our great forefathers join Eliyahu Hanavi in interceding on our behalf, and may the call soon issue forth, "Go and assemble the elders of Israel and say to them: Hashem the God of your fathers, the God of Avraham, Yitzchak, and Yaakov, has appeared to me and said, 'I have taken note of you.'" May we merit to see wonders as we did in the days we left Egypt, and may the *avodah* return to its place speedily in our days.

Shabbos Chol Hamoed

TWENTY-SEVEN

Behold! He Stands Beyond Our Wall

Shir Hashirim is customarily read in public—across many of our communities—on Shabbos Chol Hamoed Pesach. Many devout Jews also read *Shir Hashirim* after completing the Seder.

Many creative explanations are offered connecting *Shir Hashirim*, referred to by Chazal as "Holy of Holies,"[1] to the unique spiritual character of Pesach.

Rabbeinu Ovadia Seforno, in his introduction to *Shir Hashirim*, writes:

> *This entire book relates the sentiments of Hashem's people to Him, particularly at times of distress. And His response—explaining why His judgment extends more readily to them than to others...*

Unexpectedly, the yearning and expressions of longing that saturate the *pesukim* of *Shir Hashirim* specifically represent our relationship with Hashem at times of challenge and suffering. Hashem and His people are presented as lovers who, despite their efforts to find each other, are unsuccessful. In despair, we fear that our Beloved has abandoned us entirely.

---

1 *Yadayim* 3:5.

But, no—the *pesukim* of *Shir Hashirim* reassure us—He is not far at all. We may not be able to see Him, but He is there, just beyond the wall, peering through its cracks.[2]

As the Seforno adds:

> *He is not far at all; He is close by to anyone who calls to Him. He is but hiding, so that we remain unaware of His presence until we are aroused to call out to Him.*

Our Beloved wishes to hear that cry—"Make your voice heard to me!"[3] This call, according to the Seforno, is a direct instruction to us to call out to Him and beg for salvation. Hashem is indeed present at all times—lingering beyond the wall. But He wishes to hear our voice, the prayer that acknowledges our yearning for Him, before He reveals Himself to us.

Our sojourn in Egypt was the first of many bitter exiles, and *yetzias Mitzrayim* was the archetype of future redemptions. At the Seder, recounting the miraculous salvation millennia ago, we long for Hashem to reveal His mercy and bring us a complete and final redemption. We open *Shir Hashirim*, so replete with the fullest expressions of Hashem's love for us, even as He hides Himself just beyond the wall and awaits our call.

---

2 *Shir Hashirim* 2:9.

3 Ibid., 14.

Shevi'i Shel Pesach

TWENTY-EIGHT

This Is My God!

A people enslaved for centuries do not become free men and women overnight. While we commemorate the miracles and events of *yetzias Mitzrayim* at the Seder, on the eve of the fifteenth of Nissan, our ancestors' true transformation from servitude to freedom only came about a week later. As they stood on the banks of the Yam Suf, surveying the remnants of Pharaoh's decimated army, every Jew experienced the Divine Presence with a clarity that exceeded even that of the greatest prophet.[1] Finally, internalizing their new status as a free people, the former slaves were inspired to intense and joyous song.

What changed at the sea? Why did they sing now—and not a week earlier, when Hashem led them out of Egypt with a mighty hand?

The Ibn Ezra[2] and Seforno[3] offer similar explanations. So long as the Jewish People knew Pharaoh was pursuing them, they were still slaves fleeing their masters. Emotionally and psychologically, they could not be free—even as they were physically beyond Egypt's reach. Nor were they confident they could evade Pharaoh. Chazal recorded their fears that "just as we will cross to other side of the sea, so will the Egyptians."[4]

1 *Mechilta, Beshalach* 15:2.
2 *Ibn Ezra, Shemos* 14:30.
3 *Seforno, Shemos* 6:6.
4 *Pesachim* 118b.

Only upon seeing with their own eyes that Pharaoh and his army could no longer harm them, could our ancestors think of themselves as free people, a new nation with a new song: "And Hashem saved on that day...Then, Moshe and B'nei Yisrael would sing..."

Beyond their fear of Egypt, however, was a deeper issue. Chassidic thought suggests that the Jewish People were still tainted by the spiritual impurity of Egypt. Fleeing from Egypt, our ancestors looked back and saw "that Egypt was pursuing them." Rashi interprets the singular use of "Mitzrayim—Egypt" to indicate that "they saw Egypt's spiritual representation (*Sar shel Mitzrayim*) pursuing them." Egypt's spiritual environment and pagan culture still pervaded the minds and hearts of the escaping slaves, dissipating only when they saw its army's complete devastation.

B'nei Yisrael may have departed Egypt on the eve of Pesach, but Egypt did not leave them until a week later, on the seventh evening of Pesach. It took the miraculous salvation at the sea, the destruction of Pharaoh's army, and a once-in-history Divine revelation for the darkness of Egypt to lift from their souls.

Upon concluding the *Maggid* section of our Seder, during which we retold the story of *yetzias Mitzrayim* in all its glory, we thank Hashem for bringing about "our salvation and our souls' redemption." Our bodies were extracted from physical subjugation, on the first evening of Pesach; our souls were salvaged from the impurity of Egypt a week later. For these, we owe a double expression of gratitude.

TWENTY-NINE

I Shall Sing to Hashem

"Then, Moshe and B'nei Yisrael sang"—this is what is meant by "Your throne is established from then."[1] *Rabbi Berechiah said in the name of Rabbi Abbahu: Even though You have existed forever, Your throne was not established, and You were not known in Your world, until Your children sang a song. Thus it says, "Your throne is established from then"...*

Additionally, "Then, Moshe and B'nei Yisrael sang"—this is what is meant by "She opened her mouth in wisdom, and words of grace were on her tongue."[2] *From the day that the Holy One, blessed be He, created the world, we do not find anyone singing to Hashem, but Yisrael [at the sea]. He created Adam, who did not sing; He saved Avraham from the furnace and from the kings, and he did not sing; Yitzchak from the knife and he did not sing; Yaakov from the angel, from Eisav, and from the people of Shechem*

1 *Tehillim* 93:2.

2 *Mishlei* 31:26.

and he did not sing. When Yisrael arrived at the sea and it split—they immediately sang before the Holy One, as it says, "Then, Moshe and B'nei Yisrael sang." Thus, "She opened her mouth in wisdom"—said Hashem, "for these I have been waiting"...[3]

What is so unique about this song that Hashem so anxiously awaited its expression?

Rashi's comments are also intriguing. "Then Moshe and B'nei Yisrael sang: 'then'—when he saw the miracle it occurred to him that he should sing a song (*alah b'libo she'yashir*)." Rashi is struggling with the odd verb tense used by the Torah to describe Moshe's song. "*Az yashir Moshe*" should be literally translated as "Then, Moshe will sing," in the future, while the entirety of the event is otherwise described in the past tense. To address this somewhat jarring inconsistency, Rashi suggests that the future "will sing" describes the thought process that led to Moshe's song.

But, as the Maharal and other commentators point out, Rashi's solution merely begets another question: what is the significance of such mention altogether? All human action must be preceded by some degree of intent or thought. Why is Moshe's intention here any more worthy of acknowledgment than the myriad other things done by him and so many others throughout the Torah?

The Maharal explains that B'nei Yisrael's song after the miracles at the sea was not the result of a calculated decision. They were not merely articulating appreciation for Hashem's wondrous intervention with nature on their behalf. *Shirah*, song, is the intense emotional outpouring of a heart overflowing with joy. In the aftermath of the splitting of the sea and Egypt's destruction, the Jewish nation were so overwhelmed

---

3 *Shemos Rabbah* 23.

by Hashem's manifest love that song burst forth from their hearts. The future tense "*yashir*—he will sing," reflects not so much the act of singing itself, but rather the joy filling their souls—emotions that would, in short order, see full expression in glorious and prophetic song.[4]

Song flows from intense inner joy; joy is the confidence that ensues when one sees the wholeness and perfection of Hashem's world. In observing a series of events and understanding their respective causes and effects, one can sense the completeness of Hashem's master plan. As the recently freed slaves stood trembling on the banks of the Yam Suf, trapped between the sea and their Egyptian pursuers, they despaired. Looking back, all they could see was Pharaoh's army closing in on them. All was dark. A short while later, they had safely crossed the sea and the mighty Egyptian army was in ruins. Suddenly, all was illuminated. The years of suffering and Pharaoh's intransigence had all been leading to this moment—when Hashem would reveal His might to the world, exacting a fitting punishment upon Egypt and declaring B'nei Yisrael His chosen people. Their swirling doubts and confusion now dissipated; B'nei Yisrael saw a new world—a world of clarity and purpose, a world of song.

Centuries earlier, Yaakov wrestled all night with a stranger. Chazal tell us that this was in fact Eisav's spiritual representation, Eisav's "angel," and, when morning arrived, this angel, like all others, had to return to his place to recite his song. Accordingly, he begged Yaakov, who now held on to his defeated opponent, to release him. The Kozhnitzer Maggid explains that Eisav's spiritual mission is to challenge Yaakov and to be defeated by him. When Yaakov successfully subdued Eisav's angel, the latter's mission was complete—it was now time for his song.[5]

Let us return to the midrash we began with. From the time of Creation, Hashem eagerly awaited Man's song. But each of the events described by Chazal fell short of the closure and clarity that facilitate song. Indeed, Adam, Avraham, Yitzchak, and Yaakov, all praised Hashem and thank Him for His kindness, but they were not inspired to *shirah*. At the sea,

4 See *Maharal, Gur Aryeh, Shemos* 15:1.

5 *Avodas Yisrael, Vayishlach.*

having finally arrived at a culminating event, the newly created nation was able to express its joy in song.

As we noted earlier, we recite *Hallel* at the Seder despite a normative ruling that *Hallel* is only said during the day.[6] While it is true that *Hallel* cannot be "read" at night, our *Hallel* at the Seder is no regular recitation—it is *shirah*—song. Song is not read, nor can it be contained or limited to the daylight hours. A heart filled with joy—the joy of clarity and closeness to Hashem—is moved to song of its own accord.

6 See responsa *Chasam Sofer*, *Orach Chaim* 51 and *Turei Even*, *Megillah* 14b.

THIRTY

For He Has Triumphed

...I will sing to Hashem, for He has triumphed gloriously (ga'oh ga'ah), horse and its rider He hurled into the sea.[1]

Simply interpreted, the verb "*ga'oh*—he triumphed" is doubled for emphasis; hence our translation, "He has triumphed gloriously." The *Kli Yakar* suggests that we read more deeply into the words. Hashem not only defeated Pharaoh on this occasion, rather, He allowed Pharaoh, who already ruled over a large empire, to become so dominant and sure of his own power that his ultimate downfall was all the more spectacular.

Similarly, when we mention the apparent success of evil people, we note that "the wicked flourish like grass; evildoers blossom...to destroy them forever."[2] Sinners may do well in the short term, but the higher their temporary success takes them, the more calamitous will be their fall when it inevitably occurs.

1 *Shemos* 15:1.

2 *Tehillim* 98:8.

Chazal presented this idea poetically:[3]

> *Let the Adir come and exact punishment for the adirim from the adirim in the adirim. Let the Adir come, this is the Holy One, blessed be He, as it is written: "Adir ba'marom Hashem—Hashem on high is mighty."*[4] *And exact punishment for the adirim, these are the Jews, as it is stated: "V'adirei kol cheftzi bam—The excellent in whom is all My delight."*[5] *From the adirim, these are the Egyptians, as it is written: "Tzalelu ka'oferes b'mayim adirim—The mighty sank as lead in the waters."*[6] *In the adirim, these are the waters, as it is stated: "Above the voices of many waters, adirim mishbarei yam—the mighty breakers of the sea."*[7]

Our experience throughout the course of Jewish history has demonstrated this notion time and again. Generation after generation, our tormentors have always risen to great heights, only to be eventually obliterated. Hashem sustains the wicked and allows them to flourish—thereby magnifying their final downfall.

---

3 *Menachos* 53a.

4 Ibid., 93:4.

5 Ibid., 16:3.

6 *Shemos* 15:10.

7 *Tehillim* 93:4.

THIRTY-ONE

Sing to Him, Praise Him

We already cited Chazal's assertion that the Jewish nation were the first to introduce the world to *shirah*—song:

> *From the day that the Holy One, blessed be He, created the world, we do not find anyone singing to Hashem, but Yisrael [at the Sea]. He created Adam, who did not sing...*[1]

This comment is surprising, and seemingly inconsistent with Chazal's teaching elsewhere that Adam composed the chapter of *Tehillim* that begins: "*Mizmor shir l'yom HaShabbos*—A song of praise for the Shabbos."[2] Did Adam sing or not?

Perhaps the answer is that *shir* (שיר) and *shirah* (שירה) are not the same thing. Adam sang, but his song was a *shir*. *Shirah* is a higher level. Hashem's name is present in the word itself (שר-י״ה), alluding to its function of uniting Man with the Divine. Hence, the loftier *shirah* was not brought into the world until the Jewish nation sang after crossing the sea.

In the Beis Hamikdash, the Levi'im would sing *shirah* to accompany the daily service—a mandatory component thereof, according to some opinions.[3] Service (עבודה—*avodah*) is not always pleasant. Indeed,

1 *Shemos Rabbah* 23.
2 *Tehillim* 92. See *Midrash Shocher Tov* ad loc.; *Zohar*, vol. 2, 138:1; and *Pirkei D'Rabbi Eliezer* 19.
3 *Arachin* 11a.

removing the letters of Hashem's name, *vav* and *hei* (ו"ה), from the word *avodah* (עבודה) leaves only *eved* (עבד), a slave. While a slave is miserable and dejected, service of the Almighty is empowering and joyous. Singing their *shirah*, the Levi'im bring together the *yud-hei* of *shirah* and the *vav-hei* of *avodah* to complete Hashem's name, underscoring the ability of Divine service to keep the world together.

THIRTY-TWO

Torah or Shirah?

The Holy One, blessed be He, sought to designate Chizkiyah as the Mashiach and to designate Sancheriv as Gog and Magog. The attribute of justice said before the Holy One, blessed be He, "Master of the Universe, if David, king of Israel, who recited several songs and praises before You, You did not designate as the Mashiach, Chizkiyah, for whom You performed all these miracles, and he did not recite praise before You, will You designate him Mashiach?" It is for that reason that the mem was closed, because there was an opportunity for redemption that was thwarted.[1]

Chizkiyah, who was acknowledged by the *Nevi'im* and Chazal as the most righteous king, could not realize his potential as Mashiach because he failed to say *shirah*. Why did Chizkiyah not say *shirah*? Moreover, why would a king who was responsible for

1 *Sanhedrin* 94a.

a nationwide religious renaissance lack sufficient merit to claim that which was rightfully his?

Chazal provide a hint: "Chizkiyah was meant to say *shirah*...but his heart was too elevated to recite *shirah*." Instead, he believed that his Torah would rectify his failure to sing *shirah*.[2]

Shirah requires absolute submission and self-nullification in the face of Hashem's overwhelming kindness. This demands far more than the *Hallel* expressing gratitude does. Even one who believes in his or her own power can thank others for their assistance. But they cannot sing *shirah*. Only when one realizes that they are utterly powerless on their own, entirely dependent on Hashem's kindness, can he or she be moved to song.

Chizkiyah, for all his piety and accomplishment, did not attain the level of humility needed to sing *shirah*. Indeed, extreme humility is a critical attribute for our kings. The Rambam writes, concerning this very topic:

> *In the same way that Scripture has given him great honor, and everyone is obliged to give him honor, so has he been commanded to be of a subdued and unpretentious heart...he must not act overly haughty toward Israel...he must be merciful and compassionate to the small and great with regard...he must show respect for even the lowest of the low. When he speaks to the entire congregation together, he is to speak sensitively...he must always behave with extreme modesty...he must suffer their burdens and criticisms and anger...*[3]

Certainly, if every king of Israel is meant to be humble and unpretentious, how much more so must be the one who is to become Mashiach. Chizkiyah did not meet this description, so he could not be the Mashiach.

Earlier, we learned Chazal's teaching that Hashem's throne was somehow not fully established until the moment B'nei Yisrael sang on

2 *Shir Hashirim Rabbah* 4:3.

3 *Mishneh Torah*, Laws of Kings 2:6.

the banks of the Yam Suf. *Shirah* is thus not merely a component of our devotion to Him, but rather a critical part of fulfilling the world's purpose. Along these lines, the Ramban writes that the purpose of Creation, and Hashem's only desire of us, is that "Man should know and thank his God Who created him."[4] If such is the very purpose of creation, it is no wonder that "Hashem's throne was not established until B'nei Yisrael sang."

If the ultimate role of Mashiach is to bring the entire world to recognize Hashem's Kingship and realize His purpose in creating the universe, we can surely understand why Chizkiyah's failure to say *shirah* disqualified him as Mashiach. He was a great king, one who not only learned so much Torah himself, but who was also single-handedly responsible for ensuring that every one of his subjects learned Torah as well. But he could nevertheless not be Mashiach. Mashiach must sing *shirah*.

---

4 *Ramban*, end of *Parashas Bo*.

THIRTY-THREE

Draw Me after You

And Hashem went before them by day in a pillar of cloud to direct their way.[1]

And Hashem's angel, who went in front of the camp of Israel, moved and traveled behind them. The pillar of cloud traveled from in front of them and stood behind them.[2]

The Zohar teaches further: At the time when B'nei Yisrael are doing Hashem's will, He walks in front of them; when they are not doing His will, He walks behind them.[3]

Rabbi Moshe of Pshevorsk would explain with the following illustration: A king once had a loyal servant, who tended to his master faithfully and did his bidding without hesitation. This king had no qualms about walking in front of his servant, fully confident that the devoted assistant would follow him wherever he

1 *Shemos* 13:21.

2 *Shemos* 14:19.

3 *Zohar, Shelach*, vol. 4, 166a.

went. On the other hand, when one has a servant who is disloyal and fickle, the master must walk behind the servant and maintain constant supervision to ensure the servant does not meander and run off.

When we fulfill Hashem's will, He can march before us, as does the confident master; when we falter, He walks behind us.

Later, Hashem tells the Jewish People, "Behold, I am sending an angel before you to guard over you on the way,"[4] exhorting them to conduct themselves such that the angel might remain in front of them. Similarly, "After Hashem, your Hashem, you should walk"[5]—follow Him devotedly, and He will have no reason to walk behind you.

Most poetically, this idea was expressed in Yirmiyahu's prophecy:

> *I remembered the kindness of your youth, the love of your betrothal—your following Me in the wilderness, in a barren land.*[6]

We strive to be the loyal servant, whose loyalty is never doubted for a moment. As the dutiful servant or the longing lover, we follow Him blindly: "Draw me after you; we shall run."[7] But sometimes we stumble. In a moment of doubt, we asked, "Are there not enough graves in Egypt?" Having shown ourselves to be incomplete in our loyalty, Hashem's angel promptly became a guard, marching behind us to ensure we remain on the correct path.

---

4 *Shemos* 23:20.

5 *Devarim* 13:5.

6 *Yirmiyahu* 2:2.

7 *Shir Hashirim* 1:4.

THIRTY-FOUR

Why Do You Cry Out to Me?

As Pharaoh drew near, the Israelites caught sight of the Egyptians advancing upon them. Greatly frightened, B'nei Yisrael cried out to Hashem…but Moshe said to the people, "Have no fear! Stand by and witness the deliverance that Hashem will work for you today; for the Egyptians whom you see today you will never see again. Hashem will battle for you, and you shall remain silent." Hashem said to Moshe, "Why do you cry out to Me? Tell the Israelites to go forward. And you lift up your rod and hold out your arm over the sea and split it, so that the Israelites may march into the sea on dry ground."[1]

1 *Shemos* 14:10–16.

As many commentators have noted in surprise, Hashem's response to Moshe on this occasion is most puzzling. Trapped between the sea and Pharaoh's army, B'nei Yisrael cried out to Hashem, as have our ancestors through millennia of suffering. Why did Hashem object to this prayer, instead directing Moshe to lead the people forward in silence?

Rather, on some occasions, even prayer is not appropriate. At such moments, nothing Man does, including beseeching Hashem, has the power to change the outcome. The only remaining avenue of salvation is to hold steady to one's faith, to strengthen one's belief in Hashem, and to follow Him confidently. B'nei Yisrael at the sea had arrived at such a moment.

Rav Chaim Volozhiner writes that, indeed, their unwavering faith on this occasion would effect a different outcome.

> *Therefore, at the time of the splitting of the Red Sea, The Holy One, blessed be He, said to Moshe, "Why are you crying out to Me? Speak to the Israelites that they should start moving," as if to say that it depends on them. That if they will be in the mode of faith and belief, and they would travel, going and proceeding to the sea absolutely certain and without fear, out of their mighty belief that it will undoubtedly split before them, then as a result they will cause an awakening above, so that a miracle should happen and it will split before them.*[2]

My teacher, the Klausenberger Rebbe, *zt"l*, would likewise often share this idea in the name of Rabbi Pinchas of Koretz.

These great eighteenth-century masters, Rav Chaim Volozhiner and Rabbi Pinchas of Koretz, were not the first to suggest that *emunah*, complete faith, has transformative power to impact existence on a most fundamental level. We find a very similar thought in the *Ohr Hachaim*'s comments:

---

2 *Nefesh Hachaim*, *shaar* 1, ch. 9.

> *"Why are you crying out to me?" Meaning, the matter is not in My hands. Although I wish to perform a miracle on their behalf, the attribute of justice is preventing it, as they are not worthy. Mercy cannot prevail over justice. Therefore, Hashem advised that the Israelites should strengthen themselves with faith. If they would do so, and demonstrate their complete faith by traveling into the sea even before it splits, they will empower the attribute of mercy, and I will be able to do a miracle for them.*[3]

Ultimately, the concept has its roots in the *Zohar*:

> *Rabbi Yehudah taught in the name of Rabbi Yitzchak that Pharaoh was more knowledgeable than all his magicians. He looked at every aspect of the spiritual world and saw no hope for Israel...he did not understand that there was still the path of faith, which overpowers all else. Therefore, he hardened his heart.*[4]

Emunah can transcend even seemingly immutable realities of spiritual existence. Thus, Pharaoh, correctly discerning that B'nei Yisrael could not be salvaged from Egypt's clutches per any available intercession, hardened his heart and strengthened his resolve to oppress the Jewish slaves. Pharaoh was unaware that, through their unshakeable faith in Hashem, the Jewish People would be able to alter outcomes that appeared completely fixed.

In a certain sense, the events at the Yam Suf were the apex of B'nei Yisrael's development in *emunah*, a process that began with the ten plagues more than a year earlier. While one function of the plagues was to mete out suitable punishment to the Egyptians for oppressing the Jewish People, a parallel purpose was to reinforce to the soon-to-be-freed slaves themselves that Hashem's rule extends to every facet of creation and there is no true power but Him.

---

3 *Ohr Hachaim, Shemos* 14:15.

4 *Zohar*, vol. 2, 52b.

At the Seder, we mention Rabbi Yehudah's mnemonic for the Ten Plagues: "*d'tzach adash b'achav* (דצ"ך עד"ש באח"ב)." The commentators point out that these groupings are not arbitrary or simply convenient. The ten plagues were indeed divided into three sets, extending upward from the lowest part of creation to the heavens and demonstrating Hashem's dominion over each. Blood, frogs, and lice all developed out of the dirt or the water; wild animals, pestilence, and boils affected animals and humans that occupy the level above the ground; while the final four originated in the heavens. Locusts were brought in by a powerful wind, hail descended from the sky, and the dimming of the sun and moon plunged Egypt into paralyzing darkness. Finally, with human death in the final plague, Hashem's reach to—and absolute power over—all corners of nature was shown with absolute clarity.

Now, at the sea, it fell to the Jewish People to internalize those lessons and commit themselves to full belief and trust in Hashem. "Do not cry out to me," Hashem told Moshe, "instead, let B'nei Yisrael show their faith." Proceeding into the sea as instructed, they demonstrated their faith, thereby altering the course of nature and history.

Even when prayer is called for, its extent and scope must depend on the person's faith in Hashem. Chazal teach that not all prayer is meant to take the same form:

> *Rabbi Eliezer taught: The Holy One, blessed be He, said to Moshe, "My children are in peril—the sea is closing in on them, while the enemy pursues—and you are standing in prayer! Why are you crying to me!" As Rabbi Eliezer would say, there is a time to pray at length and a time to shorten one's prayer: "Hashem, please heal her" [Miriam, from her affliction]—this is a short prayer; "I fell before Hashem as in the beginning, for forty days" [asking Hashem to forgive the Jewish People after sinning with the Golden Calf]—this is a long prayer.*[5]

5 *Mechilta, Beshalach* 3. See also a very similar teaching in the *Sifri* at the end of *Parashas Behaalosecha*, and in *Berachos* 34a.

Yet, Chazal did not illuminate any further. They did not elaborate as to why Moshe's approach varied in the respective circumstances, and they certainly did not provide us with a formula to employ when deciding whether one's prayers should be of the longer variety or if brevity is preferred.

Indeed, that formula is *bitachon*, trust, an outgrowth of our unshakeable faith in Hashem. As we learned above, there are occasions whereby faith must supplant prayer, and in those cases, faith is Man's only recourse. Likewise, even when prayer remains appropriate, its form will depend on the believer. Prayer serves to create a "pipeline" through which Hashem's mercy can flow to the requestor—*berachah*, meaning "blessing" derives from the same root as *breichah*, meaning "pool"[6]—and this stream is made stronger through the power of faith.

Moshe interceded with Hashem to heal Miriam's illness, but Miriam, a righteous woman, doubtless had complete faith in Hashem. As such, Moshe's prayer could be short, the briefest expression of trust and submission to Hashem's will. On the other hand, turning to Hashem and begging forgiveness for a nation whose actions had just exposed a lack of faith, Moshe recognized the need for intense and lengthy supplication.

Here, at the sea, B'nei Yisrael had to demonstrate their faith. Accordingly, Hashem told Moshe, "This is not a time for lengthy prayer!" Critically, the Jewish nation must provide an antidote to the lack of faith they had just exhibited by suggesting that they were taken out of Egypt only to die at the sea. At that moment, their only course of action was to plunge into the sea, display their complete trust in Hashem, and transform themselves into a nation worthy of miraculous salvation.

6 See *Rashba*, responsa, vol. 5, 51.

THIRTY-FIVE

A Maidservant's Vision

Yetzias Mitzrayim could only happen to the Jewish nation if they would rise to a higher spiritual level than the one they occupied at that moment. The Arizal famously taught that on the first night of Pesach, B'nei Yisrael were endowed with an unearned degree of spiritual greatness. This was needed for them to be extracted from Egypt's impurity; immediately after that first day, however, they lost their stature and returned to their earlier state. Time was needed, from Pesach and for the ensuing seven weeks, for B'nei Yisrael to develop themselves and rightfully claim the Torah in their own merit.

Our job during the weeks of Sefiras Ha'omer, according to the Arizal's teaching, is to replicate our ancestors' growth over this time. While our work builds on the spiritual "injection" of Pesach, we must harness that energy into organic growth that we can call our own.

In truth, this matter requires further clarification. If indeed, as we just cited, B'nei Yisrael lost their stature immediately after the first day of Pesach, necessitating weeks of effort to regain it, how are we to understand the great prophetic revelations that occurred on the seventh day of Pesach? According to Chazal, every single participant in the splitting of the Yam Suf, even the maidservants, became privy, at that moment, to prophetic clarity rivaling that of the prophet Yechezkel's visions. Such lofty descriptions would indicate that the nation had recaptured their spiritual heights already a few short days after losing them!

However, it would appear that not all spiritual heights are created equal. At *yetzias Mitzrayim*, the **Jewish People ascended to the spiritual heavens**, an event we reenact and reexperience at each year's Seder. In contrast, on the seventh day of Pesach **the heavens were brought down to earth**. True, the maidservant saw things that great prophets did not, but she remained a maidservant nevertheless. While B'nei Yisrael experienced tremendous revelations at the sea, this did not place them on a higher spiritual level; it certainly did not represent the growth required to receive the Torah as "a kingdom of priests and a holy people."

THIRTY-SIX

This Song

B'nei Yisrael sang *shirah* after crossing the sea safely and upon seeing the destruction of their enemies. And yet, upon receiving the Torah—which is unquestionably the heart and soul of the Jewish nation and the very purpose of existence itself—we did not sing *shirah*?[1]

Torah itself is a song, described as such in the *pasuk*, "And now, write this song (*shirah*) for yourselves."[2] *Shirah* is said for events, but not for another song. Our Torah is an everlasting song, and it is the ongoing song of all those who love and live it each day.

With this, we might better approach a difficult passage in the Gemara. Shortly after assuming responsibility for the Jewish People and leading them into the campaign to conquer the Holy Land, Yehoshua is confronted by an angel, who introduces himself as the "*Sar Tzeva Hashem*—General of Hashem." Supplementing the brief exchange recorded in the *pesukim*, Chazal add that the angel rebuked Yehoshua: "Last night you failed to bring the afternoon offering and today you neglected Torah study!" Yehoshua inquired as to which was the primary offense that had aroused the angel's ire, questioning him, "*Ha'lanu atah*—Are you with us?" *Tosafos* note that the word *ha'lanu* is meant to allude to the *pasuk*, "*Torah tzivah lanu Moshe*—Moshe commanded

1 See *Ohr Hachaim*, *Bamidbar* 21:17.

2 *Devarim* 31:19.

us regarding the Torah," so Yehoshua was asking if lack of Torah study was their main shortcoming. In response, the angel declared, "*Al atah basi*—I came for now," drawing upon a different reference to Torah: "*V'atah kisvu lachem es ha'shirah ha'zos*—And now, write this song for yourselves."[3]

This is surprising! According to Chazal, Yehoshua employed a *pasuk* about Torah study, while the angel referenced the obligation to write the Torah. But if Yehoshua was asking about Torah study and the angel was answering him about Torah study, why did they draw upon different *pesukim* and different themes?

Yehoshua and his people were engaged in a prescribed and holy campaign to conquer the Land. As such, and in accordance with the principle that one who is involved in a mitzvah is exempt from another mitzvah, they were released from the obligation to study Torah. Even during the night, which is a time not usually given over to military activity, they would be required to rest and prepare themselves for the following day's efforts.[4] Why then, were they so severely rebuked by the angel for failure to study Torah during this time?

Hashem's messenger, the angel, replied that Torah is not a regular mitzvah. While technically there might be a formal exemption from Torah study while the people are engaged in the timely obligation to capture and settle the Land, how could the nation forgo the song of Torah? Song must burst forth at all times from the hearts of those who carry it! Yehoshua attempted to invoke a *pasuk* about Torah study and observance—after all they were formally exempt while conducting battle. The angel was not satisfied: you may be exempt from *learning* at this moment, but how can you neglect the *shirah* of Torah?

---

3 *Megillah* 3a.

4 See *Sotah* 42b.

THIRTY-SEVEN

Shevi'i Shel Pesach

We were created for a single ultimate purpose:

> *The people I formed for Myself; they will declare My praise.*[1]

Rashi and the Radak point to the conditional relationship between the *pasuk*'s two phrases. Hashem created us in order that we shall praise Him for the miracles He did and will do for us. Our mission as a people is to experience Hashem's kindness and praise Him for it. We cited the Ramban's comments above, but these are well worth repeating here:

> *All mitzvos are meant to bring us to believe in Hashem and acknowledge that He created us. This is the intent of Creation. For there is no other available explanation for Creation, and the Almighty has no need for mortal beings—other than so that Man should know and thank his Maker.*[2]

Man's purpose, per the Ramban, includes two elements—to "know" Hashem and to "thank" Him. Step one is to know Hashem, to recognize that Man is not his own master. Not only must he answer to a Higher Power, but his accomplishments are the gifts of Hashem's beneficence, not automatic products of his own efforts.

---

1 *Yeshayahu* 43:21.

2 *Ramban*, end of *Parashas Bo*.

Nature—and the routines it imposes on us—all too often serve to dull our awareness of the Divine Presence. We internalize the patterns of cause and effect we see in the natural world and apply those rules to our activities, concluding that the outcomes we realize are commensurate with the efforts we contribute. Shlomo HaMelech, however, already assured us that this way of viewing Hashem's world is hardly correct, or wise.

> *I have further observed under the sun that the race is not won by the swift, nor the battle by the valiant; nor is bread won by the wise, nor wealth by the intelligent, nor favor by the learned. For the time of mischance comes to all. And a man cannot even know his time. As fishes are enmeshed in a fatal net, and as birds are trapped in a snare, so men are caught at the time of calamity, when it comes upon them without warning.*[3]

Rashi adds:

> *Like them, [men] are snared: with a small and weak trap, like the weak net and the snare. People stumble at the time of the visitation of their evil, when their time comes for evil to fall upon them suddenly, in an inferior trap.*

Neither the mightiest nor the wisest of men can avoid the inevitable vicissitudes of life, much less evade every man's ultimate fate. Instead, he would do well to recognize his Maker, Who sees and sustains every minute detail of Creation.

In turn, we should then develop true gratitude. With an awareness of Hashem's presence and manifest control over all existence should also come tremendous gratitude to Him for sustaining life and enabling us to flourish. We must avoid falling prey to Moshe's description of a "dull and witless people," who do not appreciate the "Father Who created you, fashioned you, and sustained you."[4]

---

3 *Koheles* 9:11–12.

4 *Devarim* 32:6.

Genuine gratitude is not constrained to internal recognition. When we truly appreciate Hashem's kindness, we enthusiastically seek to proclaim His greatness throughout the world. Our daily actions and speech are all meant to reflect David HaMelech's sentiment: "My mouth shall speak Hashem's praises, and all mankind will bless His Holy Name for eternity."[5]

Chazal instructed us that when praying we must offer thanks for Hashem's past kindness, and, in addition, beseech Him to provide our future needs.[6] Suggesting a surprising qualification to this approach, the Chasam Sofer writes that the above is only appropriate with respect to one's spiritual needs. Regarding material concerns, he argues, it is preferable to make do with the barest minimum, and prayers should only include gratitude for the past, not requests for one's future desires. In part, the Chasam Sofer infers this limitation from the absence of any supplication for the future in the *Modim* section of the *Amidah*. Only in the *Modim D'Rabanan*, which according to the Chasam Sofer pertains to one's spiritual life, is it appropriate to add, "So shall You continue to sustain us."[7]

I have difficulty understanding the Chasam Sofer's approach. Surely, asking Hashem to provide one's material needs is an essential component of the mitzvah to pray. Even when making do with the barest minimum, one is dependent on Hashem's kindness. It appears clear that Chazal's guidance—to thank Hashem for the past and ask for future needs—applies equally to both the physical and spiritual realms of one's life.

Moreover, the distinction between *Modim* and *Modim D'Rabanan*—that the former addresses the physical and therefore cannot include future needs—leaves me unconvinced. In fact, it would appear that the concluding phrase of *Modim* is indeed a prayer for the future. We say

---

5 End of *Ashrei*, *Tehillim* 145:21.

6 Mishnah, *Berachos* 9:4.

7 *Derashos Chasam Sofer*, *Parashas Behaalosecha*, vol. 2, p. 409.

"He Who is good, Whose mercy never stops, and the Merciful Whose kindness never ceases," appealing to His everlasting mercy.

Alternatively—and this would, in fact, seem to be a more straightforward answer—we follow *Modim* with the prayer of *Sim Shalom,* in which is in its entirety supplication for the future and His ongoing beneficence. By contrast, since *Modim D'Rabanan* is said by the congregation without any following prayer, it needs to conclude with an internal prayer.

A powerful lesson arises here. After her fourth son was born, our matriarch Leah thanked Hashem, giving the child a name that reflected her gratitude. However, her words, "This time I will thank Hashem," are immediately followed by the Torah's comment, "Therefore she called his name Yehudah, and she stopped bearing children."[8] The Chozeh of Lublin would teach that since Leah's words only expressed gratitude for the past, but did not include a prayer for the future, she effectively stopped the spiritual flow of grace from on High, and thus stopped having children. The Ibn Ezra already identified this allusion in the *pasuk*, commenting, "Like one who says, 'I thank Hashem for giving me all this and it is enough for me,' which is why she stopped having children."

Let us be sure to both recognize Hashem's great kindness in everything He has provided us thus far and entreat Him to continue granting us the resources to serve Him faithfully and wholeheartedly.

8 *Bereishis* 29:35.

THIRTY-EIGHT

Shevi'i Shel Pesach II

Pesach spans a total of seven days (or eight, outside Eretz Yisrael), with days of full Yom Tov at both the beginning and end. But whereas the Yom Tov at the conclusion of Sukkos is deemed a separate holiday entirely, named Shemini Atzeres, the final day(s) of Pesach are intrinsically part of the Pesach holiday. Why then is Pesach divided into two portions, with the first day commemorating our exit from Egypt and the final day commemorating the splitting of the sea, when these are simply two of the events comprising *yetzias Mitzrayim*?

Perhaps the two miracles are meant to be memorialized separately as two distinct events, each with an individual message for the Jewish nation. Several halachic authorities discuss whether or not one might discharge the daily obligation to remember *yetzias Mitzrayim* by reciting the *Shiras Hayam*, the "Song of the Sea."[1] In the eyes of those who ruled that one does not fulfill the obligation to remember *yetzias Mitzrayim* with the Song, the events are distinct miracles, and their commemorations are not to be conflated.

Moreover, David HaMelech, naming the events that occurred to the Jewish People from the day Yaakov descended with his family to Egypt and through the miracles associated with our eventual deliverance

1 See disagreement between the Magen Avraham and Rabbi Akiva Eiger (quoting the Chasam Sofer), in their comments to *Shulchan Aruch, Orach Chaim* 67.

from slavery, concludes his list before reaching the splitting of the sea.[2] This omission further reinforces the idea that the latter miracle is not subsumed within the miracles of *yetzias Mitzrayim*, but is its own event.

In fact, *yetzias Mitzrayim* was complete before our ancestors reached the sea. Hashem had already disrupted nature numerous times and dramatically took them out of Egypt's grip. *K'rias Yam Suf* had its own purpose: to demonstrate Hashem's love for His people and to implant deeply within their hearts firm trust in Him. Only following this miracle do we learn that each Jew saw Hashem's presence with such clarity that they could point to Him and say, "This is my God!"

Apparently, the experience at the sea was needed. Chazal tell us that as B'nei Yisrael stood on the banks of the Yam Suf, its governing angel refused initially to split it, arguing, "These are idolators and these are idolators!"[3] This is a shocking statement—how could the Jewish nation, witnesses to and beneficiaries of Hashem's incredible miracles in Egypt, still be idolators?

Furthermore, the Arizal famously taught that Hashem rushed to extract us from Egypt in great haste. Had we lingered there any longer, we would have succumbed permanently to its spiritually debased environment and become irredeemable. Hashem saved us from reaching this "fiftieth level of impurity" by rushing us out.[4] Once again, the question begs—how could a nation surrounded by miracles directed at their salvation be so unaffected as to remain vulnerable to the "fiftieth level of impurity?"

And, as we cited above, even as they were crossing the sea on dry land, the Jewish People worried that "just as we are to cross the sea on this side, so shall the Egyptians."[5] Indeed, the *pasuk* in *Tehillim* expresses criticism of them regarding this fear: "Our fathers did not discern Your wonders in Egypt, they did not remember your abundant kindness, and they rebelled at the sea."[6]

---

2 *Tehillim* 105.

3 *Midrash Tehillim* 15.

4 *Siddur HaAri, Seder Haggadah.*

5 *Arachin* 15a.

6 *Tehillim* 106:7.

Apparently, fearing their Egyptian masters and knowing they were being pursued, the just-freed slaves could not readily throw off their shackles. Their bodies were not in Egypt, but their minds were still enslaved—they could not, under such conditions, truly become believers. Only upon seeing the utter defeat of their former tormentors would they be able to "trust in Hashem and His servant Moshe."

Only once they were physically, mentally, and emotionally free of Egypt's bondage, they were indeed able to fully appreciate all that Hashem had done for them. Through newly opened eyes of faith and trust, they could see Hashem's love for them in the many wonders He had introduced to the world, solely on their behalf.

THIRTY-NINE

A Partner in Creation

*One who eats matzah properly for seven days—it is as if he becomes a partner to Hashem in creating the universe. As the pasuk states: "Matzos shall be eaten for the seven days." Not "seven days" but "**the** seven days"—the seven days of Creation.*[1]

What does matzah have to do with Creation? Why does eating matzah elevate one to the status of Hashem's partner in Creation? Finally, matzah is only required on the first night of Pesach, at the Seder. There is no mitzvah to eat matzah the entire week. What then is meant by "one who eats matzah properly (*k'hilchasah*)"?

Perhaps the comment was never intended to be limited to eating matzah, but rather to the requirements of Pesach overall. This would be consistent with an idea we learned earlier from the Ramban:

> *All mitzvos are meant to bring us to believe in Hashem and acknowledge that He created us. This is the intent of Creation.*

1 *Sefer Rokeach*, Laws of Pesach 291.

> *For there is no other available explanation for Creation, and the Almighty has no need for mortal beings—other than so that Man should know and thank his Maker.*[2]

Creation's very purpose is to facilitate recognition of Hashem: "The people I formed for Myself; they will declare My praise."[3] It is the Jewish nation's mission to sanctify Hashem's Name by making His presence known throughout the world, as we proclaim so many times each day: "*Yehei shemei rabba mevorach l'alam*—May His Great Name be blessed forever." We are uniquely positioned to fulfill this goal. Through many centuries we have developed great capacity to see light peeking through the darkest of clouds, to recognize Hashem's guiding hand even when all seems hopelessly disjointed and chaotic.

This is why we are known as the Jewish nation—*Yehudim*—descendants of Yehudah. Although we are obviously not all his offspring, as each of Yaakov's twelve sons produced an entire tribe, nevertheless our essence reflects Leah's pronouncement when she named Yehuda. "Now I will thank Hashem"—at all times and under all circumstances, the Jew recognizes and appreciates Hashem's kindness.

The Ramban, in his comment above, teaches us that we must fulfill the requirements of Pesach such that we remember and reflect upon the miracles of *yetzias Mitzrayim*. Still, where is the link—suggested both in the Ramban's teaching, as well as in the above assertion that eating matzah makes one a partner in Creation—between *yetzias Mitzrayim* and Creation?

Concerning the mitzvah of Pesach Sheini, the author of *Sefer Hachinuch* offers the following insight:

> *At the root of this commandment is that the Pesach offering is a powerful and clear sign to all regarding the creation of the world. For at the time [of the Exodus], Hashem, blessed be He, performed great miracles and wonders for us and changed the nature of the world in the eyes of many nations. And [so] all the*

---

2 *Ramban*, end of *Parashas Bo*.

3 *Yeshayahu* 43:21.

> *peoples of the earth saw that His providence and power is over the lower [earthly] beings. And then at that time, everyone believed and all who came after them believed that He, blessed be He, created the word ex nihilo at the time that He chose—and that was the well-known time. Even though creation ex nihilo is impossible according to the nature, so too is splitting the depths of the sea to allow the passage of a great assemblage of people on dry land and returning them to their place, as is sustaining a large and numerous people for forty years on bread that would descend from the sky every day, and all the other signs and wonders that He performed for us at that time, as they all were novel and went against the laws of nature. This is the firm pillar of our faith and our Torah, for people who believe in the eternity of the universe have no Torah and no share in the World to Come. This thing is well known and there is no need to elaborate on well-known matters. Therefore, it was His will, blessed be He, to allow every man of Israel to participate in this important commandment, and that an accident or distance not impede him from fulfilling it. Rather, "If trouble will occur to him" and he is prevented in the first month and he did not do it with the earlier ones, he may do it in the second month. And since this is a great fundamental principle in our religion, the obligation even extends to a convert who converted between the first Pesach and the second, and to a child who reached maturity between the two Pesachs—that they are obligated to bring the Pesach Sheini offering.*[4]

Thus, indeed, one who eats matzah on Pesach, engages in remembering and reinforcing the lessons of *yetzias Mitzrayim*, and fills his heart with gratitude to the Almighty, fulfills the world's mission and becomes Hashem's partner in its Creation.

---

4 *Sefer Hachinuch*, mitzvah 380.

Sefiras Ha'omer

FORTY

From Pesach to Shavuos

Examining the purpose and meaning of Pesach Sheini, the "second chance" for those who were unable to participate in the *korban Pesach* on the fourteenth of Nissan, the author of *Sefer Hachinuch* writes:

> *At the root of this commandment is that the Pesach offering is a powerful and clear sign to all regarding the creation of the world. For at the time [of the Exodus], Hashem, blessed be He, performed great miracles and wonders for us and changed the nature of the world in the eyes of many nations. And [so] all the peoples of the earth saw that His providence and power is over the lower (earthly) beings. And then at that time, everyone believed and all who came after them believed that He, blessed be He, created the word ex nihilo at the time that He chose—and that was the well-known time. Even though creation ex nihilo is impossible according to nature, so too is splitting the depths of the sea to allow the passage of a great assemblage of people on dry land and returning them to their place, as is sustaining a large and numerous people for forty years on bread that would descend from the sky every day, and all the other signs and wonders that He performed for us at that time, as they all were novel and went against the laws of nature. This is the firm pillar of our faith and our Torah, for people who believe in*

> *the eternity of the universe have no Torah and no share in the World to Come. This thing is well known and there is no need to elaborate on well-known matters. Therefore, it was His will, blessed be He, to allow every man of Israel to participate in this important commandment, and that an accident or distance not impede him from fulfilling it. Rather, "if trouble will occur to him," and he is prevented in the first month and he did not do it with the earlier ones, he may do it in the second month. And since this is a great fundamental principle in our religion, the obligation even extends to a convert who converted between the first Pesach and the second, and to a child who reached maturity between the two Pesachs—that they are obligated to bring the Pesach Sheini offering.*[1]

Pesach is so significant to the Jewish identity that, unlike any other obligation, the Torah provides an accommodation to ensure that each and every Jew has an opportunity to participate fully.

The Ramban adds that the severity of Pesach's various obligations, and the recurrence of mitzvos that are intended to remind us of *yetzias Mitzrayim*, further emphasize how central its commemoration is in our national and religious psyche:

> *And [the Torah] was very strict in this regard, assigning kareis to one who eats chametz or neglects the Pesach offering, requiring that we write down our recollection of these events and place the scroll daily on our arms and between our eyes and on our doorposts...*[2]

And yet, for all its importance, Pesach—and *yetzias Mitzrayim* itself—is but preparation for the even more sublime holiday of Shavuos (*Chag Ha'atzeres*). As the author of *Sefer Hachinuch* stresses:

---

1 *Sefer Hachinuch*, mitzvah 380.

2 *Ramban*, end of *Parashas Bo*.

> *...[T]he Torah, which is the great principle for which they were redeemed, and it is their ultimate good. And it is a great matter for them, more than freedom from slavery. And hence Hashem made a sign of their leaving Egypt for the receiving of the Torah—as we always make what is secondary into a sign for what is the essence. And because of this—that it is [the] essence of Israel, and because of it were they redeemed and went up to all of the greatness to which they rose—we were commanded to tally from the morrow of the holiday of Pesach until the day of the giving of the Torah; to show about ourselves the great desire [we have] for the honored day, which our hearts yearn [for] like "a slave seeks shade" and always tallies when the yearned-for time will come in which he will go free. As the tally shows about a man that all of his deliverance and all of his desire is to reach that time.*[3]

Pesach is thus a first step toward our destination, Shavuos, when we commemorate our acceptance of the Torah and transformation into a holy nation.

So lofty and all-encompassing is the holiday of Shavuos, that it does not have any dedicated obligations or any mitzvah that is unique to Shavuos alone. Whereas Pesach and Sukkos have special mitzvos to capture each holiday's essential character, Shavuos, on which we received the entire Torah, cannot be condensed into a single mitzvah.

On this holy day, our ancestors stood at the foot of Har Sinai and declared, "*Naaseh v'nishma*—We will fulfill and we will listen," lovingly accepting upon themselves Hashem's demands. Each year, we, too, have the opportunity to reenact this moment, dedicating ourselves anew to observing Hashem's Torah and hearing His word. Rabbi Levi Yitzchak of Berditchev taught that on Shavuos, every Jew can again hear "*Anochi*—I am Hashem" and "*Lo yiheyeh lecha*—You shall not have other gods" directly from the Divine Source, just as our ancestors did thousands of years ago at Sinai.

---

3 *Sefer Hachinuch*, mitzvah 306.

Chazal, in both the *Bavli* and *Yerushalmi*, alluded to the annual receiving anew of the Torah. In a cryptic statement, Chazal ruled that one should not engage in medicinal bloodletting on the day before Shavuos. Doing so incurs peril on account of a particularly dangerous wind (*zika*), which threatened the Jewish People at Sinai and would have killed them had they not accepted the Torah. If Chazal were concerned that this ancient harmful force renews itself yearly, then certainly it follows that the entire event with all its tremendous spiritual content and opportunity is likewise recreated each year.

Additionally, Chazal point out that although the prescribed offerings for Shavuos implicitly include a sin-offering (*chatas*), as does every holiday, the *pasuk* enumerating the offerings on Shavuos does not use the word *chatas*, "sin." Chazal explain that "the Holy One said to the Jewish People, 'Since you accepted the yoke of Torah upon yourselves, I consider it as if you had never sinned.'"[4] This, despite the fact that Shavuos occurs every year, and, during the times we have a Beis Hamikdash in which to offer them, the same offerings are brought each year. Yet, our acceptance of the Torah is renewed each year—and our sins pale in the face of our commitment to fulfill Hashem's commandments and do His will.

---

4 *Yerushalmi, Rosh Hashanah* 4:8.

FORTY-ONE

Counting Days, Counting Weeks

The mitzvah of Sefiras Ha'omer, counting the days from Pesach until Shavuos, requires counting both the individual days as well as the weeks. We fulfill the latter requirement, starting with the seventh day, by noting in our count how many complete weeks and days of the incomplete week have passed.

What is behind the requirement that our count is to include both days and weeks?

Sefiras Ha'omer, as a time period, is characterized through two different paradigms. One approach describes these forty-nine days as preparation to receive the Torah, associating the days with the forty-eight attributes Chazal insisted must be present in a person who is to acquire Torah.[1] Another view, rooted in the *Zohar*, sees the seven weeks as analogous to the seven clean days a *zavah* requires prior to regaining ritual purity.[2]

Indeed, these are not diverging explanations that disagree with one another. Rather, the first perspective addresses the count of days—each day is a growth step toward becoming a worthy vessel for Torah.

1 In the following chapter, we will address the obvious inconsistency between forty-nine days and forty-eight *kinyanei haTorah*.

2 See *Zohar, Emor* 175 and *Rabbeinu Yerucham, Sefer Toldos Adam V'Chavah, Nesiv* 4, sect. 5.

Additionally, we must also go through a purification process, one that elevates us from the impurity of Egypt to the holiness of Torah. The mitzvah to count seven weeks, seven being the unit of time required in advance of purification throughout the Torah, reminds us of this aspect of our transformation over the duration of Sefiras Ha'omer.

At the culmination of our count, we reach Shavuos. Having counted forty-nine days and their seven weeks, we are now ready to receive Torah in purity—thus realizing Man's ultimate goal.

FORTY-TWO

You Shall Count For Yourselves

Each day of Sefiras Ha'omer is unique, with its own individual energy and potential. Simply read, the Torah commands, "*U'sefartem lachem*—Count for yourselves," but the word "*u'sefartem*" can also be related to "*sapir*," a precious, brightly shining jewel. Each day of our count is precious.

We cited above those who understand that the forty-nine days of Sefiras Ha'omer parallel the forty-eight "*kinyanei haTorah*"—the requisite character traits one must develop to acquire Torah.[1] To prepare to receive the Torah, one must focus each day on one of these areas of growth.

Of course, the glaring discrepancy cannot be avoided. Chazal listed forty-eight character traits, while Sefiras Ha'omer spans forty-nine days. Why is there an extra day, and, in keeping with a paradigm whereby Sefiras Ha'omer is meant to afford us an opportunity to work on these traits, what is one meant to do with the additional day?

Both Rabbi Yisrael Salanter[2] and the *Chiddushei HaRim*[3] offer a similar answer. Day forty-nine is dedicated for review and introspection,

1 *Pirkei Avos*, ch. 6.

2 Quoted in the name of Rav Elyah Lopian.

3 *Chiddushei HaRim Al HaTorah*.

to ensure that no area of potential growth opportunity was overlooked during the preceding forty-eight days.

Perhaps there is an additional element to the forty-ninth day. Describing a dialogue between Rabbi Yehoshua ben Chanania and the people of Alexandria, the Gemara teaches that one who seeks to grow in Torah wisdom must, alongside diligent and focused efforts to study, pray to He Who is the Source of all wisdom.[4] While surely, one must work hard and apply himself to his learning, he cannot succeed in acquiring Torah without Divine assistance.

In the evening prayer at the conclusion of Shabbos, we add a basic Havdalah formula to the fourth blessing of the *Amidah*. Its opening, however, appears to simply restate the beginning of the blessing it is nested in. We always begin the blessing with the words, "*Atah chonein l'adam daas*—You grant Man intelligence"; when adding Havdalah we then follow with, "You have granted us the ability to know Your Torah." Why do we repeat this introduction when we recite the Havdalah insertion?[5]

Rabbi Mordechai Yaffe, author of the *Levush*, suggests that there are indeed two distinct types of intelligence that Hashem has granted to Man. One is the elemental human intelligence, that which sets Man apart from the rest of Hashem's Creation. It is this ability we acknowledge in the opening words of the blessing, "You grant Man intelligence." Beyond the basic human facility, however, Hashem conferred upon His people the wisdom of Torah, an ability to connect with Divine knowledge through the medium of Torah. When, at the conclusion of Shabbos, we are called upon to recognize the distinction between the holy and the mundane, labels assigned only by the Torah, we must use the Torah wisdom to do so. Thus, we introduce Havdalah with an acknowledgment of this additional gift Hashem has granted us: "You have granted us the ability to know Your Torah."[6]

---

4 *Niddah* 70b.

5 See *Beis Yosef*, *Orach Chaim* 294.

6 *Levush Malchus* (*Levush Hachur*), *Orach Chaim* 294:1.

Torah is truly unlike any other discipline. While other fields of knowledge can be mastered through the natural methods of diligence and perseverance, Hashem's word is likened to fire.[7] Just as fire cannot be naturally grasped by human hands, so too can Torah only be acquired supernaturally: "Hashem gives wisdom and understanding."[8]

Chazal teach that each Jew, while still in utero, is taught the entire Torah by an angel who then, right before birth, causes the child to forget everything it has learned.[9] What is the value of learning the entire Torah, only to forget it before entering the world? The Vilna Gaon[10] and *Noam Elimelech*[11] both explain that without the Torah we learn in utero we would be unable to master Torah when we attempt to do so in this world. Thus, the *Zohar* describes that when one studies Torah diligently, he is "reminded what he learned in his mother's womb."[12]

Thus, Torah wisdom is a Divine gift, one that we are granted only by Hashem's desire to elevate His children and share His wisdom with them. One cannot achieve growth in Torah merely through natural human efforts. Rather, he must pray to the Source of all knowledge to grant this special gift.

Rabbi Yerucham Levovitz, the Mirrer Mashgiach, told the story of a *sefer*, written by a Rishon, named *Baruch She'amar*. According to the legend, its author was orphaned at a young age. With nobody to teach him, all he had learned was the prayer *Baruch She'amar*, which he would repeat whenever he went into shul to pray. Yet, Hashem heard his prayer and he eventually became a leader of his generation.[13]

After Moshe Rabbeinu's death, the Jewish People were bereft. In their mourning, they forgot 1,700 different Torah rulings he had taught them. Chazal tell us that Osniel ben Kenaz was able to restore the lost

---

7 *Yirmiyahu* 23:29.

8 *Mishlei* 2:6.

9 *Niddah* 30b.

10 Quoted in *Chochmas Betzalel, Niddah* 30b.

11 *Parashas Chayei Sarah.*

12 *Tikkunei Zohar, tikkun* 8.

13 See *Daas Torah, Maamarim, Balak.*

halachos through his skilled exposition of the relevant *pesukim*.[14] But I do not think Osniel's success was a product solely of his superior ability and innate talent. As Chazal themselves note there:

> *And from where do we derive that Hashem answered him? As it is written: "And Yaavetz (Osniel) called on the God of Israel, saying, 'If You will bless me indeed, and enlarge my border, and that Your hand may be with me, and that You will work deliverance from evil, that it may not pain me!' And Hashem granted him that which he requested."*[15] *"If You will bless me indeed," regarding Torah. "And enlarge my border," regarding students. "And that Your hand be with me," that my studies not be forgotten from my heart. "And that You will work deliverance from evil," that I will find friends like me. "That it may not pain me," that the evil inclination should not prevent me from studying. "If You do so, good; and if not, I will go depressed to my grave."*

Osniel ben Kenaz beseeched Hashem to grant him success in learning and teaching Torah, declaring that failure would cause him to die of grief. This prayer made him worthy of the highest stature—to restore the Torah that was lost with the passing of Moshe Rabbeinu.

As mentioned above, Rabbi Yehoshua ben Chanania gave two pieces of advice to the people of Alexandria who wished to acquire Torah knowledge. The first one—to labor diligently over one's studies, without distraction—is the work of the first forty-eight days of Sefiras Ha'omer; the forty-ninth day should be dedicated to his second instruction—to beg for success from the Source of all wisdom.

Even Moshe Rabbeinu himself, the greatest of all prophets, acquired Torah as a gift:

---

14 *Temurah* 16a.

15 *Divrei Hayamim I* 4:10.

> *Rabbi Yochanan taught: throughout the forty days that Moshe spent on the mountain he would learn Torah and forget it. Finally, it was granted to him as a gift.*[16]

Chazal strengthened us with this lesson, teaching that we must never give up or, conversely, take our ability to study Torah for granted. Alongside our efforts, we must lift our eyes to the Giver of Torah that He grant us success in our learning and show us the path of greatness.

16 *Horayos* 18b.

FORTY-THREE

Man's Mission in This World

We presented several ways to understand how the forty-ninth day of Sefiras Ha'omer is to be utilized if the period is otherwise meant to parallel the forty-eight traits necessary to acquire Torah. These approaches, thus far, have all focused on the final day of our count as the "extra" day, designating it either for renewed introspection or as a day devoted to prayer.

Alternatively, we might suggest that it is specifically the first day of the count that is not associated with one of the forty-eight traits, available instead for some other emphasis. The Ramchal organized his great work, *Mesilas Yesharim*, according to the spiritual-growth map famously charted by Rabbi Pinchas ben Yair.[1] Yet, there is one important difference between the two. Whereas Rabbi Pinchas ben Yair begins his journey with "Torah leads to caution (*zehirus*)," the Ramchal did not dedicate a section to "Torah," but rather presents *zehirus* as step one.

Indeed, the Ramchal did not identify Torah as a trait, one of many, that a person is expected to develop. Rather, Torah is the very essence of the mission, the cause for and purpose of all the work that is to follow. When a person is given a critical mission, he must first and foremost,

1 *Avodah Zarah* 20b.

before he even begins gathering the necessary resources, internalize its importance and the stakes involved in its success or failure. Only having done so, can he be expected to set forth with resolute determination to realize his goal.

To illustrate this, we can picture a king who urgently summons the leader of his army and tasks with an incredibly difficult mission. The general is to lead his soldiers across mighty rivers and through difficult terrain, and to capture a heavily protected fortress. In response, the general began to detail the items he will need to carry out the mission, but, before he could do so, the king interrupted him. "Before you tell me what you need, listen closely to your mission's significance. Know that the entire kingdom is in peril, your life and that of your family's is in danger, and only successful completion of this mission will save us all from death and destruction. Only if you appreciate and understand this can you succeed."

Likewise, before embarking on the lifelong mission the Ramchal sets out in his work, the reader is called to understand the very essence of Man's mission in this world—Torah. Thus, the first chapter of *Mesilas Yesharim* is named "*Klal Chovas Ha'adam B'Olamo*—Man's General Obligation in This World."

Before we begin tackling the forty-eight traits Chazal tell us are needed to acquire Torah, we need to spend the first day of Sefiras Ha'omer reflecting on the magnitude of the mission, the importance and centrality of Torah to everything in our world and through all of existence. With such clarity and focus, one can turn to the work that follows—developing and perfecting one's character, over each of the forty-eight subsequent days.

FORTY-FOUR

Complete Weeks

And you shall count for yourselves, from the day after Pesach, beginning with the day you bring the Omer, seven weeks—they shall be complete. Until the day after the seventh week, you shall count fifty days.[1]

Above, we discussed the different paradigms through which we might approach the work of Sefiras Ha'omer—the count of forty-nine days, during which we are meant to acquire the forty-eight traits needed for Torah, and the count of seven weeks, which parallel the seven days needed for purification.

Both ideas are reflected in the Kabbalistic practice to recite the chapter of *Tehillim*, "*La'menatzei'ach B'neginos,*" after counting the omer each day. This chapter, *Tehillim* 67, is comprised of seven *pesukim* containing seven words each, for a total of forty-nine—evoking contemplation on our counts of both days and weeks. Acquiring the character traits of Torah on the one hand, and purifying our souls on the other, are thus intertwined in this recitation.

1 *Vayikra* 23:15.

To both frameworks must be added a crucial element—the Torah's insistence on "*temimos*—completeness." Preserving the forty-nine days as a single, complete unit is deemed so important that, as a practical matter, many authorities (beginning with the *Halachos Gedolos*) ruled that if one misses even a single day's count, he fails entirely to fulfill the mitzvah. Central to all growth is the complete commitment and diligent focus in pursuit of one's goals.

All service in the Beis Hamikdash is centered around the three primary vessels: the *Menorah*, *Mizbei'ach*, and *Shulchan*. These parallel the three pillars of existence: Torah, *Avodah*, and *Chessed*. In its instructions governing each of the *keilim*, the Torah insists on constancy. A light was maintained at all times on the *Menorah*, the *ner maaravi*, which served as the source from which the other lights were lit;[2] the Torah requires that a fire burn constantly on the *Mizbei'ach*;[3] and bread was to be present at all times on the *Shulchan*.[4] No true spiritual accomplishment is possible without determination and uninterrupted, consistent effort.

Rabbi Chaim Shmuelevitz sees this idea in the famous story about Rabbi Akiva:

> *Rabbi Akiva was the shepherd of ben Kalba Savua, whose daughter saw that he was humble and refined. She said to him, "If I betroth myself to you, will you go to the study hall?" He said to her, "Yes." She became betrothed to him privately and sent him to study. Her father heard and removed her from his house, prohibiting her from benefiting from his property. Rabbi Akiva went and sat for twelve years in the study hall. When he returned, he brought twelve thousand students. He heard an old man saying, "For how long will you lead the life of a widow of a living man?" She said to him, "If it were up to me, he would sit for another twelve years." When Rabbi Akiva heard this he*

---

2 *Shabbos* 22b.
3 *Vayikra* 6:6.
4 *Shemos* 25:30.

> *said, "I have permission to do this." He went back and sat for another twelve years in the study hall.*

Why did Rabbi Akiva immediately turn around and return to his studies? Why did he not enter his home, even briefly, to greet the family he had not seen for twelve years? If nothing else, should he have not gone inside to thank his wife for her devotion and support?

Rabbi Chaim Shmuelevitz answers that had Rabbi Akiva done so, he would have lost the potential inherent in twenty-four years of consecutive study. Instead, his learning would have been split into two parts, twelve years followed by another twelve years. In Torah, the total is not merely the sum of its parts; quality of Torah study is inestimably enhanced by the focus and uninterrupted constancy.

Hence, the Torah commands us to count seven complete weeks, with forty-nine complete days. Torah growth and purity of mind and soul must be achieved through persistent and focused effort, without interruption.

FORTY-FIVE

That Which I Have Damaged

Many Chassidim and other Kabbalistically-oriented traditions have the custom to recite a prayer associating each day's count in Sefiras Ha'omer with a particular realm in the system of *Sefiros*. Anchored in the teachings of the Arizal, the framework assigns to each week of Sefiras Ha'omer one of seven *Sefiros* and, in turn, each of the seven *Sefiros* is further broken down into the same seven *Sefiros*. Thus, each of the seven *Sefiros*—*Chessed*, *Gevurah*, *Tiferes*, *Hod*, *Yesod*, and *Malchus*—is composed of all seven, for a total of forty-nine unique combinations, each corresponding to one of the forty-nine days.[1]

These are lofty ideas. Let us grasp that which is relevant—on our level—to one's growth during this time.

The Kabbalists taught us that Hashem's control of the universe is exercised through a system that spans four distinct realms—*Atzilus*, *Beriah*, *Yetzirah*, and *Asiyah*—with Hashem's will cascading downward from its most refined spiritual essence (*Atzilus*) until its impact is felt in the tangible, material world (*Asiyah*). Yet, although we are rooted

1 See *Shaar Hakavanos*, *Shaar Sefiras Ha'omer*, *derush* 11.

entirely in the "lowest" world, *Asiyah*, our actions can affect the "higher" realms as well.

A total of ten *Sefiros* represent a more specific breakdown of the process we just described. These *Sefiros* are attributes that describe Hashem's interaction with Creation—how He runs the universe, as it were—and their impacts occur at different points. *Kesser*, *Chochmah*, and *Binah*—the highest *Sefiros*—belong to the world of *Atzilus*; *Chessed*, *Gevurah*, and *Tiferes* are associated with *Beriah*; *Netzach*, *Hod*, and *Yesod* with *Yetzirah*. *Malchus* is the realm in which we function, the material world of *Asiyah*. In this world, Hashem's purpose in Creation is realized—that His created beings should recognize and submit to His Kingship (*Malchus*).

If Man is created in Hashem's image, then Man, like Hashem, operates within a framework of *Sefiros* as well. While the "upper" three *Sefiros* operate at too high a plane for us to consider, we do recognize Man's God-like power to build and destroy worlds using the attributes from *Chessed* and on. It is our shortcomings in these areas that we have an opportunity to rectify during the weeks of Sefiras Ha'omer. And, when we embrace the possibility of correcting our failing in our exercise of these traits, we inspire healing of the *Sefiros* throughout Creation, even where we may have previously caused damage through our errors.

We know that each of the *Sefiros* also corresponds to one the Jewish nation's great shepherds—Avraham—*Chessed*, Yitzchak—*Gevurah*, Yaakov—*Tiferes*, Moshe—*Netzach*, Aharon—*Hod*, Yosef—*Yesod*, and David—*Malchus*. Our great forefathers, despite having surely achieved perfection in all areas, each excelled in one particular area that characterized his uniqueness.

This should greatly inspire and encourage us to seek our own individual paths to greatness. If our holy ancestors were so differentiated in their relationship with Hashem and themselves, surely, we, on our own much humbler level, must do our part to develop and grow in those areas we identify in ourselves as requiring the most attention, striving to our own unique perfection.

FORTY-SIX

For Failing to Honor One Another

They said that Rabbi Akiva had twelve thousand pairs of students from Gevas to Antipatris and they all died in one period, because they did not treat each other with respect. The world was desolate until Rabbi Akiva came to our rabbis in the south and taught them: Rabbi Meir, Rabbi Yehudah, Rabbi Yossi, Rabbi Shimon, and Rabbi Elazar ben Shamua. And these are the very ones who upheld Torah at that time. It is taught that all [the original students] died from Pesach until Shavuos.[1]

A harsh punishment indeed! Surely, their offenses did not constitute violation of any Torah prohibition that carries a death penalty. Why were Rabbi Akiva's students all wiped out?

1 *Yevamos* 62b.

I submit that their proximity to Rabbi Akiva placed a greater demand on his students' conduct toward each other. As his students, they should have internalized, in the most meaningful possible sense, Rabbi Akiva's teaching "'You shall love your fellow as yourself'—this is a great principle in the Torah."[2] They should have been living testimony to Rabbi Akiva's declaration, "Desirable is Man, for he was created in Hashem's image...desirable are B'nei Yisrael, for they are called Hashem's children..."[3] As his students, their failure to embody the great master's ethos in their own interpersonal behavior was thus all the more glaring, a shortcoming that claimed a high and tragic price and nearly wiped out an entire generation of Torah.

Indeed, Rabbi Akiva's sensibilities reached further. True, each and every Jew must be afforded the dignity befitting Hashem's child, but Torah scholars must be treated with even greater reverence and honor. Rabbi Akiva identified an extra word—"*es*"—in the *pasuk* that commands us to revere Hashem, an addition that serves to expand the *pasuk*'s reach to include Torah scholars: "*Es Hashem Elokecha tira*—You must revere Hashem, your God"—this includes Torah scholars.[4]

My great teacher, the Klausenberger Rebbe, *zt"l*, would often recall the following story. As a young child, he was once sitting on his father's lap. Seeing his father, the great Rav Tzvi of Rudnik, sobbing, the little boy innocently inquired as to the source of his father's anguish. "I cry because I envy you," replied Rav Tzvi. Bewildered, the boy wondered, "How is it possible that Father, a distinguished and highly regarded Rav and community leader, could be jealous of a young child?" Rav Tzvi answered, "I envy you because you never saw the great *Divrei Chaim* of Tzanz!" This confused the child even more, who replied, "Surely then, I should be jealous of you—you had the privilege of serving that holy *tzaddik*!"

"No," answered Rav Tzvi, "since you never saw the *Divrei Chaim*, the expectations from you will be lower. But I, who grew up in the presence

---

2 *Bereishis Rabbah* 24:7; *Sifra, Kedoshim* 2:4; *Yerushalmi, Nedarim* 30b.

3 *Avos* 3:14.

4 *Pesachim* 22b; *Kiddushin* 57a; *Bava Kama* 41b; *Bechoros* 6b.

of such greatness, will have to answer for failing to live up to the lofty heights I was exposed to!"

Along with the privilege of associating with greatness comes tremendous responsibility. Toward the end of the Torah's rebuke and ominous foreshadowing of the punishments B'nei Yisrael are to incur when they stray from Hashem's will, is a confusing *pasuk*. "And I will remember My covenant with Yaakov, and My covenant with Yitzchak, and also My covenant with Avraham I shall remember."[5] Purportedly, this *pasuk* presents itself as a note of comfort—within all the terrible calamities that are to befall us, Hashem assures us He will not forget His promise to our forefathers. Yet, the Torah then immediately reverts to its harsh rebuke and the litany of woes that our intransigence will lead to. Why is an isolated glimmer of positivity buried in *pesukim* otherwise devoted to describing the plethora of tragedies we will face?

The *Shelah Hakadosh* (*Shnei Luchos Habris*) explains that this *pasuk* is not intended to offer solace—it is part of the Torah's criticism of our actions. As children of Avraham, Yitzchak, and Yaakov, our conduct should have reflected our great lineage. Instead, we betrayed our roots and the covenant Hashem sealed with our forefathers. As Chazal expressed:

> *The Sages said to Rabbi Pereida, "Rabbi Ezra, a grandson of Rabbi Avtolus, who is a tenth-generation descendant of Rabbi Elazar ben Azaryah, who is a tenth-generation descendant of Ezra, is standing at the gate." Rabbi Pereida said to the Sages, "What is all this detail for?" Rabbi Pereida elaborated, "If he is a man of Torah, he is worthy. If he is a man of Torah and a man of lineage, he is worthy. But if he is a man of lineage and not a man of Torah, fire should devour him."*[6]

A man who fails to live up to the precedents set by an illustrious lineage is worse off than someone who was never exposed to such

---

5 *Vayikra* 26:42.

6 *Menachos* 53a.

inspiration—in the eyes of the Torah, the expectations of the former are uncompromising.

Rabbi Akiva's students, on their level, were somehow remiss in their interpersonal conduct. But, as students of Rabbi Akiva—who had so stressed the great care one must take when interacting with any human being, especially Torah scholars—they were expected to live up to the highest possible standard. Their failure to do so was calamitous.

Rabbi Akiva's students, according to the Gemara's report, perished because they "did not treat each other with respect." Chazal are silent as to whether or not the students indeed respected and loved each other. What is significant—and what they were punished for—was their outward conduct.

Let us delve into this a bit further. We are all familiar with Rabbi Akiva's pronouncement, "'You shall love your fellow as yourself'—this is a great principle in the Torah."[7] However, Ben Azzai's disagreement with Rabbi Akiva, although recorded in the original sources, is less well known:

> *"You shall love your fellow as yourself"—Rabbi Akiva said, "This is a great principle in the Torah." Ben Azzai said, "'Zeh sefer toldos adam—This is the book of Man's history'—this principle is greater than the first."*[8]

While Rabbi Akiva's position is instinctively appealing and plausible as a great fundamental precept of Torah values, Ben Azzai's claim is difficult to understand. What is the principle inherent to the words "this is the book of Man's history"?

Perhaps Rabbi Akiva and Ben Azzai are debating which element is more central to the formation and preservation of a Torah society. Is love for one's fellow the primary value, or does our social fabric hinge on individuals treating one another with respect? Rabbi Akiva's answer is "Love your fellow as yourself!" In the Torah's view, reciprocal love is

---

7 *Bereishis Rabbah* 24:7; *Sifra, Kedoshim* 2:4; *Yerushalmi, Nedarim* 30b.

8 Ibid.

the foundation of an enduring culture. Ben Azzai, on the other hand, invoked a different *pasuk*, perhaps a more modest approach, yet one that appears deeply embedded in Creation. "This is the book of Man's history; on the day God created Man, He formed him in the image of God," underscores Man's origin and essential character—his creation in the Divine image.

Ben Azzai reminds Rabbi Akiva of the latter's other teaching, that "beloved is Man, for he was created in the Divine image." In Ben Azzai's view, this second teaching supersedes—and is indeed more fundamental to—the call to love one's fellow man. Why? Ben Azzai recognized that love, as an emotion, cannot be demanded. One is naturally inclined to loving certain individuals more so than others; he cannot be expected to love all people equally, nor can everyone else love him in the same measure. But behavior can be prescribed. The Torah can indeed demand that I treat every single person with equal respect, regardless of my love for them, or theirs for me.

Writing very forcefully and poignantly, the Netziv addresses our obligation to respect one another—no matter what:

> *By praising Hashem as "just" (yashar), the Torah acknowledges the Holy One, blessed be He's judgment being meted out toward the generation who lived during the destruction of the Second Beis Hamikdash, who are described as a perverse and twisted generation.*[9] *We explained that though they were righteous and pious, toiling in Torah study, they were not upright in their societal behavior. And so, due to the baseless hatred for one another residing within their hearts, they suspected anyone who was not religious in accordance with their viewpoint to be a Sadducee. This led to rampant bloodshed along with a transgression of all the other evils in the world, causing the Beis Hamikdash's destruction. Thus, the acknowledgment of Hashem's justice: the Holy One, blessed be He, is just (yashar), intolerant of those types of righteous*

---

9 *Devarim* 32:5.

> *individuals. Rather, he favors those who act in a way that is socially upright (yashar)—unlike those who act in a perverse manner, even when their actions are performed for the sake of Heaven. Such can lead to the destruction of creation and the ruin of civilization.*[10]

Harsh critique indeed! Righteous individuals, sages and Torah scholars, failed to respect others, treating those who disagreed with them as adversaries and heretics. Hashem does not tolerate such *tzaddikim*. Failure to treat one's fellow with respect led to the death of Rabbi Akiva's twenty-four thousand students and to the destruction of the Beis Hamikdash.

10 Introduction to *Haamek Davar*.

FORTY-SEVEN

Ahavas Re'im and Kevod Chaverim

For Hashem has greater interest in one's mitzvos that also fulfill the needs of others, than mitzvos that are strictly between Man and Hashem.[1]

To love one's fellow Jew is indeed a great mitzvah, a foundation of *bein adam l'chaveiro,* as Rabbi Akiva taught, "You shall love your neighbor as yourself—this is a great principle in the Torah."

But we are also obligated to treat each other with respect. This is a separate requirement. Even in a situation where "love your neighbor" proves exceedingly difficult—and it often does—the requirement remains to treat everyone with the dignity befitting a fellow human being.

We noted above that Rabbi Akiva's students did not die because they did not love each other. They were punished for dismissive and contemptuous actions and speech toward one another. Whatever feelings

1 *Rosh*, Mishnah, *Peah* 1:1.

of love or hatred they may or may not have harbored, Chazal were careful to tell us that the punishment was for the disrespect.

Chazal stressed the severity of preserving a fellow person's dignity: "One should rather throw himself into a fiery furnace than publicly embarrass his friend."[2] And, conversely, they noted the tremendous stature of someone who scrupulously preserves his or her friend's dignity. When Rabbi Pinchas ben Yair split the river that was blocking his way, successfully crossing it on dry land, his students asked whether they might cross as well. He responded that only those individuals who are certain they never treated another Jew lightly may do so.[3]

Fully developed, one's sensitivity for the feelings and dignity of others can extend to truly staggering proportions. Such concern is clearly evident in Rabbi Chanina bar Chama's actions following the death of his great teacher, Rabbi Yehudah HaNasi, known as Rebbi.[4]

Rebbi's death was imminent; the Jewish People down on earth were struggling with the celestial forces summoning the great leader back to Heaven. Rebbi called for his colleagues, the sages of the academy, to whom he would entrust his final instructions. Prescient and Divinely inspired, his words are predictive as much as they are prescriptive:

> *Yosef Chafni and Shimon Efrasi attended to me in my life—they shall attend to me in my death. They [the Chachamim] thought he meant in this world. When they saw that their [Yosef's and Shimon's] biers preceded his, they said, "Now we understand that he meant in the other world."*

Rebbi then named successors to the positions he held:

> *My son Shimon shall be the leading Torah authority, my son Gamliel shall be the Nasi, and Chanina bar Chama shall sit at the head of the academy.*

---

2 *Bava Metzia* 59a.

3 *Yerushalmi, Demai* 4a.

4 *Kesubos* 103a.

And yet, despite the explicit command of his holy teacher, Rabbi Chanina bar Chama refused to take his seat at the head of the academy. Instead, he deferred the honor to Rabbi Efes, who was two-and-a-half years his senior. How are we to understand Rabbi Chanina's actions? Chazal, elsewhere, tell us how scrupulously Rabbi Chanina venerated his master, cherishing every word he learned from Rebbi.[5] Yet, here he blatantly rejects Rebbi's last will, instructions so clearly laden with Divine inspiration! Apparently, in Rabbi Chanina's eyes, the possibility of offending Rabbi Efes was unimaginable. Better to face the consequences of defying his teacher's wishes than risk hurting his fellow sage and senior colleague!

But Rabbi Chanina's sensitivity to Rabbi Efes's feelings hardly resolves our question. After all, surely, the great Rebbi—at the time of his passing no less—would be equally attentive to Rabbi Efes's honor. Indeed, we learn that his statements regarding Yosef Chafni and Shimon Efrasi were specifically intended to preserve their dignity. Certainly, Rebbi's sensibilities in the area of his fellow man's dignity were not inferior to Rabbi Chanina's in any way. And, nevertheless, Rabbi Chanina demurred and did not take his seat as leader of the academy, setting aside his teacher's instructions.

Perhaps Rabbi Chanina bar Chama really did want to fulfill Rebbi's instructions. In his mind, he was fully aware of all the above and wished to submit to his master's instructions, just as he had throughout Rebbi's life. But he was unable to. So carefully had Rabbi Chanina honed his sensitivity to the feelings of others, that his noble character would not allow him to proceed with an action that could possibly offend Rabbi Efes. And, as per the general rule that one who is unable to perform a mitzvah is exempt from its obligation, Rabbi Chanina, under such duress, was excused from attending to Rebbi's command.

Meticulous attention to preserving a fellow man's dignity is a great mitzvah—a "fundamental principle of the Torah"—and a lofty character trait. But Chazal also describe its awesome power. Years after

---

5 *Yerushalmi, Niddah* 2:7. See also *Shabbos* 153a: "Who is deserving of a place in the World to Come? One who finds favor in the eyes of his teachers."

the events above, when asked why he had lived such a long life, Rabbi Chanina identified as the source of his merit his extreme care for Rabbi Efes's honor.[6] Moreover, Chazal tell us that Rava, the towering giant of his generation and teacher to the leaders of the next, attained his stature in the same merit:

> *When Rava took leave of Rav Yosef, he would walk backward, until his legs were bruised and the threshold of Rav Yosef's house was bloodied. They said to Rav Yosef, "This is what Rava does." He said to him, "May it be God's will that you lift your head over the entire city..."*[7]

Rashi interprets "lift your head over the entire city" to mean that Rava will become the head of the academy; Rabbeinu Chananel defines the promise as an assurance that the halachah will always follow Rava's opinion. Indeed, both became true. Rava's stature was due not only to his remarkable efforts to acquire Torah, which similarly caused him to spill his own blood,[8] but was earned through the greatness of character exemplified in his extreme deference to Rav Yosef.

Rabbi Chanina's refusal to occupy the position designated for him when doing so might damage the dignity of another person, was not without precedent. Moshe Rabbeinu himself, whose greatness would never be disputed, showed the same degree of concern. Rashi, reading this theme into Moshe's words to Hashem at the *sneh* (burning bush), writes:

> *Neither from yesterday nor from before yesterday: This teaches us that for an entire period of seven days Hashem had been endeavoring to persuade Moshe at the thornbush to go on his mission, for the terms "mitmol—yesterday" and "shilshom—before yesterday" and "me'az dabercha—since you spoke" imply three days, and the thrice-stated "gam—also"*

---

6 *Yerushalmi, Taanis* 4:2.

7 *Yoma* 53a.

8 See *Shabbos* 88a.

> *point to three extensions of the period, making six in all, and therefore he had now reached the seventh day when he further said to Him, "Send, I pray, by the hand of him whom You will send"—until Hashem became angry with him, and he accepted the mission. All this reluctance was because he was unwilling to assume any dignity that would make him superior to his brother Aharon who was older than he and was also a prophet, as it is said that the man of God spoke to Eli, the high-priest, in Hashem's name, "Surely I revealed myself to the house of your father when they were in Egypt"—"your father" means Aharon. Similarly, "And I made myself known to them in the land of Egypt…and I said to them…," and that prophecy was spoken to Aharon.*[9]

Hashem Himself has instructed Moshe to lead His people out of Egypt, yet Moshe hesitates to assume a role that might suggest he is superior to his older brother. Did Moshe consider his own sensitivity to Aharon's feelings to be more refined than Hashem's? Surely, Hashem's decision implicitly incorporated all such considerations—what right did Moshe have to question it?

Moshe, like Rabbi Chanina centuries after him, was not refusing to do Hashem's will. He was telling Hashem that he simply could not physically take an action that might hurt his brother in any way. Fully aware of the tremendous opportunity in front of him, Moshe was claiming the exemption of one who is incapacitated and cannot perform the obligation on hand. Only upon receiving Hashem's assurance that Aharon's feelings would not be hurt, rather—on the contrary—"he will see you and rejoice," was Moshe satisfied that no barrier stood in front of him.

---

9 *Rashi, Shemos* 4:10.

FORTY-EIGHT

Love Your Fellow As Yourself

Rav Moshe Leib Sassover would tell his chassidim that he learned the true meaning of the Torah's commandment to love one's fellow as one's self, from a conversation between two peasants that he happened to overhear. One gentile asked his friend, "Do you love me?" Somewhat surprised, the other replied, "Of course I do! We have been best friends for twenty years! How could you ask me whether I love you?" "If you truly love me," retorted the first, "then tell me which tooth hurts me right now!"

How can one claim to love his fellow Jew if he does not feel his friend's every pain, if his heart does not fill with joy at his neighbor's success? To love another human being is to be bound together with the other's soul, to experience a friend's pain and happiness as if it were his own.

Rav Moshe Leib's teaching is true to the Baal Shem Tov's tradition. Each blade of grass and every moment of time is governed by Divine

Providence, and there is something to learn from the most ostensibly mundane and insignificant event. Life teems with meaning and opportunity—and, in this case, Rav Moshe Leib's chance encounter is Divinely orchestrated to provide deep insight into an all-important mitzvah.

Nevertheless, the concept—that love entails sharing the other's every emotion—appears elsewhere as well. A midrash, cited by *Tosafos* and other Rishonim, relates the following story about Shlomo HaMelech:

> *Ashmedai once produced from the ground a man with two heads in the presence of Shlomo HaMelech. The man married and had children, some with two heads, like their father, and others with one head, like the mother. When the time came for them to divide their father's estate, those with two heads demanded a double portion, claiming that they were two people, and their case came before Shlomo HaMelech.*[1]

Other versions of the story include Shlomo's reaction:

> *In his wisdom, Shlomo covered one head and poured boiling water on the other. When both heads cried out in pain as one, Shlomo concluded that it was a single person with two heads and should only be counted as one.*[2]

As Chazal famously characterized the wanton nature of revenge:

> *This would be like someone who was cutting meat and accidentally cut his hand. Would he in turn cut the other hand?*[3]

Hurting another Jew is no different than one hand striking back at the other. B'nei Yisrael share a single body, and we are meant to experience our fellow's ups and downs as our own. As Rav Moshe Leib of Sassov recounted the peasant's words, "If you truly love me you should know which tooth hurts me!"

---

1 *Tosafos, Menachos* 37a (s.v. "*oh kum galei*").

2 See *Shitah Mekubetzes* ad loc.

3 *Yerushalmi, Nedarim* 30b.

Pesach Sheini

FORTY-NINE

Why Should We Lose Out?

And there were men who were impure from handling a dead body, and they were unable to offer the Pesach on that day, and they approached Moshe and Aharon on that day. These men said to him, "We are impure from handling a dead person—why should we lose out by not offering Hashem's offering in its appointed time along with B'nei Yisrael?"[1]

Pesach Sheini is an entirely unique mitzvah. No other commandment came in direct response to a request for such an obligation. These individuals were exempt from the Pesach offering that year because they were impure. Only after their plaintive demand—"Why should we lose out on the opportunity to offer the Pesach?"—did Hashem respond in kind with the mitzvah of Pesach Sheini.

1 *Bamidbar* 9:6–7.

Approaching Hashem with such a demand is bold. Yet, when animated by pure intentions, such boldness can be holy[2] and has the power to generate new Torah—in this case, the mitzvah of Pesach Sheini.

This theme reappears later in the Torah. Moshe says to the people, "On this day you became a nation to Hashem your God,"[3] yet no date is given, nor is the comment identified with any particular catalyzing event. Commenting on a different *pasuk*, Rashi provides us with the context of these words:

> *I have heard that on the day when Moshe gave the Book of Torah to the sons of Levi, as it is written, "And he gave it to the priests the sons of Levi," all Israel came before Moshe and said to him, "Our teacher, Moshe, we, too, stood at Sinai and accepted the Torah, and it was given to us; why, then, do you give the people of your tribe control over it, that they may tomorrow say to us, 'Not to you was it given, but to us was it given?'" Moshe rejoiced at this matter and in reference to this he said to them, "This day you became a nation," meaning, on this day I came to understand that you are attached to and have a desire for Hashem's closeness.*[4]

Amazingly, it was not on the day that B'nei Yisrael solemnly declared, "*Naaseh v'nishma*—We will fulfill and then we will listen," that they "became a nation." That moment only arrived forty years later. When they cried out, "We too stood at Sinai and received the Torah—do not withhold it from us," they demonstrated their wholehearted passion for Hashem and His Torah. On that day, they truly became Hashem's people.

---

2 *Sanhedrin* 105a—"*Chutzpah*, even towards Heaven, can succeed."

3 *Devarim* 27:9.

4 *Rashi, Devarim* 29:3.

Rabbi Yaakov Emden provides a surprising explanation for Pesach Sheini:

> *The reason Pesach Sheini was established in Iyar was revealed to me from Heaven: this was the day they finished consuming the bread they took out of Egypt...therefore the miracles of yetzias Mitzrayim continued until then...*[5]

Acknowledging that this is a novel, previously unheard idea, Rabbi Yaakov Emden teaches us that by eating the matzos, our ancestors continued to draw down the spiritual nourishment and energy of *yetzias Mitzrayim*. Although the matzah was baked entirely naturally, its essence evoked the pathos of both slavery and redemption—the "poor man's bread" alongside their hurried exit from Egypt—thereby continuing their miraculous existence. Fittingly, Pesach Sheini was designated for the final day those wondrous experiences of *yetzias Mitzrayim* still permeated their consciousness.

5 *Siddur Beis Yaakov, Chodesh Iyar.*

FIFTY

Lag Ba'omer

They said that Rabbi Akiva had twelve thousand pairs of students from Gevas to Antipatris and they all died in one period, because they did not treat each other with respect. The world was desolate until Rabbi Akiva came to our rabbis in the south and taught them: Rabbi Meir, Rabbi Yehudah, Rabbi Yossi, Rabbi Shimon, and Rabbi Elazar ben Shamua. And these are the very ones who upheld Torah at that time. It is taught that all of them died from Pesach until Shavuos.[1]

On the thirty-third day of Sefiras Ha'omer we celebrate, noting that on this day the plague that devastated the ranks of Rabbi Akiva's students came to a stop.[2] Why did the deaths end on the day we now refer to as Lag Ba'omer?

Earlier, we cited the *baalei mussar* who taught that each day of Sefiras Ha'omer corresponds to one of the character traits listed by Chazal as

1 *Yevamos* 62b.

2 *Shulchan Aruch, Orach Chaim* 493:1.

necessary attributes for acquiring Torah.[3] Each day from Pesach until Shavuos has its unique calling, an opportunity to grow in that day's character trait in preparation for receiving the Torah.

Details always matter, and nothing is a coincidence. If we examine this one-to-one relationship between the forty-eight attributes and their days in Sefiras Ha'omer, we discover that day thirty-two corresponds to the requirement that one who is to acquire Torah must "love all creatures." Thus, we would suggest that Rabbi Akiva's students, sensing their collective burden as soon as the plague struck, immediately set to work on their love for one another. On day thirty-two they felt they had succeeded—they now were bound together in mutual love and respect—and, indeed, the plague was over the following day, day number thirty-three.

That said, Chazal's description of this character trait—love for all creatures—demands our attention. The Torah commands us to love our fellow Jews. For all the regard we are meant to have for Hashem's creation, nowhere in the Torah are we instructed to love all creatures. Yet, Chazal used this term, apparently drawing upon Rabbi Akiva's teaching that "man is beloved, for he was created in Hashem's image."[4] Every person, regardless of stature or importance, was created in the Divine image and is worthy of respect. Chazal insisted on each individual's dignity, no matter whom, even in the face of serious halachic implications, noting that "one's honor is so great that it can override a Torah prohibition."[5]

Rabbi Moshe of Lechovitch would relate the words of Rav Mannela, a prominent *chassid*, who commented, "When I say the words '*B'fi yesharim tisromam, u'b'sifsei tzaddikim tisbarech, u'v'leshon chassidim tiskadash, u'v'kerev kedoshim tishalal*—In the mouths of upright ones You will be elevated, on the lips of righteous ones You will be blessed, in the words of the pious You will be sanctified, and among holy ones You will be praised,' I do not see myself included. Can I claim to be even 'upright,'

---

3 *Avos* 6:6.

4 Ibid., 3:14.

5 *Berachos* 19b.

let alone righteous or pious? However, then I continue, *'u'v'makhalos rivevos amecha beis Yisrael*—and among the multitudes of thousands of Your people Israel.' In that group I belong!" And Rav Moshe would add, "I do not even know that I meet that description. But when I then say, *'She'kein chovas kol ha'yetzurim*—For it is the obligation of all creatures,' I am certainly included." We are all Hashem's creations and are beloved—and deserving of honor—for that reason alone.

Chazal strongly urged us to adopt a position of humility and deference toward others:

> *The Sages in Yavneh were wont to say: I am God's creature and my counterpart is God's creature. My work is in the city and his work is in the field. I rise early for my work and he rises early for his work. And just as he does not presume to do my work, so I do not presume to do his work. Lest you say: I do a lot, while he does little, it has already been taught: One who brings a substantial offering and one who brings a meager one—as long as he directs his heart toward Heaven.*[6]

Each person has his or her individual mission, innate abilities, and unique challenges. No person can know what is in the heart or mind of another, what their fellow man is struggling with, or most important, who is indeed greater than whom. What one must know is that "I am Hashem's creature and he is Hashem's creature"—each of us was formed in Hashem's image and is thus deserving of respect. Beyond that—"one who brings a substantial offering and one who brings a meager one—as long as he directs his heart toward Heaven."

Many thousands of Rabbi Akiva's students died between Pesach and Shavuos. It is fair to posit that, as students of that holy Tanna, however deficient their interpersonal conduct may have been, their quarrels were not over trivialities. It is unlikely, indeed, that their offenses

---

6 Ibid., 17a. Note that according to many interpretations, this passage contrasts one who studies Torah—"my work is in the city"—to a laborer who has little time for Torah—"his work is in the field," yet Chazal insist that any such comparison is inappropriate.

were animated by competition over money or fame. Surely, we must assume that their disagreements concerned matters of the spirit—diverging opinions in Torah, halachah, and service of Hashem—and, in their zeal and pursuit of truth they did not treat one another with the fullest respect.

Chazal alluded to this, commenting (in a separate account of the plague), "that they envied each other's Torah."[7] Although their intentions were pure and their zeal driven by sincere desire to serve Hashem properly, they incurred a terrible punishment. Torah scholars bear the added burden of representing peace and mutual respect in a fragmented world—they must not be the ones fueling division and discord.

We already quoted the Netziv's harsh words, which are worth repeating here:

> *...[T]he generation who lived during the destruction of the Second Beis Hamikdash, who are described as a perverse and twisted generation.*[8] *We explained that though they were righteous and pious, toiling in Torah study, they were not upright in their societal behavior. And so, due to the baseless hatred for one another residing within their hearts, they suspected anyone who was not religious in accordance with their viewpoint to be a Sadducee. This led to rampant murder along with a transgression of all the other evils in the world, causing the Beis Hamikdash's destruction. Thus, the acknowledgment of Hashem's justice: the Holy One, blessed be He, is just (yashar), intolerant of those types of righteous individuals. Rather, he favors those who act in a way that is socially upright (yashar)—unlike those who act in a perverse manner, even when their actions are performed for the sake of Heaven. Such can lead to the destruction of creation and the ruin of civilization.*[9]

---

7 *Koheles Rabbah* 11.

8 *Devarim* 32:5.

9 Introduction to *Ha'amek Davar*.

When love of Hashem leads one to hate his fellow man, something has gone awry. One who loves Hashem, loves His children as well; when someone hates a Jew, he does not truly love Hashem. Rashi explicitly states the same:

> *Those who hate You: those who hate Israel. For anyone who hates a Jew, hates the One Who spoke and created the world...*[10]

In sequencing their forty-eight character traits, Chazal suggest an order that reflects this idea, with "loves the Almighty" preceding "loves all creatures." Love of Hashem must organically and necessarily expand to love for one's fellow man. Hashem has declared B'nei Yisrael His children—if I love the Father, love for the children who were created in His image must follow.

---

10 *Rashi, Bamidbar* 10:35.

FIFTY-ONE

Love Your Fellow—A Great Principle in Torah

Rabbi Akiva taught: "'You shall love your fellow as yourself'—this is a great principle in the Torah."[1]

During this time of year, as we mourn the great loss of Torah that was wrought by neglect of this mitzvah and Rabbi Akiva's teaching, we are called upon to consider its message and pursue growth in this area.

Let us recall. Rabbi Akiva led twenty-four thousand students, all of whom died in a few short weeks for their failure to treat each other with proper respect. Bereft, Rabbi Akiva sought out new students to whom he might impart his Torah, individuals who would be of nobler character than their predecessors. Identifying "the masters from the south" as such individuals, he began teaching his Torah to Rabbi Meir, Rabbi Yehudah, Rabbi Yossi, Rabbi Shimon, Rabbi Elazar ben Shamua, and Rabbi Nechemia.[2] As the Midrash teaches, in his first instruction

---

1 *Bereishis Rabbah* 24:7; *Sifra, Kedoshim* 2:4; *Yerushalmi, Nedarim* 30b.

2 See *Yevamos* 62b and *Koheles Rabbah*, ch. 11. The two versions complement each other,

to these great men, Rabbi Akiva warned them, "I just lost twenty-four thousand, who died because they envied each other's Torah. You must not be like them."[3]

We discussed above the bewildering severity of this event—thousands of Torah scholars, wiped out for an offense that surely does not carry a death penalty. For all its importance, we are unaware of any hint in the Torah that the mitzvah to love one's fellow man can generate such a punishment. As we noted, these individuals were obviously held to an unusually high standard. True disciples of Rabbi Akiva would doubtless have heard him many times reinforce the greatness of every man—"Beloved is Man for he was created in the Divine image"—and the consequent "great principle of the Torah" that one must love his fellow as one loves himself. Their proximity to Rabbi Akiva and his worldview imposed upon his students exacting demands in this area, expectations that they, unfortunately, did not meet.

Perhaps their deaths should not be understood as punishment for their behavior. After all, as mentioned, nowhere in the Torah is it suggested that failure to honor one's fellow man is a capital offense. Rather, their fate was intertwined with the Divine plan for Rabbi Akiva himself. Rabbi Akiva's Torah was intended to serve as the primary transmission of *Torah She'baal Peh*—the Oral Law, the central *mesorah*—the tradition that would travel with the Jewish People far into the future. His students would be a crucial link in that chain, and, as such, their character had to be impeccable, their Torah pure and fully representative of Rabbi Akiva's loftiest teachings. Failing to live up to these standards, Rabbi Akiva's first group of students forfeited their place in the development and transmission of Torah.

Their place was taken by the giants we named above, who, in due time, indeed became the primary transmitters and teachers of authoritative *Torah She'baal Peh*, as we know it to this day:

---

whereby Rabbi Nechemia is mentioned only in the latter text, as are Rabbi Akiva's instructions to the new students.

3 *Koheles Rabbah*, ch. 11.

> *An unattributed Mishnah is Rabbi Meir, an unattributed Sifra is Rabbi Yehudah, an unattributed Sifri is Rabbi Shimon, and an unattributed Tosefta is Rabbi Nechamia—all in accordance with Rabbi Akiva.*[4]

Let us consider another striking phenomenon. The Rambam, in his introduction to the Mishnah, identifies the complete chain of Torah transmission, from Moshe Rabbeinu through completion of the Talmud. If we count each individual, with Moshe Rabbeinu as the first, number thirty-two will be none other than Rabbi Akiva, and his students—Rabbi Shimon, etc.—are the thirty-third link. This, I feel, alludes to the celebration of Lag Ba'omer as Rabbi Shimon's day, acknowledging his centrality—along with his peers—to the perpetuation of Rabbi Akiva's Torah.

Rabbi Akiva's second group of elite students not only carried his Torah in the forms of Mishnah and midrash, but they also remained faithful to his very first instruction to them. Their own teachings reflect Rabbi Akiva's insistence that each man and woman be treated with the dignity befitting a representation of the Divine image:

Rabbi Meir taught:

> *One who blesses a Jew is considered to have blessed the Divine Presence.*[5]
>
> *Be exceedingly humble in the presence of all people.*[6]

Rabbi Yehudah stated:

> *One who greets his fellows is considered to have greeted the Divine Presence.*[7]

Rabbi Yossi declared:

> *Throughout my days, I never disregarded the words of my colleagues. I know that I am not a Kohen, yet, if they would*

---

4 *Sanhedrin* 86a.

5 *Midrash Tanchuma, Vayechi* 2.

6 *Avos* 4:10. Rabbi Meir's own nobility of character is seen also in *Yerushalmi, Sotah* 1:4.

7 *Shir Hashirim Rabbah* 2:15.

> *instruct me to go up to the platform [and offer the Priestly Blessing], I would go up.*[8]

> *Even if one taught his fellow only a single Mishnah, he becomes his teacher.*[9]

Rabbi Shimon famously taught:

> *One should rather throw himself into a fiery furnace than publicly embarrass his friend.*[10]

Rabbi Elazar Ben Shamua expressed sentiments clearly inspired by his master:

> *Your student's honor should be as dear to you as your own, your peer's like your teacher's, and awe of your teacher as the awe of Heaven.*[11]

Finally, Rabbi Nechamia, who, according to one version is included in the list of Rabbi Akiva's students, stressed the horrific impact of unjustified hatred (*sinas chinam*).[12]

Such was the spirit of Rabbi Akiva's later students, men whose names would eventually be synonymous with the traditions of *Torah She'baal Peh* for all future generation. Only those whose hearts and minds overflow with an abundance of love and care for the honor of others can serve as links in an unbreakable chain.

Various reasons are given for the customary celebration on Lag Ba'omer, practices that are codified in *Shulchan Aruch*.[13] Many assign to this day the events surrounding Rabbi Shimon ben Yochai's passing, and the secrets of Torah he shared with his students on that day. Others write that Lag Ba'omer was the day Rabbi Akiva began teaching his new

---

8 *Shabbos* 118a.

9 *Bava Metzia* 33a.

10 Ibid., 59a.

11 *Avos* 4:15.

12 *Shabbos* 32b.

13 *Orach Chaim* 493:2.

group of students.[14] And, among others, the Meiri asserts that the plague which devastated the ranks of Rabbi Akiva's students stopped on Lag Ba'omer.

If, as the *baalei mussar* taught, the days of Sefiras Ha'omer correspond to the forty-eight character traits expected of one who is to acquire Torah, then day thirty-two represents the requirement to "love all people." On day thirty-two, Rabbi Akiva's students successfully mastered this trait, conquering the obstacles they previously confronted in their interpersonal encounters. The plague then ended and day thirty-three became a day of celebration—Lag Ba'omer.[15]

Rabbi Akiva's students perfected their love for each other on day thirty-two and the plague thus stopped on day thirty-three. Likewise, in our times—when each day brings new challenges and dangers—we must strengthen ourselves and grow in our love and respect for our fellow.

---

14 *Chida, Maris Ayin* 493.

15 See below, where we discuss the different reasons given for Lag Ba'omer and explain why we would celebrate if Rabbi Akiva's students all died.

FIFTY-TWO

I Can Absolve the Entire World of Any Judgment

Lag Ba'omer is a special day. In the *Shulchan Aruch*, the Rama tells us that "[the custom is to] add joy somewhat and we do not say *Tachanun*."[1]

What happened on Lag Ba'omer? Several explanations are offered, as we briefly mentioned above. According to Rabbi Chaim Vital, the day's significance is prescribed by the holy Tanna Rabbi Shimon bar Yochai, who referred to it as "our day of joy."[2] Many understood that to be the day of his death, on which he transmitted myriad secrets of Torah to his closest disciples. Some Rishonim however, maintained that Lag Ba'omer brought an end to the plague afflicting Rabbi Akiva's students, making the day a joyous one.

This latter suggestion begs an obvious question. What is there to celebrate? According to Chazal, Rabbi Akiva had twenty-four thousand students, all of whom died in a short period of time owing to their inadequate interpersonal conduct. If indeed they all died, how is the plague's end cause for celebration? The deaths stopped simply because there were no remaining students!

1 *Orach Chaim* 493:2.

2 *Shaar Hakavanos, Derushei Pesach* 12.

In a startling explanation, the Rama MiPano writes that in fact the Divine decree had initially demanded Rabbi Akiva's own death. Out of an abundance of mercy, Rabbi Akiva was spared—but his twenty-four thousand students were taken instead. Eventually the deaths ceased, and we celebrate the fact that all was not lost—Rabbi Akiva remaining among the living, seeking out new students with whom to share his Torah.

An additional answer might be suggested according to an alternate description of the events following the plague. Our text of the Gemara reads: "The world was desolate until Rabbi Akiva came to our rabbis in the south and taught them..."[3] Rav Sherira Gaon's version is different. He states: "The world was desolate until they came to our rabbis in the south and learned from them." Perhaps the five (or six) great students, who went on to become the backbone of our tradition, were already part of Rabbi Akiva's initial group of students. On Lag Ba'omer we celebrate the fact that they did not meet the same tragic fate as their peers.

We also mentioned the Chida's position, which challenges the tradition that Rabbi Shimon bar Yochai passed from this world on Lag Ba'omer. Nor does he adopt the view that the celebration can be tied to the plague's end. Rather, suggests the Chida, Lag Ba'omer was the day Rabbi Akiva started teaching his new students, the great Tanna'im who transmitted his Torah to future generations.[4] Following the death of twenty-four thousand scholars, Rabbi Akiva's world was devastated, his surroundings doomed to become a spiritual wasteland. On Lag Ba'omer, Rabbi Akiva's Torah was reenergized—the spiritual future of our nation was to be rebuilt.

Perhaps these approaches are essentially all one and the same. The plague indeed was over on Lag Ba'omer, and Rabbi Akiva remained alive. Immediately, he sought to rebuild what had been lost, and he began teaching his new students. We celebrate on Lag Ba'omer the gift

---

3 *Yevamos* 62b.

4 *Maris Ayin* 493.

of Torah—Torah that will never be lost from the Jewish nation. And this was the source of Rabbi Shimon bar Yochai's claim to the day as his day of joy—after all, Rabbi Shimon was the one who declared, "Heaven forbid! Torah will never be forgotten by the Jewish People, as it says: 'For it will not be forgotten from the mouths of his descendants.'"[5]

Let us turn to Rabbi Shimon bar Yochai's enigmatic pronouncement: "I am able to absolve the entire world from judgment."[6] How so? The Ben Ish Chai, in his work *Ben Yehoyada*, offers a fascinating explanation.

Chazal tell us that when a person reaches the Heavenly court after his time on earth comes to an end, Hashem will judge him for any misdeeds committed while alive. An argument will ensue, however. The body will declare that it is not the sinner—after all, since the time of death, the body has lain tranquilly in the grave, committing no transgressions. Certainly, the soul must be the true culprit! And yet, turning to the soul, Hashem hears a similar claim—the soul could not have been at fault, as evidenced by the fact that since the person's death, the soul has been soaring through the universe without nary a stumble.

Such a conundrum can only be resolved by taking the approach of the metaphorical king. This king had a prized and beautiful orchard that he wished to protect, but he struggled to find trustworthy guards who would not be suspected of stealing its fruit. Finally, the king reached a solution. He commanded a cripple and a blind person to serve as the orchard's guards—the cripple might be tempted by the fruit, but would be unable to walk, while the blind man, though he could walk, would not be drawn to fruit he could not see. However, as time went on, the cripple communicated to his counterpart how succulent and attractive the fruits of the orchard were and they devised a scheme—the cripple would ride on the blind man's shoulders, directing him to the fruit, which they then partook of heartily.

Eventually, the king discovered their crime and put them on trial. Each guard claimed he was not—and could not have been—the thief.

---

5 *Shabbos* 138b.

6 *Sukkah* 45b.

Understanding their ploy, the king placed the cripple on the blind man's shoulders and punished them as if they were one.

So too, Hashem will reunite the body and soul, and punish them together as one unit for the sins they jointly committed.

A well-known halachah teaches that when two people jointly perform a forbidden act on Shabbos, they are exempt from punishment, as neither individual executed a complete violation.[7] Yet, if it is an act that requires two people to complete, the two are indeed both liable. Rabbi Shimon bar Yochai, however dissents, ruling that they are both exempt. Consistent then with his ruling—that two coconspirators are exempt even when both their efforts are needed—Rabbi Shimon bar Yochai would maintain that the body and soul can indeed each successfully evade punishment by pointing to their individual inability to complete any action!

---

7 *Shabbos* 90b.

FIFTY-THREE

Let Me See Its Wonders

For many generations, the widespread practice to visit Rabbi Shimon bar Yochai's grave and celebrate there on Lag Ba'omer has been met with skepticism, occasionally with outright condemnation. The Chasam Sofer famously challenged some of the conduct that took place at Meron,[1] and Rabbi Yosef Shaul Nathanson went so far as to argue that during the lifetimes of the Arizal and Rabbi Yosef Karo such celebrations certainly did not take place.[2]

This last claim is incorrect. Rabbi Chaim Vital testified that the Arizal himself would celebrate on Lag Ba'omer at Rabbi Shimon bar Yochai's grave. Moreover, Rabbi Chaim Vital relates the shocking story of a certain pious man, a contemporary of the Arizal, named Rabbi Avraham HaLevi. Rabbi Avraham had a personal practice to recite the "*Nacheim*" prayer every day of the year, including Lag Ba'omer, out of distress that the Beis Hamikdash still lay in ruins. Rabbi Shimon bar Yochai appeared to the Arizal, angry that Rabbi Avraham would say *Nacheim*, a symbol of mourning, on his day of joy, and warned that Rabbi Avraham would indeed require "*nechamah*"—comfort. So it was that thirty days later Rabbi Avraham's son died, and the bereaved father

1 *Sh'eilos U'Teshuvos Chasam Sofer, Yoreh Deah*, 233; *Derashos Chasam Sofer*, vol. 2, p. 390.

2 *Sh'eilos U'Teshuvos Shoel U'Meishiv, Mahadura Hei* 39.

accepted "*tanchumim*" from those who came to comfort him. Clearly, Rabbi Shimon bar Yochai wished for the day to be one of joy.[3]

Likewise, Rabbi Immanuel Chai Rikki, an early eighteenth-century Italian Kabbalist, writes:

> *It is a mitzvah to rejoice with Rashbi, and if one lives in the Land of Israel, he should go to his grave, and there he should celebrate with great joy.*[4]

Thus, the practice of visiting Meron on Lag Ba'omer and the celebrations that took place there, were indeed longstanding traditions. Above, we discussed several possible reasons for the unique status enjoyed by Lag Ba'omer. Many identify it as the day of Rabbi Shimon's death, others named it as the day Rabbi Akiva's students stopped dying, and we mentioned the suggestion that on this day Rabbi Akiva began transmitting his Torah to his new students, those who serve as the next link in the chain of *mesorah* (tradition). In such matters, of course, it behooves us to recognize that "*eilu v'eilu divrei Elokim chaim*—these are all the words of the Living God."[5]

Rabbi Yaakov Emden, however, introduces us to a completely new idea:

> *Now the custom is established to make this day [Lag Ba'omer] a holiday. I believe this is because it is entirely judgment, just like a court in which all judges seek to convict.*[6]

Preceding Rabbi Yaakov Emden by several centuries, Rabbi Avraham Saba writes:

> *In truth, Lag Ba'omer is the strongest possible judgment (din), alluded to in the words, "Eid ha'gal ha'zeh—This mound shall bear witness..." Similarly, we find this in the pasuk, "You control the mighty seas; when its waves threaten (b'so galav)*

---

3 *Shaar Hakavanos, Derushei Pesach* 12.

4 *Mishnas Chassidim, Maseches Iyar–Sivan* 1:7.

5 *Kaf Hachaim* 494:26.

6 *Siddur Beis Yaakov, Chodesh Iyar* 27.

> *You will break them up." The days of the Omer are like a raging sea; Hashem, in His mercy, tames the mighty sea. And when the waves threaten, He silences them...this is "galav—its waves"—Lag Ba'omer, which has the power of judgment.*[7]

Lag Ba'omer, according to this idea, is not celebrated in connection with any historical event. Rather, its very spiritual essence represents unchecked forces of *din* (judgment). Mysteriously, that looming threat of judgment is eliminated through Hashem's mercy, and the day is converted to one of joy. Rabbi Yaakov Emden likens the process to that of a court in which not a single judge advocates for acquittal. All indications point to conviction—yet the halachah is that such a case must be dismissed, and the accused is acquitted.

Indeed, there is something magical about Lag Ba'omer, an energy Rabbi Shimon bar Yochai insisted to the Arizal that we must attune ourselves to. Many thousands of Jews are uplifted every year by this spirit, visiting Rabbi Shimon's grave on Lag Ba'omer and rejoicing in Rabbi Shimon's Torah. Even those who are unable to visit Meron in person on Lag Ba'omer should dedicate the day to learning Rabbi Shimon's Torah. Such was the practice of my master and teacher, the Klausenberger Rebbe, *zt"l*, who would speak at length and delve into Rabbi Shimon's Torah each year at the Lag Ba'omer *tish*. Rabbi Menachem Nachum of Chernobyl taught that engaging in a particular *tzaddik*'s Torah is akin to visiting that individual's grave, affording one the opportunity to connect with and draw energy from the *tzaddik*.[8]

---

7 *Tzror Hamor, Emor.*

8 *Yismach Lev, Shabbos.*

Sheloshes Yemei Hagbalah

FIFTY-FOUR

And They Traveled from Refidim

And they traveled from Refidim, and they came to the Sinai wilderness, and they encamped in the wilderness. Israel set up camp there, opposite the mountain.[1]

The *Ohr Hachaim* explains that three stages of preparation for Torah are embedded in the description above:

The Torah wanted to acquaint us with three essential steps in preparation for receiving the Torah. With these, Hashem became willing to entrust the beloved Torah to the Jewish People as an eternal inheritance.

The first step was for the Israelites to strengthen themselves and to study the Torah diligently. Laziness is like a weed that leads one to forfeit whatever achievements in Torah insights one has acquired. You will observe that whenever Hashem mentions the Torah, He is careful to use such attributes as

1 *Shemos* 19:2.

> *strength or intensity (chazak) as well as fortitude and vigor (ometz)...In our pasuk, the Torah alludes to this by saying that the Israelites "moved away from Refidim." If the Torah had wanted us to know from which location the Israelites journeyed toward the desert of Sinai, this would have been stated earlier. The Torah meant that the Israelites moved away from their neglect of Torah (rifyon yadayim)...and prepared themselves for effort of Torah.*
>
> *The second step the Israelites had to take in preparation for Torah was to be modest and humble. Our Sages say that only people who are humble can be certain that they will not forget their Torah knowledge. Thus, the pasuk states: "They camped in the wilderness," meaning they made themselves like the wilderness that anyone can trample over...*
>
> *The third step required to be taken by the Israelites in preparation for the giving of the Torah was sincere cooperation between Torah scholars and genuine exchange of insights. This way, they sharpen each other and address one another with grace...Therefore, the pasuk uses the singular, "Va'yichan—And [Israel] camped," as one—now they were worthy of receiving Torah.*[2]

Let us examine each of these three components in B'nei Yisrael's preparation for receiving the Torah and, of course, consider how we can apply them to our own growth during this time.

I. Effort and Diligence

Acquiring Torah entails hard work, efforts that weaken the body but energize one's soul. In fact, Chazal taught that the more we labor in Torah, the greater its power to sustain us.[3]

Chazal were very explicit that physical sacrifice and an austere lifestyle are inherent to spiritual growth:

---

2 *Ohr Hachaim, Shemos* ad loc.

3 *Yerushalmi, Peah* 3a.

> *Such is the way of Torah: you shall eat bread with salt, and rationed water shall you drink; you shall sleep on the ground, your life will be one of privation, and in Torah shall you labor. If you do this: "Happy shall you be, and it shall be good for you"—"Happy shall you be" in this world, "and it shall be good for you" in the World to Come.*[4]

The Rambam echoes and expands upon this theme:

> *The words of the Torah do not remain permanently with one who is indolent in acquiring them, nor with such who study the Torah in an environment of luxury and amidst eating and drinking, but with one who sacrifices his life for them and constantly suffers his body and does not yield sleep to his eyes nor dozing to his eyelids. The Sages commented, by way of allusion: "This is the law, when a man dies in a tent," the Torah does not remain with any save with him who sacrifices his life in the tents of the wise. And so did Shlomo in his wisdom say: "If you were weak in the day of adversity, your strength is small indeed," and he, moreover, said: "Also*[5] *my wisdom stood by me"—only the wisdom that I studied in suffering stood by me.*[6]

The need to approach Torah study as a difficult and demanding pursuit is embedded in a striking event described by Chazal:

> *Rabbi Elazar ben Arach went there [to Phrygia and Deyomses]. He was drawn to their lifestyle and forgot his learning. When he later got up to read from a Torah, instead of reading, "Ha'chodesh ha'zeh lachem," he read, "Ha'cheresh hayah libam."*[7]

---

4 *Avos* 6:4.

5 In the original: אף חכמתי עמדה לי. The word "*af*" is typically translated as "also," but in the present text it is read to connote frustration or anger, i.e., the wisdom Shlomo HaMelech acquired through adversity.

6 *Mishneh Torah*, Laws of Talmud Torah 3:12.

7 *Shabbos* 147b.

When the great Tanna Rabbi Elazar ben Arach found himself indulging in the luxuries of the surrounding culture, his error in reading Torah was itself a prophetic intervention. Reading, "Their hearts were deaf," he was reminded that material pleasures dull one's spiritual capacity. Shlomo HaMelech asked Hashem for a "hearing heart"[8] as the precursor to success in Torah. An unhearing heart, developed by overinvestment in the pleasures of the flesh, is impervious to the wisdom and depth of Torah.

The Rambam captures this tension between body and soul in a pithy comment:

> *To acquire wisdom, one must imagine that the soul is destroyed by the care for the body, and the soul is nourished through destruction of the body.*[9]

II. Humility

The second critical step in preparation for a life of Torah is developing humility, a trait Chazal pointed to repeatedly when describing an individual who masters Torah.

> *Torah is like water: just as water leaves a high place and finds a low place, so too words of Torah only maintain themselves within a person who is subdued.*[10]

> *Words of Torah are only maintained within a person who makes himself like a wilderness.*[11]

> *The people of Simonia came before Rebbi. They said to him, "We want you to give us a man to serve as preacher, judge, reader, teacher, and to do all the things we need." He gave them Levi bar Sissi. They set up a great stage and seated him on it. They came and asked him, "A woman without arms—with what does she remove the shoe for chalitzah?" And he did not answer. "What if*

8 *Melachim I* 3:9.

9 Introduction to his commentary on Mishnah. See also *Tamid* 32a.

10 *Taanis* 7a.

11 *Eruvin* 54a.

> *she spit blood?" And he did not answer. They said, "Perhaps he is not a master of the law. Let us ask him something in Aggadah." They came and asked him, "What is the meaning of the pasuk, 'But I will tell you what is inscribed in the book, in truth?' If it is truth, why is it inscribed? And if it is inscribed, why is it truth?" He did not answer them. They came back to Rebbi and said to him, "Is this a mason of your mason's guild?" He said to them, "By your lives! I gave you someone who is as good as I am." He sent and summoned him and asked him. He said to him, "If the woman spit blood, what is the law?" He answered him, "If there is a drop of spit in it, it is valid." "A woman without arms—how does she remove the shoe?" He said to him, "She removes the shoe with her teeth." He said to him, "What is the meaning of the pasuk, 'But I will tell you what is inscribed in the book, in truth?' If it is truth, why is it inscribed, and if it is inscribed, why is it truth?" He said to him, "Before a decree is sealed, it is described as inscribed. Once it is sealed, it is described as truth." He said to him, "And why did you not answer the people when they asked you these same questions?" He said to him, "They made a great stage and seated me on it, and my spirit became haughty." He recited concerning him the following pasuk: "'If you have been foolish, exalting yourself, or if you have been devising evil, put your hand on your mouth'; what caused you to make a fool of yourself in regard to teachings of Torah? It was because you exalted yourself through them."*[12]

Moshe Rabbeinu, the greatest of all prophets, who learned Torah directly from its Divine Source, and who reached the loftiest spiritual heights available to Man, is identified by the Torah as "the most humble of all men."[13]

I heard that on one occasion the Chasam Sofer was teaching and, in his comments, rejected the position of Rabbi Meshulam Igra, his

---

12 *Yerushalmi, Yevamos* 69a.

13 *Bamidbar* 12:3.

predecessor as Rav of Pressburg. Suddenly, the Chasam Sofer lost his train of thought, became confused, and was unable to continue his presentation. Immediately attributing his faltering to a possible offense against the honor of Rabbi Meshulam Igra, he rushed out to the cemetery to beg forgiveness. Having done so, he returned to his students and continued teaching.

Stories such as those recounted above should trouble us greatly. Rabbi Elazar ben Arach and Rabbi Levi bar Sissi, who were truly towering Torah scholars, individuals of stature hardly imaginable to us, lost their Torah on account of slight indiscretions—the former visited a bathhouse, the latter was proud of his new appointment. Yet, we, who surely indulge in far more serious lapses in the areas of simplicity and humility, do not experience the same immediate consequences they did. Why would that be?

Their Torah, like that of all the Tanna'im, was of a quality and purity that exceeds our understanding. So refined was their learning and so developed were their characters that the smallest mistake had an immediate and dramatic effect. Much in the same way that if one were to add a little bit of water to fine wine the wine would be ruined, while the same mixture in inexpensive grape juice makes little difference. Likewise, the pure and high-quality Torah of the Tanna'im could not be diluted with even a small measure of imperfect conduct, but our Torah, far from such lofty levels, is not nearly as sensitive to our human weaknesses.

III. Love of One's Fellow

The *Ohr Hachaim*'s third step, learned from the singular "and he camped," is the need for strong bonds between scholars, relationships that breed robust and respectful dialogue. When Torah is clarified in such spirit of brotherhood, all participants benefit and the Torah is uplifted.

As the Amora Rabbi Chanina would declare:

> *I have learned much from my teachers, even more from my peers, and the most from my students.*[14]

---

14 *Taanis* 7a.

FIFTY-FIVE

Sheloshes Yemei Hagbalah

We discussed already at length the importance of the days between Pesach and Shavuos as preparation to receive the Torah anew on Shavuos. We described the potential and opportunity inherent in each day of Sefiras Ha'omer to focus on one of the forty-eight attributes expected of one who is to acquire Torah. With the approach of Shavuos, it behooves us to narrow our focus to the final stage in that journey—the Sheloshes Yemei Hagbalah, the three days immediately prior to Shavuos. At Sinai, these days brought with them very concrete instructions, but those were specific to the momentous events that were to follow. They are not directly or apparently relevant to us. Yet, we still mark these days. What then is their significance, and what is expected of us on these days?

In a preceding essay, we examined the *Ohr Hachaim*'s discourse on three essential areas of growth needed before one can receive Torah. Developing this idea further, let us proceed to associate the three days of final preparation with the three items identified by the *Ohr Hachaim*.

> *The Torah wanted to acquaint us with three essential steps in the preparation to receive the Torah. With these, Hashem became willing to entrust the beloved Torah to the Jewish People as an eternal inheritance.*
>
> *The first step was for the Israelites to strengthen themselves and to study the Torah diligently. Laziness is like a weed that*

> *leads one to forfeit whatever achievements in Torah insights one has acquired. You will observe that whenever Hashem mentions the Torah He is careful to use such attributes as strength or intensity (chazak) as well as fortitude and vigor (ometz)...In our pasuk, the Torah alludes to this by saying that the Israelites "moved away from Refidim." If the Torah had wanted us to know from which location the Israelites journeyed toward the desert of Sinai, this would have been stated earlier. The Torah meant that the Israelites moved away from their neglect of Torah (rifyon yadayim)...and prepared themselves for effort of Torah.*
>
> *The second step the Israelites had to take in preparation for Torah was to be modest and humble. Our Sages say that only people who are humble can be certain that they will not forget their Torah knowledge. Thus, the pasuk states, "They camped in the wilderness," meaning they made themselves like the wilderness that anyone can trample over...*
>
> *The third step required to be taken by the Israelites in preparation for the giving of the Torah was sincere cooperation between Torah scholars and genuine exchange of insights. This way, they sharpen each other and address one another with grace...Therefore, the pasuk uses the singular "va'yichan and [Israel] camped," as one—now they were worthy of receiving Torah.*[1]

Three fundamentals are absolutely critical features of an individual or a nation that is to receive Torah—effort, humility, and seeking truth while united with others. B'nei Yisrael could not approach Sinai without perfecting themselves in these areas. I believe Chazal alluded to effort, humility, and interdependent truth-seeking in their description of the conditions under which Torah was given:

---

1 *Ohr Hachaim, Shemos* ad loc.

> *Torah was given under three conditions: fire, water, and the wilderness.*[2]

Fire is mightily potent with absolute destructive force. Yet, properly harnessed, its energy brings us light and warmth. So it is with one's physical exertions to study Torah—they may take their toll on the body, but, done effectively, they illuminate one's soul.

Chazal invoked the properties of water in the context of Torah quite explicitly:

> *Torah is like water: just as water leaves a high place and finds a low place, so too words of Torah only maintain themselves within a person who is humble.*[3]

What about the third condition, wilderness? In the *Ohr Hachaim*'s comments, wilderness was an additional association to humility. But other interpretations support the idea that "wilderness" can be a reference to the productive exchange between peers who all seek to arrive at the Divine truth. Chazal teach:

> *What is meant by the pasuk, "From midbar (wilderness) to matanah"? When a person makes himself available to all [like the wilderness], it is given to him as a gift (matanah).*[4]

Rashi explains that one makes oneself "available to all" by teaching Torah to anyone with no demand for compensation.

And, in a similar passage:

> *If one makes himself like a wilderness that all can use freely, Torah is given to him as a gift.*[5]

Wilderness then reflects the value of engaging with peers and students in a mutual quest for wisdom. By teaching Torah to all who seek

---

2 *Bamidbar Rabbah* 1:7.

3 *Taanis* 7a.

4 *Nedarim* 55a.

5 *Eruvin* 54a.

Divine knowledge, the student of Torah expands the circle of those who are likely to assist him in arriving at truth.

Other interpretations of these last two passages are consistent with the *Ohr Hachaim*'s premise that "wilderness" refers to humility.[6]

In light of our three fundamental criteria for greatness is Torah, ceaseless effort, humility, and engagement with others, I propose that we might better understand the fascinating events surrounding Rabbi Eliezer's famous dispute with his colleagues.

> *They taught: On that day, Rabbi Eliezer answered all answers in the world, but they did not accept his position. He said to them, "If the halachah is in accordance with my opinion, this carob tree will prove it." The carob tree was uprooted from its place one hundred cubits, and some say four hundred cubits. They said to him, "One does not cite proof from a carob tree." He then said to them, "If the halachah is in accordance with my opinion, the stream will prove it." The stream turned backward. They said to him, "One does not cite halachic proof from a stream." He then said to them, "If the halachah is in accordance with my opinion, the walls of the study hall will prove it." The walls of the study hall leaned to fall. Rabbi Yehoshua scolded the walls and said to them, "If Torah scholars are contending with each other in halachah, why are you involved?" They did not fall because of deference due Rabbi Yehoshua, but they did not straighten because of the deference due Rabbi Eliezer, and they still remain leaning. He then said to them, "If the halachah is in accordance with my opinion, Heaven will prove it." A Divine voice emerged and said, "Why are you differing with Rabbi Eliezer, as halachah is in accordance with him in every place?" Rabbi Yehoshua stood on his feet and said, "It is not in heaven." What does "It is not in heaven" teach? Rabbi Yirmiyah says, "Since the Torah was already given at Mount Sinai, we do not*

6 See *Ran*, *Nedarim* 55a.

> *regard a Divine voice, as You already wrote at Mount Sinai, in the Torah, 'After a majority to incline.'"*[7]

Rabbi Eliezer invoked three separate witnesses to uphold his position—the carob tree, the stream, and the walls of the study hall. Each of these, I believe, corresponds to one of the three essential values necessary for Torah, all of which Rabbi Eliezer exemplified. The carob tree symbolizes a life of austerity and physical difficulty, reminding us of Rabbi Shimon bar Yochai and his son in hiding, whose sustenance was provided solely by a carob tree.[8] The stream, as seen above, alludes to humility—Torah, like water, always descends to the lowest spot it can rest. Finally, Rabbi Eliezer calls upon the walls of his study hall, a place where scholars gather to engage with each other and sharpen their understanding of Torah.

Only upon these three pillars—physical sacrifice, humility, and valuing the contribution of others—can Torah be firmly established, and toward them we must direct our attention during the final three days before Shavuos and *kabbalas haTorah*.

---

7 *Bava Metzia* 59b.

8 *Shabbos* 33b. See also *Taanis* 10a, regarding Rabbi Chanina, who survived on carobs alone.

FIFTY-SIX

Your Life and the Length of Your Days

As the count of Sefiras Ha'omer brings us inexorably closer to Shavuos, it behooves us to seize every available moment and ready ourselves for this transcendent day. How does one prepare to receive Torah, to become, once again, transformed by Torah as our ancestors were thousands of years ago?

First, we must appreciate how unique Torah is. It is not a discipline or even a source of wisdom like any others. More than even a lifestyle, it is life itself: "For it is your life, and in this way you will live long lives."[1] The Jewish soul is empty without Torah: "The lives of people of wisdom and those who seek it are like death if they do not entail Torah study."[2]

We are well versed, from the youngest ages, in Rabbi Akiva's famous and engaging illustration:

> *One time, the evil empire [Rome] decreed that Israel may not engage in Torah. Pappos ben Yehudah came and found Rabbi Akiva, who was convening assemblies in public and engaging in Torah. He said to him, "Akiva, are you not afraid of the empire?" Rabbi Akiva answered him: "I will relate a parable:*

1 *Devarim* 32:47.

2 *Rambam, Mishneh Torah*, Laws of a Murderer 7:1.

To what can this be compared? A fox was walking along a riverbank when he sees fish fleeing from place to place. The fox said to them, 'From what are you fleeing?' They said to him, 'From the nets that people cast upon us.' He said to them, 'Do you wish to come up onto dry land, and we will reside together just as my ancestors resided with your ancestors?' They said to him, 'You are the one of whom they say, he is the cleverest of animals? You are not clever; you are a fool. If we are afraid in our habitat which gives us life, in a habitat that causes our death, all the more so!' So too, now that we sit and engage in Torah, about which it is written, 'For that is your life, and the length of your days,' we fear to this extent; if we proceed to idle from it, all the more so!"[3]

Rabbi Akiva's point is clear: to imagine life without Torah is to imagine something other than life. Yet, despite our familiarity with this story, or perhaps because of it, we fail to fully contemplate Rabbi Akiva's metaphor. At second glance, the fox's suggestion, that the fish should join him on land, just as his ancestors and theirs once shared a habitat, is odd. When did the fox and fish ever live together? Even during the Flood, the fish remained—unscathed—in the raging water outside the ark. The fish would have done well to respond to the fox that he is not only a fool, but also a liar, for his very premise is completely false! Not only did the fish and fox never live together, but they cannot. One is a land animal; one lives in water. Creation's boundaries assign different habitats to the different creatures.

Indeed, the fox was attempting to blur this very distinction. He argued that for all the obvious differences, surely they all have enough in common that the fish can accustom themselves to a different life. Objecting sharply, the fish replied that such an argument is the height of foolishness. There is no commonality between a fox and a fish, creatures that by their very nature, are nourished by and thrive in completely different environments. We too, as Jews, similar as we appear,

3 *Berachos* 61b.

our source of nourishment diverges from that of other humans. From the very first moment Moshe Rabbeinu descended the mountain with our Torah, we can only survive when immersed in Torah.

Sadly, we hear the fox's argument all too often. In every generation, there are those who would propose that we leave the study hall, just for a little bit. Ostensibly seeking our benefit, they suggest that we might do well to overcome some of the differences between the Jew and his surrounding culture. Our answer must always be clear: our ancestors never did occupy the same habitat as yours. Yaakov and Eisav were brothers, but they could not live together. A Jew can only live in the environment designed for his soul, steeped in and surrounded by Torah.

Simply learning Torah, however, is insufficient. To truly tap in to the life-sustaining nature of Torah, one must toil and work diligently. Only through passionate, unrelenting devotion does Torah become the Jew's elixir of life. Chazal emphasized this level of commitment in several places in *Yerushalmi*:

> *When is it your life? When you toil in it.*[4]

To fully grasp what such "toil" entails, we can learn from the Gemara's teaching that Torah is an "elixir of life" only for those who "take it to the right—*meyaminim bah*" while it is poisonous for those who "go to the left—*masmilim bah.*" Rashi explains "take it to the right" as a reference to the hand of greater strength:

> *Those who engage in it with all their energy and are preoccupied with understanding its secrets.*[5]

Two distinct elements characterize true all-consuming devotion to Torah study. First is the directing of one's entire physical and mental capacity toward engagement with Torah. Second, one must be so emotionally invested in the material that any gap in knowledge or

---

4 *Yerushalmi Peah* 2, *Shavuos* 3, *Shabbos* 11, *Sukkah* 18, *Kesubos* 51.

5 *Shabbos* 88b.

understanding causes distress. Such is the Torah that enlivens and sustains a Jew.

Rashi appears to make a parallel comment elsewhere:

> *"And you shall teach them to your children"—so that the words of Torah should be well versed in your mouth, review them and inquire after their depth.*[6]

"Review them" expresses the constant application of one's energies to Torah study, and "inquire after their depth" alludes to that unstoppable quest for truth that is the mark of one who is deeply connected to the subject and its Giver.

Torah is acquired only through these efforts, applied consistently and persistently. The great Torah scholars of all times attained their stature this way, always exemplifying the spirit of an untiring quest for riches—the word of Hashem.

But this labor of love is not the exclusive domain of Torah giants—it is meant for each of us:

> *Rabbi Elazar taught: just as a baby needs to nurse at all hours of the day, so too, every Jew must labor in Torah at all hours of the day.*[7]

---

6 *Kiddushin* 30a.

7 *Yerushalmi, Berachos* 9:5.

FIFTY-SEVEN

Prepare Yourselves for the Third Day

And Hashem said to Moshe, "Go to the people and warn them to stay pure today and tomorrow. Let them wash their clothes. Let them be ready for the third day (la'yom ha'shlishi); for on the third day Hashem will come down, in the sight of all the people, on Mount Sinai."[1]

And he said to the people, "Be ready for the three days (l'shloshes yamim): do not go near a woman."[2]

"For the third day"—means be ready by the end of three days, that is, by the fourth day, for Moshe added a day of his own accord to the time appointed by Hashem. This is the opinion of Rabbi Yossi. But according to the opinion that

1 *Shemos* 19:10–11.

2 Ibid., 19:15.

the Ten Commandments were given on the sixth of the month, Moshe did not add anything...[3]

Implicitly, Rashi suggests that Moshe's choice of "*l'shloshes yamim*—for the three days" in the later *pasuk*, rather than the more intuitive "*la'yom ha'shlishi*—the third day," supports the view that Torah was in fact given to the Jewish nation on the seventh of Sivan. According to this opinion, Moshe added a day of preparation of his own accord, delaying the giving of the Torah from the third day—as seemingly intended by Hashem in the earlier *pasuk*—to the day following three full days of preparation, i.e., the fourth day.[4]

If we adopt this position and then reconstruct the full chronology of events starting from *yetzias Mitzrayim*, we find that the revelation at Sinai occurred on the seventh day of Sivan, a day later than the holiday on which we commemorate that same event—Shavuos. While it may be somewhat troubling to celebrate an event on the "wrong" date, the truly difficult issue is that we insist it is the right day. Throughout Shavuos, in all the prayers and during Kiddush, we declare the day—the sixth of Sivan—to be "the time we received the Torah." Why do we identify Shavuos as the day we received the Torah if it is not, and, moreover, why indeed was the holiday established a day early?[5]

Beyond these questions, which have been previously raised by many authorities, I have difficulty with the entire premise that Moshe added a day and thereby delayed the revelation at Sinai. Hashem had unambiguously stated earlier that "*ba'yom ha'shlishi*—on the third day," He would appear to the people. It seems very unreasonable to suggest that Hashem's words, as recorded in the Torah, were not fulfilled.

Addressing the actual institution of Shavuos on the sixth of Sivan, the Maharsha makes a fascinating suggestion:

---

3 *Rashi*, ibid.

4 *Shabbos* 86b.

5 See *Magen Avraham* 493, for a discussion of the first question, and *Maharsha*, *Avodah Zarah* 3b.

> *Since Israel was not worthy then of receiving Torah, as they had not yet cleansed themselves of Egypt's impurities...the purification required a seven-week process, followed by day fifty—numbers that we see elsewhere as having holy significance, such as Shabbos, shemittah, and yovel. Since their purification was complete on day fifty, as evidenced by the fact that we received Torah on day fifty-one, Hashem fixed Shavuos on that fiftieth day, as fear of Heaven must precede wisdom, temporally and conceptually.*[6]

We celebrate on Shavuos, according to the Maharsha, our successful preparation and purification, not the giving of Torah itself. This approach resolves one question—why we commemorate the "wrong" day—but it still leaves unanswered the problem with our liturgy. Why do we repeatedly assert that Shavuos is the day we received the Torah if it is not?

The key, I believe, can be found in the details of *Hilchos Geirus*—the laws governing conversion to Judaism. Chazal derived these procedures from the events at Sinai, extrapolating the individual's acceptance of Torah from our collective covenant at Sinai. Just as the latter incorporated circumcision (*milah*), ritual purity (*tevilah*), and an offering (*korban*), so must all subsequent personal journeys to Torah include these three elements.

But these three are only the *actions* required to complete one's conversion. In addition, and perhaps more centrally, the individual seeking to convert must accept upon himself or herself "*ol malchus Shamayim*—the yoke of mitzvos." Normative practice establishes two components to this acceptance. The first is an acknowledgment of and commitment to abide by the Torah's commandments. This is the fundamental commitment to join the Jewish People and live in accordance with Hashem's will. Second, Chazal required that the prospective convert must be taught several mitzvos, some "easy" mitzvos (*kalos)* and some "hard"

---

6 *Maharsha, Avodah Zarah* 3b.

ones (*chamuros*), following which he or she once again reaffirms a desire to live as a Jew.[7]

Now comes our opportunity for a reverse inference: if the conversion procedure entails these two phases of acceptance, it follows that our ancestors at Sinai experienced the same. We would thus suggest that on the sixth of Sivan they accepted upon themselves wholeheartedly to fulfill Hashem's will, as it would be revealed to them in the Torah they were yet to learn. Agreeing, as Chazal teach, to be buried under the mountain should their commitment be lacking in any way, they had already completed the first stage of the covenantal transformation. This initial acceptance, their initiative, is what we commemorate on Shavuos.

On the following day, Hashem revealed Himself to His nation and they heard the Ten Commandments directly from Him. This was the second stage, the teaching of "several mitzvos" that occurs in the final phase of conversion.

With this, we might also offer additional insight into the enigmatic passage we sing at the Seder: "Even if He had brought us close to Sinai, but not given us the Torah, it would have been sufficient." Even before Hashem gave the Torah to us, on the seventh of Sivan, we had already begun our entry into His covenant on the sixth of Sivan with our acceptance of Hashem's will and commitment to Him as our King.

Surely, then, we are justified in declaring the sixth of Sivan "the day we received our Torah."

Indeed, Hashem had assured Moshe, months earlier, that when the nation leaves Egypt, they "shall serve Hashem on that mountain." What service did they perform at Sinai? Listening to Moshe's voice as he repeated the Ten Commandments does not strike us as very demanding work! It must be, rather, that their service consisted of bringing themselves to the point at which they would be able to, in advance of receiving it, wholeheartedly and steadfastly promise to accept Hashem's Torah.

---

7 See *Chemdas Shlomo, Yoreh Deah* 29–30.

Shavuos

FIFTY-EIGHT

He Chose Us among All Nations

Each holiday has a soul, a unique character and spiritual energy that it draws down from the highest spheres, uplifting and enriching all of creation. We allude to these attributes on each such occasion, when we declare Pesach as the "time of our freedom," Sukkos as the "time of our joy," and Shavuos as the "time our Torah was given." And, while we are commanded by the Torah to rejoice on all the holidays, our joy is flavored by the day's special character.

If so, how do Shavuos and Simchas Torah, both celebrations of Torah and our relationship with it, differ from one another?

On Shavuos we rejoice for having received the Torah; on Simchas Torah we celebrate what we have done with it. Simchas Torah is the day we complete a full cycle of Torah, having read it, studied it, and grown from it, week after week, day after day, over the course of a year. Shavuos reenacts and commemorates the moment Hashem chose us, a small nation among many, to be His chosen people.

While Shavuos, in its entirety, celebrates our good fortune in being chosen by the Almighty, we note this fact more often. Daily, in *Birkas HaTorah*, we mention "that He chose us from all the nations," and weekly, when reciting Kiddush, we similarly declare "that You chose us and sanctified us above all nations." What is common to these two obligations—to study Torah and to observe Shabbos—that their respective blessings share a formula reflecting the theme of "chosen-ness"?

I submit that both mitzvos highlight the distinction between the Jewish nation and all other inhabitants of the world. Both exclude gentiles from participation: a non-Jew may not observe Shabbos,[1] nor may he study Torah the way a Jew does.[2] Our uniqueness as a people is expressed when we observe these mitzvos, and, hence, in the blessings that introduce them.

In one teaching, however, Chazal seem to suggest that this uniqueness is less than complimentary:

> *It was taught in the name of Rabbi Meir: "Why was Torah given to the Jewish nation? Because they are bold." Rashi adds: "They are bold—and Torah was given to them so they should toil in it and it will weaken and subdue them."*[3]

Superficially, this comment appears to be derogatory. Rather than as a sign of their greatness, Torah was given to the Jewish People as an antidote to their overly bold and stubborn nature. Yet, it is clear that Rabbi Meir's question should not be read this way. Of course, Hashem gave the Torah to us, His beloved and chosen children. But why, if so, did He give us a Torah that can only be mastered through unnatural effort and physical sacrifice?

I would thus interpret the passage differently. We know that the very purpose of creation was to sanctify Hashem's great Name. A king must have subjects; when these subjects willingly and lovingly acknowledge and bless their king, his kingdom is complete in a way that could not be achieved without the existence of a physical world. Rabbi Meir taught that only the Jewish People are of such a tenacious nature that, despite all the difficulties and challenges attendant to living a life of Torah, they will still sanctify His name in this world. Torah could only be given to a people who would use it to realize Hashem's original intent in Creation itself.

---

1 *Sanhedrin* 58b.

2 Ibid., 59a.

3 *Beitzah* 25b.

FIFTY-NINE

Hashem Came from Sinai

And he said, "Hashem came from Sinai, and rose from Seir unto them," and it is written: "Hashem comes from Teiman and the Holy One from Paran…" What did He require in Seir and what did He require in Paran? Rabbi Yochanan says, "This teaches that the Holy One, blessed be He, took the Torah around to every nation and language, but they did not accept it, until He came to the Jewish People and they accepted it."[1]

Do Chazal really mean to suggest that Hashem would possibly have given the Torah to another nation? Did Rashi not tell us, right at the very beginning of *Bereishis*, that Torah was created *for* the Jewish People? Focusing on the first word of the Torah, "*Bereishis*," Chazal taught that the world was created for Torah and the Jewish nation, both of which are referred to as "*reishis*—first." Our relationship with Torah was encoded in Creation itself; would Hashem

1 *Avodah Zarah* 2b.

have changed His intention and given the Torah to any nation that acquiesced to it?

Rather, Hashem never actually considered giving the Torah to any nation other than the Jewish People, His beloved children. All the same, He offered it to others as well, to eliminate any future argument that they had no opportunity to serve Hashem. But, indeed, as cited above, the Jewish soul and Torah, by their very nature belong together.

The singular compatibility between Torah and the Jewish nation also explains Moshe's intention in breaking the first set of *Luchos*—the tablets upon which were engraved the Ten Commandments. At first blush, Moshe's actions appear highly objectionable. After all, it was not Moshe's Torah. Hashem had entrusted him to deliver the Torah to the Jewish nation. When Moshe descended the mountain and found his people in the apparent throes of a grave sin, worshipping a Golden Calf, we would expect him to turn back and return the Torah to its Giver. Hashem would then have decided what to do with the *Luchos*—perhaps He would have sought a different nation once again. What right did Moshe have to destroy the precious tablets, carved by Hashem's own Hand?

Moshe knew that Torah belonged with the Jewish People—and only with them. He understood that no other nation would be able to receive it or live up to its demands. Thus, Moshe concluded, if the Jewish nation, too, proved itself unworthy, there is no need for *Luchos* at all. He summarily smashed them at the foot of the mountain.

In an alternate version of the passage we began with, Chazal taught:

> *And he said: Hashem came from Sinai—when Hashem revealed Himself to give Torah to Israel, He revealed Himself not only to Israel, but also to all the other nations…*[2]

Hashem revealed Himself to give Torah to the Jewish People. There was never any doubt about His intention. In His kindness, however,

---

2 *Sifri, Zos Haberachah* 343.

He provided an opportunity to all other nations, should they wish to partake as well.

The Kesav Sofer, citing his father, the Chasam Sofer, beautifully illustrates the above dynamic.[3]

> *A father had several children, but one was his favorite. When the time came for the father to distribute his property among his children, he wished to designate his most prized possessions for his favorite child, but he also wanted to preserve peace between the children and not cause jealousy.*
>
> *The father owned a number of fields, several of which were fertile, well cultivated, and highly desirable. In addition, he held title to a barren piece of land that was of no interest to anyone. Privately summoning his favorite child, the father revealed that the neglected parcel held a gold deposit deep beneath its surface, and he taught the child everything he knew about how to locate and mine the valuable metal.*
>
> *At the appointed time, all the children gathered, with each choosing one of the beautiful fields. Only the favored child knew to select the overlooked, but infinitely more valuable asset as his inheritance.*

Similarly, the nations of the world did not appreciate the preciousness and beauty of Torah, and declined Hashem's offer. B'nei Yisrael, whose souls were natural counterparts to Torah, and whose minds had been filled with a love for Hashem and His mitzvos inherited from Avraham, Yitzchak, and Yaakov, were eager to receive the Torah.

---

3 *Kesav Sofer Al HaTorah, Yisro.*

SIXTY

And They Stood at the Foot of the Mountain

Rabbi Elazar said: When B'nei Yisrael declared, "We will do" before "We will listen," a Heavenly voice called out, "Who divulged this secret to my children?" This is a formula that the angels use, as the pasuk states: "Bless Hashem, His angels, mighty of strength, who do His bidding and listen to His voice." First they "do," and only after do they "listen."[1]

Rabbi Elazar's teaching suggests that the events at Sinai elevated the Jewish nation to a level that exceeded anything they had previously experienced. Even after the miracles in Egypt and their prophetic vision at the sea, where each person pointed to Hashem, they could still reach new heights. At Sinai they attained the stature of angels, using the same formula as the angels, about whom the *pasuk* states, "Bless Hashem, His angels, mighty of strength."

---

1 *Shabbos* 88a.

Chazal further tell us that, standing at Sinai, our ancestors were cleansed of an impurity injected into mankind by the primordial snake in Gan Eden. Submitting themselves to Hashem's will and declaring, with one heart and in one voice, "We will do and we will listen," they became new people, free of the snake's ancient curse.

And, as we mentioned earlier, it was this proclamation of faithfulness that earned them two crowns:

> *Rabbi Simai taught: when B'nei Yisrael declared "we will do" before "we will listen," six hundred thousand angels descended and adorned each Jew with two crowns, one for "we will do" and one for "we will listen."*[2]

B'nei Yisrael had already achieved incredible spiritual heights. What was so special about their commitment to "do and then listen" that beckoned the added recognition of crowns?

An intelligent person, acting of his or her own free will, does not commit to a binding contract before knowing its contents and associated obligations. A "blind" agreement to fulfill all clauses of an unread document, bearing unknown and potentially eternal demands, is the mark of one acting under duress. Or it can be a sign of love. B'nei Yisrael, at Sinai, of their volition and under no compulsion, expressed their immense love and joy at becoming Hashem's chosen people by committing themselves to serve Him loyally, whatever such service might entail. In their love for Him, they rejected the life of a free people, wholeheartedly subjugating themselves to Him for all time.

So powerful is this affirmation of our ancestors' desire to follow Hashem's will at all cost, that *Tosafos* struggle to reconcile "we will do and we will listen" with Chazal's parallel description of Hashem suspending the mountain over their heads, threatening their demise should they fail to accept the Torah.[3]

Tosafos suggest that Hashem was concerned B'nei Yisrael would become fearful at Sinai, with the Divine voice ringing out amidst fire and

---

2 Ibid.

3 *Tosafos* ad loc.

escalating sounds of a blowing shofar. To stop them from retreating in panic, He compelled their presence and obedience.

I would like to take another approach. Let us consider, for a minute, our ancestors' state of mind as they approached Sinai. They had witnessed, for the past year, incredible miracles wrought by Hashem on their behalf. Egypt was humbled and then destroyed, in their own land and then later at the sea. B'nei Yisrael realized Hashem's centuries-earlier promise to Avraham, that "they will then go out with great wealth." Each Jew left Egypt leading donkeys laden with the riches of Egypt, only to accumulate even more after their pursuers were drowned at the sea. Hashem was leading them through the wilderness, protecting them from its perils and providing them with miraculous food. After all this, is it really any wonder that when Hashem offered them Torah, they did not question Him or respond with anything other than enthusiasm? Why, indeed, are we so surprised at their promise to "do and then to listen?"

This is precisely why He suspended the mountain above them and demanded their acceptance!

At that moment, B'nei Yisrael, having directly experienced Hashem's kindness, their path illuminated by His brightly shining light, would have no reason not to follow Him and embrace His Torah. But becoming the chosen nation also means to accept centuries of darkness, times when Hashem's presence is all but invisible. There will be moments, days, and years of challenge, when observing Torah and mitzvos will entail great peril. To accept Torah is to accept servitude and subjugation, commitment to His will even under the most difficult conditions.

The procedure for acquiring a non-Jewish slave, when in effect, includes a final stage whereby the prospective slave immerses in the mikveh. This act represents a partial entry into the household of a Jew, which, as such, obligates the slave in many Torah commandments. Before the slave exits the mikveh, Chazal instructed that one should "place a heavy vessel on his head," symbolizing the servitude that now rests on his shoulders.[4]

---

4 *Yevamos* 46a.

Similarly, as the Jewish People accepted Torah, Hashem suspended the mountain on their heads, demonstrating that Torah is not a path to freedom and power, but to hard work and challenge. When, nevertheless, despite such severe warning, they still eagerly embraced Hashem's will, promising to fulfill it come what may, they expressed the true nature of their commitment and love for Hashem.

When a Jewish person is forced to sell himself to another Jew to pay off his creditors, the Torah prescribes an initial term of sale of six years. If, upon completion of six years, the slave wishes to remain in service to his master, they must complete a procedure whereby, among other things, the slave's ear is pierced. Chazal explain the symbolism attached to one's ear:

> *This ear, that heard at Sinai, "For B'nei Yisrael are My servants—My servants and not servant to servants," and yet went and accepted another master, should be pierced.*[5]

This objection to the individual's acceptance of slavery should apply just as readily to his initial term of service. Why is the lesson only imposed when he enters the extended period?

Originally, the man only sold himself under duress—as the only recourse available to meet his financial obligations. Choosing such a difficult step is not in direct conflict with one's subservience to the true Master. But, at the end of six years, after which point the servant will no longer receive anything in exchange for his sale, his decision can indeed be criticized. Choosing freely to remain subjugated to another human being suggests that he does not value his direct, and joy-filled, service of Hashem, electing instead to serve one of His servants.

Thus, when B'nei Yisrael crowned Hashem as their King and Master, freely and joyously committing to do His will without questioning or doubting Him, they themselves became worthy of crowns, servants to the King of kings.

---

5 *Kiddushin* 22b.

Even Pharaoh, having lost his slave-nation, recognized their exit not as escape to freedom, but as entry into an exalted, yet still demanding calling:

> *Pharaoh began crying out, "You were previously my slaves and now you are free? Surely, you are now Hashem's slaves. You should praise Him that you are His slaves." As it says: "Praise Him, praise, servants of Hashem."*[6]

Moshe Rabbeinu, who achieved the closest possible relationship Man can have with Hashem, is referred to at the end of his life and after all his accomplishments, as "Hashem's servant."[7] This seems surprising! Do Chazal not tell us that a child's stature is greater than that of a servant, that when the Jewish People faithfully adhere to Hashem's will, they are known as His children?[8] Why then is Moshe known by the seemingly lesser description of "servant?"

Rather, not all servants are equal. A servant generally occupies a lower status than a child does because the former usually acts solely out of obligation and duty. But a servant who cherishes his work and relationship with his master can be greater than a child. Thus, Chazal themselves taught that one is believed to assert that someone who acts toward him as a servant is in fact his son, on the premise that a son might "serve him like a servant would."[9] Servitude can, in such a case, represent the greatest level of affection and deference. Moshe served Hashem as a child who is eager to please a beloved parent—"Moshe will rejoice in his portion"[10]—earning him the title "servant" as a mark of the greatest honor.

Chazal tell us about Tzadok and Beitos, students of Antignus Ish Socho. When the latter taught that we must conduct ourselves like "servants

---

6 *Yalkut Shimoni, Tehillim* 113:872.

7 *Devarim* 34:5.

8 *Kiddushin* 36a.

9 *Bava Basra* 127b.

10 *Amidah* prayer for Shabbos morning.

who serve their master without expectation of reward," his students objected, "Is it possible that workers should labor all day and not be paid in the evening?" Having concluded that such an expectation is unjust, they abandoned the way of Torah. Their central mistaken premise, though, was equating the work of a daily laborer with the labor of Hashem's servants. The former most certainly deserve their wages each evening; for the latter, any opportunity to serve is payment enough.[11]

Tzadok and Beitos perpetuated this error, and, centuries later, their intellectual heirs failed to appreciate our relationship with Torah:

> *A Tzeduki saw that Rava was immersed in study and his fingers were beneath his leg and he was squeezing them, and his fingers were spurting blood. He said to Rava, "You impulsive nation, who accorded precedence to your mouths over your ears. You still bear your impulsiveness! You should listen first. Then, if you are capable, accept. And if not, do not accept!" He said to him, "About us, who proceed wholeheartedly, it is written: 'The integrity of the upright will guide them,' whereas about those people who walk in deceit, it is written: 'And the perverseness of the faithless will destroy them.'"*

I once heard the Gerrer Rebbe, the *Lev Simchah*, relate a story he heard from his father, the *Imrei Emes*, concerning an incident that happened in the court of his grandfather, the *Sefas Emes*. One Sukkos, the *Sefas Emes* noted to his *chassidim* that during *Hallel*, when reciting the words "*Ana Hashem*—Please Hashem," one can effect great things in the upper realms. These words occur several times in *Hallel*, and the *chassidim* disagreed as to which of these their Rebbe was referencing. Some *chassidim* poured out their hearts while saying the words, "*Ana Hashem hoshia na*—Please Hashem, save us," while others pronounced the following phrase, "*Ana Hashem hatzlicha na*—Please Hashem, make successful," with incredible devotion. "But," related the *Imrei Emes*, "I knew that both groups were wrong—my father meant neither. He was

11 See *Avos D'Rabi Nosson* 1, and *Rambam*, *Mishneh Torah*, Laws of Teshuvah, ch. 10.

referring to the plea, '*Ana Hashem ki ani avdecha*—Please Hashem, for I am Your servant!'"

We should hardly be surprised that these words are so laden with the potential ascribed to them by the *Sefas Emes*. The Rambam uses the phrase "great joy" to describe only two things. The joy of Sukkos, says the Rambam, exceeds that of other holidays, all of which require that one rejoice. On Sukkos, there was "great joy" in the Beis Hamikdash, owing to the Torah's command to "rejoice before Hashem for seven days."[12] Second, *Hallel* is not recited on Rosh Hashanah and Yom Kippur because *Hallel* must be said with "great joy," which is inappropriate on days of judgment.[13] Thus, the recitation of *Hallel* on Sukkos represents one of the most joyous moments in a Jew's year. When, at such a time, the Jew affirms so passionately and sincerely his single-minded identity as Hashem's servant, he will surely draw down profound spiritual impact.

There is an additional noteworthy nuance here. In both phrases, "*Ana Hashem hoshia na*" and "*Ana Hashem hatzlicha na*," the word "*ana*" ends with an *alef*, while "*ana*" in "*Ana Hashem ki ani avdecha*" ends with a *hei*. The Radak explains that *ana* with a *alef* is a request, while *ana* with the *hei* at its end expresses acknowledgment and gratitude. A servant might approach his master and beg for favors, but David HaMelech taught us to thank Hashem for the very opportunity we have to serve Him and do His will, day after day, throughout our lives.[14]

---

12 *Mishneh Torah*, Laws of Lulav 8:12.

13 *Mishneh Torah*, Laws of Chanukah 3:6.

14 *Radak, Tehillim* 116:16.

SIXTY-ONE

And You Approached and Stood under the Mountain

On the third day, as morning dawned, there was thunder, and lightning, and a dense cloud upon the mountain, and a very loud blast of the horn; and all the people who were in the camp trembled.[1]

You came forward and stood at the foot of the mountain. The mountain was ablaze with flames to the very skies, dark with densest clouds.[2]

Our ancestors, standing at Sinai, were overcome by fear. The *pesukim* describe their reaction:

All the people witnessed the thunder and lightning, the blare of the horn and the mountain smoking; and when the people saw it, they fell back and stood at a distance. "You

1 *Shemos* 19:16.

2 *Devarim* 4:11.

> *speak to us," they said to Moshe, "and we will obey; but let not God speak to us, lest we die." Moshe answered the people, "Be not afraid, for God has come only in order to test you, and in order that the fear of Him may be ever with you, so that you do not sin."*[3]

Rashi adds:

> *They stood at a distance: they moved back startled twelve mil, a distance equal to the length of their camp…*
>
> *So that His fear may be ever with you: through the fact that you see that He is feared and dreaded you will know that there is none beside Him and you will therefore fear Him and not sin.*

B'nei Yisrael experienced awe and dread at the extra-natural activity—the fire, smoke, and noises surrounding Sinai—and instinctively retreated away from the mountain. And yet, we also read the *pasuk* in *Devarim* that describes their tenacity:

> *You came forward and stood at the foot of the mountain. The mountain was ablaze with flames to the very skies, dark with densest clouds.*[4]

Not only did they not flee in terror, but they drew closer and stood, resolutely, "under" the mountain! How are we meant to think about the tension between these *pesukim*?

I believe the two reactions must coexist, side by side, then and for all time. Our ancestors did shrink back in fear, but this very same awe inspired a deeper love and a desire to draw nearer. Coming closer, they once again were frightened, but could not escape the will to see their King. So it was, fear and love alternatively animating their actions, in a self-perpetuating and ever-reinforcing cycle.

---

3 *Shemos* 20:15–17.

4 *Devarim* 4:11.

Chazal teach us the same about Avraham and Iyov:

> *Rabbi Meir says: It is stated with regard to Iyov that he was "God-fearing" and it is stated with regard to Avraham that he was "God-fearing." Just as the description "God-fearing" stated by Avraham is referring out of love, so too, "God-fearing" with regard to Iyov is out of love. And from where do we derive Avraham's love? As it is written: "The offspring of Avraham who loved Me."*[5]

Love drives awe and awe engenders love—both are crucial pillars supporting one's relationship with Hashem. Every morning, we ask Hashem to "focus our hearts to love and fear Your name," with love preceding fear, while in the *Zohar*, fear always precedes love: "*B'dchilu u'rechimu*—With fear and love." These two powerful emotions must be harnessed in service of Hashem; our ancestors at Sinai received their first such lesson, experiencing them both simultaneously as they gathered, awestruck, awaiting Hashem's message.

---

5 *Sotah* 31a.

SIXTY-TWO

Hashem Will Give Strength to His People

When the Torah was given to the Jewish People... all gathered around Bilaam the wicked, and said to him, "... [W]hat is this tumultuous sound that we have heard?" He said to them, "He has a good and precious item in His treasury, that was hidden away with Him for 974 generations before the world was created, and He seeks to give it to his children, as it is stated: 'Hashem will give strength to His people.'"[1]

Regarding that day, the pasuk states: "Hashem reigns, clothed in majesty; Hashem is clothed, He has donned strength." Strength can only mean Torah, as the pasuk says: "Hashem will give strength to His people."[2]

1 *Zevachim* 116a.

2 *Zohar*, vol. 2, 94a.

Rabbi Elazar said: When B'nei Yisrael declared, "We will do" before "We will listen," a Heavenly voice called out, "Who divulged this secret to My children?" This is a formula that the angels use, as the pasuk states: "Bless Hashem, His angels, mighty of strength, who do His bidding and listen to His voice." First they "do," and only after do they "listen."[3]

These enigmatic passages in Chazal yield several points:

- By proclaiming, "We will do," and then, "We will listen," B'nei Yisrael elevated themselves to the level of the angels.
- At Sinai, Hashem donned "new" clothes, as did B'nei Yisrael.
- These clothes represent strength, which represents Torah.
- Even Bilaam understood prophetically that Torah is strength.
- The events at Sinai are described as "Hashem gave strength to His people."

Now, let us attempt to construct a meaningful lesson from these elusive ideas.

Our great teachers, for many generations, have struggled with the apparent conflict between Man's free will and Hashem's omniscience. The Rambam famously raised the question in as many words: If Hashem knows everything that is destined to occur, and can see each person's actions and outcomes, then everything is preordained—how is it yet possible for Man to choose between good and evil? According to the Rambam's answer, humans indeed act freely, and as finite beings, qualitatively unlike Hashem, we cannot possibly understand how Hashem's knowledge functions. It is not for us to attempt to penetrate the depths

3 *Shabbos* 88a.

of this question, which, as the Rambam describes, is "longer than the earth and broader than the sea."[4]

Commenting on Rabbi Akiva's teaching in *Avos* that "everything is predicted, and permission is granted," the Rambam further states: "This teaching incorporates very lofty matters, and none other than Rabbi Akiva would say such things." According to the Rambam, Rabbi Akiva in this Mishnah is dealing with our question.[5]

So many others wrote about and grappled with this immense question.[6] We need not dwell on the topic any further here. In the final analysis, whichever path we choose to resolve the tension between free will and Hashem's omniscience, we firmly believe that Man has agency at all times to choose between right and wrong, and Hashem's knowledge in no way forces him to act. A person will be duly rewarded for choosing what is good and punished for doing the opposite.

Angels, too, were created by Hashem with free will. However, their proximity to Hashem's awesome Majesty effectively eliminates any ability they may have to contravene His will. If human eyes were similarly given a glimpse of Hashem's greatness, we too would lose our free will.

We read in *Tehillim* the call to Man to "give strength to Hashem."[7] How do we give anything, much less strength, to Hashem, Who already is Master of the universe and everything in it? I heard cited in the name of the Vilna Gaon that in one area, Hashem did indeed cede control. By granting Man free will, Hashem diminished, as it were, His own Kingdom, removing Man's actions from within His control.

Man then has the opportunity to restore these elements to Hashem's domain. By conquering one's impulses and refining one's character to the point that a particular act becomes repulsive and unthinkable, a person removes that act from the realm of free will and "restores" it to Hashem's kingdom—where it naturally belongs. In so doing, Man enlarges the Kingdom of Heaven ever so slightly and "gives strength"

---

4 *Mishneh Torah*, Laws of Teshuvah 5:5.

5 *Peirush Hamishnayos, Avos* 3:15.

6 See *Tosafos Yom Tov, Avos* 3:15, *Shu"t Rivash* 118, *Mei Hashiloach, Parshas Vayera, Takanas Hashavin* 6, *Pri Tzaddik Parshas Shelach*, and *Kovetz Hearos* 49:12.

7 *Tehillim* 68:35.

to Hashem. These are of course deep concepts, the surface of which we can only just barely scratch.

This is the inner greatness of "*naaseh v'nishma*—we will do and we will listen." A person acting freely does not obligate himself in advance. First, he or she hears what is being requested or demanded, and then chooses how to act or react. B'nei Yisrael, declaring "we shall do," promised to obey Hashem's Torah absent any knowledge of its contents, and effectively surrendered their free will, "giving strength" to Hashem.

Thus, Hashem gave Torah to His people, granting the power of choice. With the commands of Torah came our ability to decide freely whether or not to comply. In our choice to fulfill His desire, we are giving that power "back" to Hashem, as we are called to do by David HaMelech in *Tehillim*, mentioned above.

Hashem, hearing His children proclaim their willingness to cede their free will in the face of His greatness, wonders how Man came to a realization that was previously limited to angels, beings whose greatness had long since caused them to suspend their own free will. Hashem marveled at His people and declared them to be on the level of His ministering angels.

SIXTY-THREE

A Day for You

Rabbi Eliezer says, "A person must choose on a festival: he either eats and drinks or sits and learns." Rabbi Yehoshua says, "Divide the day, half of it for eating and drinking and half of it for the study hall." Rabbi Yochanan said, "Both of them learned from the same source. One pasuk says: 'It shall be an assembly for the Lord your God,' and another pasuk says: 'It shall be an assembly for you.' Rabbi Eliezer holds that it must be either entirely for Hashem or entirely for you. And Rabbi Yehoshua holds that one should split the day, half of it for Hashem and half of it for you…" Rabbi Elazar said, "All agree with regard to Atzeres [Shavuos], that we require that it be also 'for you.' Why? It is the day on which the Torah was given."[1]

1 *Pesachim* 68b.

One might have imagined that on the day we commemorate receiving the Torah, we would devote all our attention and energy toward Torah study. Indeed, we are familiar with a prevalent custom, dating back many centuries, to remain awake and learn Torah the entire night of Shavuos.[2] At the same time, we find halachic authorities commenting on the special foods customarily eaten on Shavuos.[3] How are we meant to think about the character of this special day?

Rashi, addressing the passage cited above, writes that all agree that one must indulge on Shavuos "to show that it is agreeable to us to celebrate the day that Torah was given to Israel." Our goal is to demonstrate unambiguously our abiding sense that Torah represents not only the pathway to eternal reward but also to a rich, joyful, and meaningful life in this world.

Even while advocating a simple and austere worldly existence, Chazal promised that a life of Torah will be the best way to enjoy one's years in the physical world:

> *Such is the way of Torah: you shall eat bread with salt, and rationed water shall you drink; you shall sleep on the ground, your life will be one of privation, and in Torah shall you labor. If you do this, "Happy shall you be and it shall be good for you"—"Happy shall you be" in this world, "and it shall be good for you" in the World to Come.*[4]

I often comment, in a somewhat lighter tone, that Chazal's promise that "one who studies halachos every day is assured a place in the World to Come," refers to one who only studies halachos. But a person who swims in the sea of Torah, probes its mysterious depths, and explores its myriad alleyways is guaranteed to enjoy not only a worthy portion in the World to Come, but will also delight in every moment of this world.

---

2 See *Magen Avraham* 494:1.

3 See Rama's comments, ibid., regarding the practice to eat foods made with milk and honey on Shavuos.

4 *Avos* 6:4.

Our great Sages were suffused with palpable joy of Torah:

> *Rebbi said: When I went to Rabbi Elazar ben Shamua to clarify my knowledge, and some say to clarify the knowledge of Rabbi Elazar ben Shamua, I found Yosef the Babylonian sitting before him. And every ruling was especially dear to him, until one time he said to him, "My teacher, one who slaughters the offering to leave of its blood for the next day, what is the halachah?" He said to him, "It is fit." In the evening [he asked again], and he said to him that it is fit. In the morning [he asked again], and he said to him that it is fit. At noon [he asked again], and he said to him that it is fit. Later in the afternoon, he said to him, "It is fit, but Rabbi Eliezer deems it unfit." Yosef's face lit up. He said to him, "Yosef, it seems to me that our halachos were not in agreement until now." He said to him, "My teacher, yes, I agree, but Rabbi Yehudah taught me that it is unfit, and I went around to all his disciples, seeking another who agrees, and I could not find one. Now that you have taught me that Rabbi Eliezer deems it unfit, you have returned to me that which I had lost." Rabbi Elazar ben Shamua's eyes streamed with tears, and he said, "Happy are you, Torah scholars, for whom matters of Torah are exceedingly dear." Rabbi Elazar ben Shamua recited this pasuk about Yosef the Babylonian: "O how I love Your Torah; it is my focus all day."*[5]

> *A certain noblewoman saw [Rabbi Yonah] and said,*[6] *"Old man, old man! Surely you are one of these three: either you drank wine, you are a usurer, or you raise pigs." He said to her, "This woman's spirit should be overturned, for not one of these apply to me. Rather, my study is always with me, as it states in the pasuk, 'A man's wisdom lights his face.'" Rabbi Avahu arrived at Teveria. Rabbi Yochanan's students observed that Rabbi Avahu's face was shining...Rabbi Yochanan asked him, "What*

---

5 *Menachos* 18a.

6 Commenting on his glowing countenance.

> *new Torah have you heard?" He replied, "An ancient Tosefta." Rabbi Yochanan declared, "A man's wisdom lights his face..."*[7]

Joy of Torah is not meant to remain abstract and cerebral, in the sense of "Hashem's directives are just, bringing joy to the heart." As we saw in Chazal above, this joy transforms the person and lights up his countenance.

According to the Ramban, this celebration was appropriate even at Sinai, and on many subsequent occasions whereby Torah was renewed or rededicated in some fashion:

> *"He did not raise His hand against the notables of Israel, and they saw God and they ate and drank." They drank, meaning, they rejoiced and made it a holiday. For one is obligated to celebrate upon receiving the Torah. As we see they were commanded to do upon writing the Torah on stones (when entering the Land of Israel): "And you shall slaughter offerings and eat there, and you shall rejoice before Hashem, your God."*[8] *And the pasuk states regarding Shlomo, "And the wisdom and knowledge were given to you..."*[9] *and then, immediately, "And he came to Yerushalayim and made a feast for all his servants."*[10] *Rabbi Elazar said that from here [we learn] to make a feast upon completing the Torah.*[11] *And it says that when his father David donated to the construction of the Beis Hamikdash, "And they slaughtered offerings to Hashem and they offered burnt offerings...and they drank before Hashem on that day with great joy."*[12] *Here too, on the day of [their] marriage with Torah they did the same.*[13]

---

7 *Shekalim* 13a.

8 *Devarim* 27:7.

9 *Divrei Hayamim II* 1:12.

10 *Melachim I* 3:15.

11 *Shir Hashirim Rabbah* 1:9.

12 *Divrei Hayamim I* 29:21–22.

13 *Ramban, Shemos* 24:11.

Consider also the moving and holy words of the *Ohr Hachaim*, who writes that one who truly appreciates Torah can scarcely refrain from jumping with joy and celebrating his great fortune.[14]

Even the pure joy of performing a single mitzvah can bring a person to unnatural levels of joy:

> *Abaye was sitting before Rabbah. He saw that Rabbah was overly glad. He said to him, "Does it not say in the pasuk, 'rejoice in trembling?'" He replied, "I am wearing tefillin." Rabbi Yirmiyah was sitting before Rabbi Zeira and saw that he was overly glad. He said to him, "Does it not say in the pasuk, 'From sadness there is gain?'" He replied, "I am wearing tefillin."*[15]

Rashi explains that the justification, "I am wearing tefillin," was meant to convey the wearer's true—serious—state of mind. With the tefillin on his head, there was no concern that Rabbah or Rabbi Zeira would lose himself in empty merriment. But Rabbeinu Yonah adopted a different approach, according to which the tefillin—i.e., fulfillment of a mitzvah—was itself *cause* for joy.

Chazal further recorded:

> *Rabbi Ilaah said to Ulah, "When you arrive there, inquire about my brother Rabbi Bruna in the presence of the entire group, for he is a great man and takes joy in mitzvos. One time, he prayed right after saying the blessing on redemption (samach geulah l'tefillah), and he did not stop smiling the entire day."*[16]

Our Sages did not hesitate to openly and demonstrably celebrate their relationship with Torah and its mitzvos. Any engagement in Torah study or fulfillment of Hashem's will, however seemingly small, was cause for great joy.

---

14 *Ohr Hachaim, Devarim* 26:11.

15 *Berachos* 30b.

16 Ibid., 9b.

SIXTY-FOUR

Honey and Milk

Our familiar custom to partake on Shavuos of dairy foods as well as those made with honey is well documented and codified in halachah.[1]

Drawing on the *pasuk* "honey and milk under your tongue," we seek to reinforce in our minds, in our hearts, and in those of our children, that this day—the day on which we accepted Torah—has afforded us immeasurable and never-ending sweetness.

As the *Ohr Hachaim* comments on the *pasuk*, "You shall rejoice in all the good":

> *"In all the good" refers to Torah. For if people would appreciate the sweetness of Torah and its appeal, they would go crazy and pursue it as if nothing else in the world had any other value. For it alone contains all the good in the world.*[2]

Such is the attitude and experience of someone whose very body is transformed through an appreciation for Torah and its otherworldly qualities. I recall, as a youngster, participating in a class that my Rebbe, the Klausenberger Rebbe, *zt"l*, delivered to a small group in his private office. It was an unusually brief *shiur*, at the completion of which he ushered in a well-known benefactor of the yeshiva. The Rebbe apologized

1 *Rama, Orach Chaim* 494:3, and *Be'er Heitev* 8.

2 *Ohr Hachaim, Devarim* 26:2.

profusely to his guest for delaying their meeting past the appointed time, explaining that he was suffering from terrible headaches and no medication would afford him any comfort. As his only remaining option was to invite in a group of students and study with them, he was forced to keep his guest waiting.

Rashi and Rabbeinu Yonah both taught that Hashem Himself delights in Torah study. We, charged with a life's mission to emulate Hashem, must also consider Torah to be our primary delight, even amidst the pleasures of a material world:

> *They [the tablets of stone] were the work of God—as it sounds, that He Himself made them. Alternatively, like someone who says, "So-and-so is busy only with such-and-such." So too, the Holy One, blessed be He, delights only in Torah.*[3]

How fortunate are we, that we too have the opportunity to delight and rejoice in Torah morning and evening, bringing its bright light into a world of chaos and darkness.

---

3 *Rashi, Shemos* 32:16.

SIXTY-FIVE

Return Us to Your Torah

In the weekday *Amidah*, we approach Hashem with the following request:

> *Return us, our Father, to Your Torah, and bring us close, our King, to Your service.*

Two distinct modes of relationship are invoked in this brief prayer. When mentioning Torah, we refer to Hashem as "our Father," but when we contemplate our service to Him, He is "our King." The latter is intuitive—a king is to be served loyally by his subjects. But how are we made Hashem's children specifically through the medium of Torah and its study?

Chazal saw an allusion to Torah as a familial bond in Shlomo HaMelech's words, describing the revelation at Sinai as a wedding:

> *"Go forth, daughters of Zion, and gaze upon King Shlomo wearing the crown that his mother gave him on his wedding day, on the day of the gladness of his heart." "On his wedding day" refers to the Giving of the Torah. "And on the day of the gladness of his heart" refers to the building of the Beis Hamikdash; may it be rebuilt speedily in our days.*

A midrash describes even more vividly our familial ties with Hashem and His Torah.

> *...[T]here are purchases that the one who sells them is sold along with them—the Holy One, blessed be He, said to Israel, "I sell to you My Torah, and I am sold along with it [as it were]," as it is said: "And they shall take for Me."[1] This is similar to a king who had an only daughter. One of the kings came and took her and sought to go back to his land to marry her. He said to him, "My daughter who I have given to you is my only one. I cannot bear to separate from her, but to tell you that you cannot take her is also impossible since she is your wife. Rather, do me this favor, that everywhere you go make me a small room, so that I can live with you, for I cannot leave my daughter." So said Hashem to Israel, "I have given you the Torah. I cannot bear to separate from her, and to tell you not to take her is also impossible. Rather, everywhere you go make Me one house so that I can live within it," as it is said: "And make Me a sanctuary."[2]*

We, the Jewish nation, are "taking" the Torah from Hashem for it to become our own. Hashem, unable to bear its absence, asks that we preserve a place for Him to reside—the *Mishkan* and Beis Hamikdash.

Maintaining this imagery, Chazal later continue:

> *"An inheritance (morashah)"—do not read it as "morashah—inheritance," rather as "me'orasah—betrothed." So long as he has not married his betrothed, a groom is but a guest in his father-in-law's home; once he marries her, then her father comes to visit her. So too, until the Torah was given to the Jewish People, Moshe had to go up to the mountain; after it was given, Hashem said to Moshe, "Make for Me a sanctuary."[3]*

Before the Torah was given to B'nei Yisrael, all mankind, even the most righteous among them—Moshe himself—were Hashem's servants. One could only approach Hashem as a subject, meeting Him at

---

1 ["*V'yikchu li*," which the midrash renders literally as, "They shall take Me."]

2 *Shemos Rabbah* 33:1.

3 Ibid., 33:7.

His appointed time and place. Moshe thus was required to go up to the mountain to converse with Hashem. When Hashem bequeathed the Torah to B'nei Yisrael, we became family—formalities are cast aside, and He visits us just as an earthly king might spend time with his own children.

Rabbi Akiva, even while teaching the greatness of every single human being, stressed the uniqueness of the Jew:

> *Man is beloved, for he was created in Hashem's image. Great love is due to him, for he was created in the Divine image, as it says: "He created Man in the Divine image." Israel is more beloved, for they are called Hashem's children, as it says: "You are children to Hashem, your God." Israel is more beloved, for they were given a precious item...*

Each human is great, representing the Divine image. But we, who received His Torah, are Hashem's children. In giving us His precious gift, He singled us out as "family," and, henceforth, Torah represents our unique relationship with Him as our Father. We are thus "more beloved" for the "precious item" He gave us.

Indeed, it appears that this is also the reason why a gentile who studies Torah deserves death; for woe unto the servant who masquerades as a son of the King.

"Return us, our Father, to Your Torah."

SIXTY-SIX

I Will Give You Tablets of Stone

And Hashem said to Moshe: Come up to Me on the mountain and remain there; I will give you the tablets of stone, and the Torah, and the commandments, which I have written to direct them.[1]

Here, as well as in other *pesukim*, we learn that Hashem handed Moshe two stone tablets bearing the Ten Commandments. Why two? Surely, the Ten Commandments could have been fit onto a single tablet!

Rashi stresses that the two tablets were "equal," hinting that it was their contents that divided the ten instructions across two separate pieces of stone.[2] The Ramban elaborates on this theme, outlining a well-known distinction between the first five commandments and the latter five:

1 *Shemos* 24:12.

2 *Rashi, Devarim* 9:11.

> *These Ten Commandments include five that honor the Creator and five that honor humanity. Honoring one's parents is to honor Hashem, for it was to honor Him that Hashem commanded to honor a parent, who participated in Man's creation. This leaves five that address the good of Man and his needs...*[3]

The Ramban establishes that the first five commandments, carved on one tablet, address Man's engagement with Hashem, while the instructions on the second tablet provide a framework for an upright society. With Rashi's comment, we learn that neither category is any more or less important than the other. Faithfulness to each is absolutely critical for Man to reach his own potential and for mankind to realize its purpose.

Moshe received two tablets, calling attention to the need for equal focus on both aspects of Torah. While their demands may conflict at times, it is precisely through successful mediation of this tension and rising to the opportunities it presents that Man achieves meaningful growth.

Thus, Rabbi Yisrael Salanter taught that when Moshe Rabbeinu descended the mountain and saw his people engaging in the worship of a Golden Calf, he initially wished to break only one tablet. Seeing the nation's failure in remaining faithful to a single God, he determined that they were unworthy of the first tablet, with its lofty theological and spiritual vision for humanity. But the second tablet, with its instructions for a just society and proper interpersonal conduct, was still relevant to them. These commandments were, perhaps, unaffected by their religious shortcomings. However, Hashem told Moshe that his thinking regarding this matter was incorrect. The commandments may be split across two tablets, but their soul is one—partial Torah is not Torah. "Do not kill" absent "I am your God" is not Torah.

Chazal read deeply into this message, teaching that to achieve spiritual perfection one must eschew material benefit. For nothing has the power to corrupt one's psyche and character more than pursuit

---

3 *Ramban, Shemos* 20:13.

of financial gain. To this end, they dubbed a sage who was unable to recognize a coin "holy of holies."[4]

The Rambam, in describing the attitude of those who choose to devote themselves to a life of devotion and closeness to Hashem, writes:

> *Not only the tribe of Levi, but each well-informed thinking person whose spirit moves him to devote himself to the service of Hashem, to know Hashem, and has walked uprightly as God created him after casting off his neck the yoke of many a cunning wile that men contrived, is indeed Divinely consecrated, and Hashem will forever and ever be his portion. Hashem will provide sufficiently for his needs, as He did for the priests and the Levites...*[5]

To elevate oneself in Divine service is to first "walk uprightly as God created us."

The consequences of ill-gotten property can be harsh and extreme. Chazal warned us that one who lends at interest will lose his possessions. But the harm can extend even further when one provides for his family with tainted money, raising children on a spiritually poisoned diet and potentially ensuring their distancing from Hashem and His Torah. The Klausenberger Rebbe, *zt"l*, would often quote, and included in his will, the words of the *Noam Elimelech*:

> *The great Rebbe, R' Menachem Mendel [of Rimanov] would reflect: One might wonder at those children who appear to be on the proper path—they go to study with their teachers, they pray, answer Amen and Amen yehei shmei rabba, and in general conduct themselves well. Yet, when they grow up, they develop terrible character and no longer learn or pray, etc. Where does this come from? After all, the Torah they learned as children should be pure and only lead them to*

---

4 *Sanhedrin* 53b.

5 *Mishneh Torah*, Laws of Shemittah and Yovel 13:13.

> *greater strengths! He answered that it is because their fathers supported them with stolen money, earned through dishonest dealings. They thus grew by way of forbidden food, which then became part of them, embedding within them bad traits. We see this proven in the law that a chicken's innards may not be offered as an offering because a chicken eats from anything it finds, even property not belonging to its owner. Thus, even though the chicken itself is not commanded to avoid theft, its very existence is abhorrent to Hashem.*[6]

We often look about and wonder why some of our youth seem to inexplicably turn their backs on Yiddishkeit. Rebbe Menachem Mendel of Rimanov revealed to us, in as many words, what is all too often at the root of their desertion.

---

6 *Agra D'Pirka* 126.

SIXTY-SEVEN

Your Nation Is My Nation, Your God Is My God

There is a longstanding custom to read *Megillas Rus* on Shavuos, for the rather obvious reason that the story of Rus draws on a central aspect of the day. Our ancestors at Sinai entered into the covenant and became Hashem's chosen nation on this day, and, in her own personal journey, Rus embraced the God of her mother-in-law, Naomi, and became a convert. Each year, Shavuos brings with it the spiritual potential of Sinai—for each of us to once again commit ourselves to Hashem's covenant.

In thinking about the overlapping themes of conversion and Shavuos, I am struck by the breathtaking words of Rabbi Kalonymus Kalman Shapira, the Piaseczno Rebbe, in his work *Tzav V'Ziruz*. Sharing with the reader his innermost thoughts, the Rebbe records a dialogue with Hashem: "Master of the world, with all my heart, I wish to give You something; I want to come closer to You and do Your will. But what can I yet offer? To study more Torah? I have, for the longest time, been learning with all my energy. Shall I pray more? I have always attempted to pray with the greatest intensity possible...How I wish I could convert—but, what can I do, I am already a Jew!"

The Rebbe's passion moves me to tears. So consumed with love for the Divine was his soul that he could not satisfy his yearning with anything but the transformation of conversion, whereby one casts aside his entire past and present in service of a holy future, and becomes a Jew. But, he concluded, I was born a Jew and that option is not available to me.

Perhaps, however, a Jew can indeed convert. True, he cannot be circumcised as a convert, for he is already commanded to do so; immersing in the mikveh, for all its powers of purification, cannot effect a conversion. But maybe the Jew can nevertheless stand before the great Judge in Heaven and declare, as does the prospective convert to the *Beis Din* (Rabbinical Court), his wholehearted acceptance of all the mitzvos in the Torah. And, just as halachah dictates that a convert may not withhold a single letter of Torah from his or her commitment, the Jew must reaffirm on Shavuos his complete commitment to Torah in its entirety.

We know, all too well, that through the rhythms of daily life and the habits they develop, we tacitly choose which mitzvos to "accept," and our observance becomes uneven, scrupulous in some areas and lax in others. One might focus solely on devotional obligations, directing his gaze heavenward to Godly matters and neglecting the world around him, while another might place great emphasis on interpersonal conduct, offering lackluster attention to other demands. A convert has no such luxury. He may not pick or choose. His acceptance must be unqualified and full-throated.

Imagine a candidate for conversion standing before the *Beis Din*. The presiding judge, the *Av Beis Din*, turns to the prospective convert and asks if the latter accepts upon himself to observe the entire Torah. In a barely audible whisper, the soon-to-be convert replies, "Yes—just like the *Av Beis Din*." Confused, the Rabbi angrily demands an explanation. Hesitantly and full of apology, the convert elaborates, "If I'm not mistaken, I recently overheard you, the *Av Beis Din*, speaking ill of someone else. I am able to convert if I, too, can speak as freely as you." Ashamed and humiliated as he may be, the Rabbi will have no choice but to acknowledge that while the candidate may be indeed qualified to serve as *Av Beis Din*, he has not met the requirements for becoming a Jew! To join the Jewish People and live in Hashem's presence, he must accept the entire Torah.

Thus, a Jew, too, can and must undergo a conversion of his own. He must stand before the Heavenly Judge and commit to fully embrace and observe all of Torah. Channeling the energy of "*naaseh v'nishma*—we will do and we will listen," our acceptance of Torah on Shavuos should be an equally unambiguous testimony to our love for Hashem and His Torah.

SIXTY-EIGHT

Torah and Beis Hamikdash

"And God spoke all these words, saying"—the Holy One, blessed be He, leads Israel in the manner of kings, as it says: "With Me from Lebanon, My bride!" Why so? In the merit that they said, "We will do and we will listen."[1]

Some have written that this is a difficult midrash to explain. But, if we examine a nearby passage in the text, it appears quite straightforward. We already cited this teaching above:

> *...[T]here are purchases that the one who sells them is sold along with them—the Holy One, blessed be He, said to Israel, "I sell to you My Torah, and I am sold along with it [as it were]," as it is said, "And they shall bring Me gifts." This is similar to a king who had an only daughter. One of the kings came and took her and sought to go back to his land to marry her. He said to him, "My daughter who I have given to you is my only one. I cannot bear to separate from her, but to tell you that you cannot take her is also impossible since she is your wife. Rather, do*

1 *Shemos Rabbah* 28.

> *me this favor, that everywhere you go make me a small room, so that I can live with you, for I cannot leave my daughter." So said Hashem to Israel, "I have given you the Torah. I cannot bear to separate from her, and to tell you not to take her is also impossible. Rather, everywhere you go make me one house so that I can live within it," as it is said: "And make me a sanctuary."*[2]

In another text, the association between Torah and the Beis Hamikdash is made even more explicit:

> *When the Jewish nation joyously assumed Hashem's rule, saying, "Everything that Hashem speaks we will do and then we will listen," Hashem immediately instructed Moshe to tell the people to make a sanctuary for Him...*[3]

And, as we also saw earlier, the midrash again reinforces the imagery of a beloved daughter leaving the home of her father, a king, as a metaphor for Hashem's desire to maintain an ongoing presence among us after giving over His Torah:

> *"An inheritance (morashah)"—do not read it as "morashah—inheritance," rather as "me'orasah—betrothed." So long as he has not married his betrothed, a groom is but a guest in his father-in-law's home; once he marries her, then her father comes to visit her. So too, until the Torah was given to the Jewish People, Moshe had to go up to the mountain; after it was given, Hashem said to Moshe, "Make for Me a sanctuary."*[4]

Matan Torah, the giving of Torah at Sinai, was a marriage between B'nei Yisrael and the Torah. Just as a marriage is celebrated by the participants and their families in the presence of those closest to them, so too Hashem wished to celebrate with us and His precious Torah, forever, in the Beis Hamikdash:

---

2 *Shemos Rabbah* 33:1.

3 *Tanna D'bei Eliyahu* 17.

4 Ibid., 33:7.

> *"Go forth, daughters of Zion, and gaze upon King Shlomo wearing the crown that his mother gave him on his wedding day, on the day of the gladness of his heart." "On his wedding day" refers to the Giving of the Torah. "And on the day of the gladness of his heart" refers to the building of the Beis Hamikdash, may it be rebuilt speedily in our days.*[5]

I would go so far as to suggest that Hashem even made a chuppah, a wedding canopy, at Sinai. This may have been the mountain itself, suspended over the people; perhaps the Clouds of Glory served the purpose of a chuppah on this special occasion. Indeed, such an idea is proposed by Rabbi Yehudah ben Yakar:

> *One wonders: what is the basis for making a chuppah? Why did Chazal establish this, given that it does not effect the marriage itself?...We can say that the chuppah hints at the protection of the Clouds of Glory that the Holy One, blessed be He, made for the Jewish People prior to giving the Torah, and then He later betrothed them there at Sinai with the Torah and mitzvos.*[6]

My dear son-in-law Rav Binyamin Beinish suggested, consistent with the above, that the sanctuary's very name points to this idea. It is referred to by the Torah as "*Mishkan Ha'eidus*—A Sanctuary of Testimony," for its primary function is to house the *Luchos Ha'eidus*—the tablets, which are the very essence of our relationship with Hashem, on account of which we deserve a sanctuary in the first place. Indeed, we are familiar with the prayer "that the Beis Hamikdash should be rebuilt speedily in our days, and You will give us our portion in Your Torah," explicitly intertwining Torah and the Beis Hamikdash.

One final point on this note. When a couple lives in harmony and love, their parents delight in visiting them and spending time with them—as does the King in our midrash. But when, God forbid, a couple are not at peace with each other, living instead in acrimony, every encounter

---

5 *Taanis* 26b.

6 *Peirush Hatefillos V'Haberachos*, p. 38.

brings great distress to the parent. All he wishes to do is extract himself from their unpleasant company.

This is the essence of Divine Presence in the Beis Hamikdash, and, sadly, its absence too.

> *May it be Your will that the Beis Hamikdash is built speedily in our days, and You give us our portion in Your Torah, and we shall serve You there in awe, as in days of old and years gone by.*

SIXTY-NINE

Lest You Forget What Your Eyes Have Seen

We are commanded to never forget the momentous and transcendent events of Sinai. In its instruction to this effect, which, according to the Ramban, is to be counted among the mitzvos of the Torah, the *pasuk* warns, "Guard yourself, lest you forget the things you saw, etc."[1]

Yet, the phrase itself is intriguing. Primarily, our experiences when receiving the Torah were auditory—we heard great thunder and the sounds of a mighty shofar, and, most importantly, we listened to Hashem's voice declare, "I am your God." Why then does the Torah emphasize that we must not forget what we *saw* at Sinai?

To explain this, we must remind ourselves of Chazal's teaching that at Sinai, our ancestors were able to "see that which is normally heard and hear that which is normally seen."[2]

There is a profound message here. Typically, of Man's five senses, the one he is most likely to trust unquestionably is his sight. That which I can see with my own eyes I am most likely to accept as factual; inputs into the other four senses can be questioned or doubted. Is that noise my imagination? Is that smell what I think it is? But I can be confident in

1 *Devarim* 4:9.

2 *Mechilta, Yisro.*

the reality of an event I observe directly. Chazal even gave expression to this idea, saying that "hearing should not be more reliable than seeing."[3]

All the same, a Jew must experience the world differently. He must know that his vision is limited and cannot grasp all of reality. Our belief in One Creator, Who created the universe and everything inhabiting it, yet He cannot be seen Himself, demands that we recognize the boundaries of physical existence. Our eyes of flesh and blood cannot apprehend true existence across its many dimensions. Only Man's soul, breathed by Hashem directly into Man but which cannot itself be seen, can truly appreciate existence for what it is.[4]

This sensitivity is not intuitive—it must be cultivated and developed. Children cannot see the angels, Hashem's messengers, that they learn about from their parents. But they accept the existence of such spiritual beings and become trained to understand that reality extends far beyond their field of physical vision.[5] Ultimately, "hearing" carries far more meaning than "seeing."

Our ancestors reached this level at Sinai. When they "saw that which is heard," they heard Hashem's message to them with the same clarity one usually experiences when seeing something. At the same time, so elevated were they that their physical surroundings became less real, a distant report—they "heard that which is normally seen," and the immediacy of vision became dulled in the face of Hashem's overwhelming presence.[6]

Perhaps we can use this lesson to understand the following passage in the Gemara:

> *Rabbi Yochanan sat and taught: In the future, the Holy One, blessed be He, will bring precious stones and pearls that are thirty cubits by thirty cubits, and He will hollow out in them ten by twenty and set them in the gates of Jerusalem. A certain student sneered at him, "Now we do not find precious stones*

---

3 *Rosh Hashanah* 25b.

4 See *Nefesh Hachaim, shaar* 3, ch. 11, and *Bnei Yissaschar, Chodesh Sivan, maamar* 5.

5 See *Ramban, Devarim* 4:9, and *Sefer Hachinuch*, introduction.

6 See also *Meshech Chochmah, Parashas Chukas*, and *Meor Einayim, Parashas Beshalach*.

> *even of the size of an egg of a dove, and yet all of this we will find?" After some time that student's ship went to sea, where he saw ministering angels sitting and sawing precious stones and pearls that were thirty cubits by thirty cubits and hollowed out in them ten by twenty. He said to them, "For whom are these?" They said to him that in the future, the Holy One, blessed be He, will place them in the gates of Jerusalem. He came before Rabbi Yochanan and said to him, "Continue to interpret, my teacher, it is fitting for you to interpret, as I saw just as you said!" Rabbi Yochanan said to him, "Empty one! If you had not seen, you would not have believed; you are mocking the statement of the Sages." He set his eyes upon him, and he was turned into a pile of bones.*[7]

Rabbi Yochanan's unnamed student was not punished when he scoffed at the original teaching. Yet, when he returned and attempted to support his teacher's words he was struck down. Why would this be?

Returning to Rabbi Yochanan and offering his eyewitness experience as evidence that his teacher was correct demonstrated that the student gave greater credence to his own vision than he did to the lessons of his master. Only the student's personal experience justified accepting Rabbi Yochanan's words. To this critical error, Rabbi Yochanan reacted so harshly, calling his student an "empty man." Thus, the student, an individual of sufficient stature to converse with angels, was turned into a pile of bones. A man of his level should have internalized the need to "see that which one hears" from the traditions of our parents and teachers.

Nor was the mode of the student's punishment incidental. Rather, his fate directly targeted his failing. A human is indeed but a pile of bones—it is only the soul he received directly from Hashem that keeps a man upright, living, breathing, and acting. This student, who over-emphasized that which he could physically see, failed to appreciate the role of that which eludes our vision. Rabbi Yochanan thus called him

---

7 *Bava Basra* 75a.

"empty," questioning him, "Are you indeed empty? Are you not aware of the soul that inhabits your body yet cannot be seen?"

Similarly, the Gemara stresses this message in another episode:

> *Rav Sheshes was blind. Everyone was going to greet the king and Rav Sheshes stood up and went along with them. A heretic found him and said to him, "Intact jugs go to the river, why do the broken shards go?" Rav Sheshes said to him, "Come see that I know more than you." The first troop passed; when the noise grew louder, this heretic said to him, "The king is coming." Rav Sheshes said to him, "He is not coming." A second troop passed; when the noise grew louder, this heretic said to him, "Now the king is coming." Rav Sheshes said to him, "The king is not coming." A third passed, and when there was silence, Rav Sheshes said to him, "Certainly now the king is coming." This heretic said to him, "How do you know this?" He said to him, "Royalty on earth is like royalty in the heavens, as it is written: 'And He said: Go forth, and stand upon the mount before Hashem. And, behold, Hashem passed by, and a great and strong wind rent the mountains, and broke in pieces the rocks before Hashem; but Hashem was not in the wind; and after the wind an earthquake; but Hashem was not in the earthquake; and after the earthquake a fire; but Hashem was not in the fire; and after the fire a still small voice.'" When the king came, Rav Sheshes began to bless him. The heretic said to him, "Do you bless someone you do not see?" And what ultimately happened to this heretic? Some say that his friends gouged out his eyes, and some say that Rav Sheshes fixed his gaze upon him, and he became a pile of bones.*

Here too, a profound message prevails. Not all knowledge can be discerned from one's sight. In fact, Rav Sheshes, relying only on his hearing, knew better than the heretic, not only about that which is hidden from physical vision, but even regarding events happening in their presence. When the heretic failed to understand this lesson and continued to mock Rav Sheshes by asking him why he would bless the king that he cannot see, he too was punished. Both versions of the heretic's punishment allude to our idea: either his eyes were gouged out, pointing to the overemphasis on physical sight, or he, like Rabbi Yochanan's unfortunate student, became a pile of bones, representing his failure to acknowledge that which cannot be seen.

At the time of our future redemption, we will likewise achieve clarity of vision through hearing, when we will all "see, each with his eye, when Hashem returns to *Tziyon*; all flesh together shall see that Hashem has spoken."[8] During *Mussaf* on each Shabbos and holiday, we recite in *Kedushah*, "And He will again in His mercy make us hear, in the presence of all life, saying..." At that time, we will be fortunate enough to rid ourselves of mundane limitations, and, once again, "see the sounds" of Hashem's revelation. To ensure we never lose our connection with those wondrous moments at Sinai, and the lofty spiritual heights we achieved, the Torah warns us, specifically to remember "that which your eyes saw" at Sinai.

---

8 *Yeshayahu* 52:8.

SEVENTY

Lest You Forget

Be sure to guard yourself very carefully, lest you forget the things your eyes saw.[1]

What is it that we saw at Sinai, the memory of which we are admonished so strongly to protect?

One critical event presents itself. In what serves, in many ways, as the very cornerstone and foundation of our tradition, the *pasuk* tells us that B'nei Yisrael witnessed Hashem conversing directly with Moshe:

> *And Hashem said to Moshe, "I will come to you in a thick cloud, in order that the people may hear when I speak with you and so trust you ever after." Moshe reported the people's words to Hashem.*[2]

Let us examine two basic approaches to this event. These will, in due course, illuminate the essence of our experience at Sinai and what it is we were warned to safeguard in our memories for all time. We shall begin with the Ibn Ezra's comment:

---

1 *Devarim* 4:9.

2 *Shemos* 19:9.

"When I speak to you"—the Ten Commandments—they will then believe that it is possible that Hashem might speak to Man and he will nonetheless survive. And "They will also believe in you," refers to the fact that you are a prophet—eliminating any doubt in their minds. Indeed, we see explicitly their declaration that "Today we saw Hashem speak with Man and live," and also, "For what other creature heard the voice of a living God speak from the fire and survive?" There, it also states: "You [Moshe] draw close and listen," a reference to their everlasting belief in you.[3]

According to the Ibn Ezra, the primary objective was to demonstrate to the Jewish nation that prophecy is both real and possible—that Hashem might indeed reveal His will to Man through the medium of a single individual, who will survive the encounter and communicate its contents to others.

The Ramban takes issue with the Ibn Ezra's premise, arguing that there was never a doubt as to the existence of prophecy. Rather, explains the Ramban, it was the criticality of establishing Moshe Rabbeinu's unique status that necessitated an elaborate setup:

What seems correct to me is the following: "I will come to you in a cloud"—you should approach the mist, so the people will hear My words. Thus, they themselves will prophetically hear My words, and they will not need to rely on others. As the pasuk later states: "Gather the people and I will cause them to hear My words, in order that they shall learn to fear Me forever." And, further, they will believe in you forever, through all generations. If a prophet or seer will later arise and contradict your teachings, they will immediately reject him, for they already saw with their eyes and heard with their ears that you reached the highest levels of prophecy. It will be clear to them about you from what is written later: "If you shall have

---

3 *Ibn Ezra*, ibid.

> *a prophet, I, Hashem, will appear to him in a vision or speak to him in a dream. My servant Moshe is unlike this—he alone is the most faithful. I will speak to him directly." Therefore, He said that the nation should hear Me speaking to Moshe, so they should hear My voice from amidst the fire and they will know that I am Hashem speaking to you. They will then believe in Me and in you forever.*[4]

The Rambam, in laying out the foundations of our tradition, offers a very similar approach:

> *Our master Moshe was not believed in by Israel because he performed wonders, for anyone who bases his belief contingent upon miracles retains suspicion in his heart, for it is possible that the miracle was delivered by means of enchantment and witchcraft. But all the miracles delivered by Moshe in the wilderness were responsive to necessities, and not as testimony for prophecy. When it became necessary to have the Egyptians sunk, he divided the sea and drowned them therein; when our need was food, he brought down for us the mann; when they became thirsty, he split open the rock for them; when Korach and his assembly denied him, the earth swallowed them up. Likewise came to pass all the other wonders. How, then, did they properly believe in him? By being present at Mount Sinai; for our own eyes saw and not through a stranger's, and our own ears heard and not that of another; the flame, the thunder and lightning, and he drew near the thick cloud and the Voice speaking to him, we heard it saying, "Moses, Moses, go and tell them thus and such"; for so he also said, "Hashem spoke with you face-to-face on the mount out of the midst of fire," and it is moreover said: "Hashem did not make this covenant with our fathers, but with us, even us." How do we know that the standing at Mount Sinai alone is the evidence that makes*

---

4 *Ramban*, ibid.

> *his prophecy true without a shadow of suspicion? Because it is said: "I will come to you in a thick cloud, in order that the people may hear when I speak with you and so trust you ever after." Evidently, hitherto they did not believe in him with an everlasting belief, but with a belief wherein there is after-thought and reflection.*[5]

The Ramban and Rambam—about both of whom was said, "From Moshe to Moshe, there was none like Moshe"—each wrote that the events at Sinai were designed to establish the primacy of Moshe Rabbeinu and his prophecy.

The Seforno, writing several centuries later, adopted the Ibn Ezra's approach, but also addressed the Ramban's objections:

> *"So that the nation shall believe in you"—they will believe in the possibility of face-to-face prophecy, that indeed you have been granted this level of face-to-face prophecy by Me, not merely a dream...This means that the prophet remains in full control of all his faculties including all parts of his body while hearing Hashem, something everyone previously imagined impossible. Now they will believe that you can prophesize this way, as the pasuk attests: "And Hashem spoke directly to Moshe," and as they themselves later said, "This day we have seen that Hashem can speak directly to Man, and Man can survive such an encounter." It is not that the people needed convincing that prophecy was possible. They knew that all the patriarchs, Moshe, Aharon, and Miriam were all prophets. However, up until this time all prophetic messages had been communicated either in a dream or in a vision, as Hashem Himself declared when saying, "I will appear to him in a vision." But that Moshe could truly communicate with Hashem while in command of his faculties was unclear to them until now—when they themselves experienced this*

---

5 *Mishneh Torah*, Laws of Foundations of the Torah 8:1.

> *kind of prophecy. Henceforth, they would believe in Moshe's prophecy and no future prophet could contradict them, for their prophecy would never be on this level.*

The Seforno acknowledges that the Jewish People surely accepted the reality of prophecy, but they were unfamiliar with the *quality* of Moshe's prophecy. The events at Sinai were thus needed to establish the possibility that Man might communicate with Hashem while fully alert and awake, a kind of experience previously unheard of and never to be repeated.

To summarize, we learned two diverging understandings of the revelation at Sinai:

- The Ibn Ezra and Seforno: to eliminate doubt regarding prophecy, either in its entirety or in its unique application to Moshe.
- The Rambam and Ramban: to establish the absolute authority of Moshe Rabbeinu and the authenticity of his prophecy for all times.

All that said, I humbly submit that the true function of the events at Sinai was to provide the entire people with an opportunity to experience, directly, the Divine Revelation in all its glory, and for each individual to ascend to the level of Hashem's ministering angels. Never would such an experience be forgotten. The awesome sights and sounds of Sinai would remain with them throughout their lives, and beyond—they would share these experiences with their children, who would in turn transmit them to all future generations.

What, then, were the commentators discussing? The Ibn Ezra, Seforno, Ramban, and Rambam were addressing a narrower question: Why was Moshe alone called to approach the mist and hear directly from Hashem, and not the entire nation? The two approaches identified above were focused on this issue alone.

Yom Tov

SEVENTY-ONE

Shabbos and Moed

On six days work may be done, but on the seventh day there shall be a pause of complete rest, a sacred occasion. You shall do no work; it shall be Shabbos for Hashem throughout your settlements.[1]

What relation is there between the Shabbos and the festive seasons? To teach you that he who desecrates the festivals is regarded as though he had desecrated the Shabbos, and that he who keeps the festivals is regarded as though he had kept the Shabbos.[2]

Shabbos and Yom Tov—our holidays, coexist, side by side, as very similar categories of special days. They are all holy days, dedicated for celebration, joy, and closeness to Hashem, and on all of them we are forbidden to work.

1 *Vayikra* 23:3.

2 *Rashi*, based on *Sifra*, *Emor* 9.

Nevertheless, for all their external similarity, Shabbos and Yom Tov are fundamentally different in essence. Shabbos was established by Hashem himself, from the very first Shabbos of Creation: "And on the seventh day, He stopped and rested."[3] Ever since, Shabbos has remained a fixed and permanent feature of reality; every seventh day is *inherently* Shabbos, simply because Hashem declared it so. Yom Tov, on the other hand, is established by us, here in the material world. When the *Beis Din* convenes and consecrates the new month, they imbue the resulting calendar days with the holiness of each holiday.

The formula we use for Kiddush and prayer reflects this distinction. On Shabbos, we conclude the Friday night Kiddush and the middle blessing of each *Amidah* prayer with "*Baruch...mekadesh haShabbos*—Blessed...He Who sanctifies the Shabbos," whereas on holidays, we say at the very same points, "*mekadesh Yisrael v'ha'zemanim*—He Who sanctifies Israel and the special times." As Chazal explain, since the holiness of the holiday is predicated on the calendar determinations of B'nei Yisrael, our own sanctification by Hashem is invoked in the blessing. Shabbos, permanently embedded directly by Hashem in Creation, is sanctified directly by Hashem without any intermediary.[4]

Thus, given their inherently distinct natures, one might mistakenly imagine that holidays can be treated more leniently. Practical halachah might give even further credence to such a position. A Shabbos violation carries the death penalty, while the same infraction on a holiday is only punishable by lashes, signaling perhaps that the latter is less important. Countering any such error, Rashi teaches, is the above *pasuk*, carefully worded to draw Shabbos and Yom Tov back together. They may be categorically separate, but their observances are equally mandated, and their soul is one: "He who desecrates the festivals is regarded as though he had desecrated the Shabbos, and he who keeps the festivals is regarded as though he had kept the Shabbos." Shabbos and Yom Tov each commemorate *yetzias Mitzrayim*, and both speak to the very foundations of our belief in Hashem and His Torah.

---

3 *Shemos* 31:17.

4 *Pesachim* 117b.

The *Sefas Emes* suggests a profound continuity between Shabbos and Yom Tov:

> *B'nei Yisrael merited the holidays owing to the power of Shabbos. Shabbos was given to them first, and it became a testament to B'nei Yisrael's acknowledgment of the Holy One. In exchange for observing Shabbos properly, they were also given the holidays, which represent Hashem's acknowledgment of B'nei Yisrael.*[5]

Shabbos is established and dictated entirely from on high, what the Kabbalists referred to as "*Isarusa d'l'eila*—an awakening from above." Yom Tov is created on earth, by us, through "*Isarusa d'letata*—awakening from below." When B'nei Yisrael embraced Shabbos and observed it as Hashem wished, they were empowered to confer similar sanctity upon other days.

As we mention in every Kiddush, each Yom Tov commemorates, in some way, our deliverance from Egypt and our birth as a nation. Shabbos, likewise, serves as a remembrance of *yetzias Mitzrayim*. But Shabbos, unlike the holidays, is also *zecher l'maaseh bereishis*—it recollects and reinforces our awareness of Creation.

When the Ten Commandments were first dictated, Shabbos, the fourth commandment, was defined solely as a reminder of Creation:

> *For in six days, Hashem formed the heavens, the earth, the sea, and all that is in them, and then He rested on the seventh day; therefore Hashem blessed the day of Shabbos and sanctified it.*[6]

In the repetition of the Commandments, Shabbos is presented differently:

> *And you shall remember that you were a slave in Egypt and Hashem took you from there with a strong hand and an*

---

5 *Sefas Emes, Emor* (5641).

6 *Shemos* 20:11.

> *outstretched arm; therefore Hashem your God commanded you to keep the day of Shabbos.*

First and foremost, Shabbos is a testimony to Hashem as Creator. It is encoded into existence along with all of Creation. Later, after B'nei Yisrael proved themselves worthy, its holiness became intertwined with the sanctity of the holidays created by us, here on earth, both now bearing witness to *yetzias Mitzrayim* and the holiness of Hashem's chosen people.

SEVENTY-TWO

Joy of Yom Tov and Joy of Mitzvah

Among the roots of this commandment—since Man is designed in a way that his nature requires rejoicing occasionally, just like it requires nourishment, and rest and sleep. And Hashem wanted to give us—"His people and the flock of His grazing"—merit. He commanded that all our rejoicing be for His sake, so that all our actions might bring us closer to Him. He fixed for us times during the year for holidays, to remember upon them the miracles and the good that He granted us. And He commanded us then at those times to indulge the physical with some of the joy that it needs. It is of great service to us that the satiation of joyous occasions can be for His sake and to remember Him; as this thought will be a fence, that we do not go further out than is enough from the straight path. And the one who has reflection without a desire to argue will find reason in my words.[1]

1 *Sefer Hachinuch* 488.

As the author of the above passage from *Sefer Hachinuch* hints, one might take exception to this reasoning for the Torah's holidays. Is it indeed appropriate to reduce our holy days to a mere need to satisfy Man's instinctive desire for the occasional celebration? Is rejoicing on Yom Tov no different than sating one's hunger and thirst with food and drink? Surely, to adopt this position is to greatly minimize the holiness and transcendent nature of our special days!

However, I submit that quite the contrary—the opposite is true. The concept proposed above enhances the importance of our holidays, placing them within the context of Hashem's wholesome and brilliant Creation. Hashem, Who gave us the Torah, is the same Hashem Who created Man, with all his weaknesses and needs. Torah is the counterpart to Man. It was created alongside him and it is the spiritual answer to Man's physical quest. Thus, Hashem created a man who needs moments of joy, and he created in His Torah opportunities for Man to satisfy those needs—in celebration of holidays and in the joy of fulfilling mitzvos. Need and fulfillment are not paired incidentally; Hashem created them simultaneously.

He, the Master Creator, embedded in Man, among the panoply of needs, desires, and impulses that animate us to do His will, also a longing for joy. This need propels us toward those opportunities He created for us in the Torah, and only through those outlets can our innermost drive for joy be truly satiated.

This, in turn, should give us pause and inspire an even deeper appreciation for the holidays and their mitzvos. For it is only through them that Man fulfills his need for celebration, and it is only because of them that Hashem imbued us with that need.

In the *Kuzari*'s eloquent presentation:

> *Our law, as a whole, is divided between fear, love, and joy, by each of which one can approach Hashem. Your contrition on a fast day is not nearer to Hashem than your joy on Shabbos and holy days, if it is the outcome of a devout heart. Just as prayers demand devotion, so too is a pious mind necessary to find pleasure in Hashem's command and law; that you should*

> *be pleased with the mitzvah itself out of love for the Lawgiver. You should recognize how much He has done for you, as if you had been His guest invited to His festive table. You thank Him in mind and word, and if your joy leads you so far as to sing and dance, it becomes worship and a bond of union between you and the Divine.*[2]

Three critical pillars support one's relationship with Hashem—fear, love, and joy. Joy is no less important than love or fear; perhaps it is even greater. Rabbeinu Bachya even suggests that the joy of a mitzvah may be more elevated than the mitzvah itself!

> *Joy is a mitzvah from the Torah. Man is commanded in this regard, for joy is a fully devotional act toward Hashem, more important even than a mitzvah.*[3]

---

2 *Sefer Kuzari* 2:50.

3 *Kad Hakemach*, "*Simchah*."

MOSAICA PRESS
BOOK PUBLISHERS
Elegant, Meaningful & Bold

info@MosaicaPress.com
www.MosaicaPress.com

The Mosaica Press team of acclaimed editors and designers is attracting some of the most compelling thinkers and teachers in the Jewish community today. Our books are available around the world.

HARAV YAACOV HABER
RABBI DORON KORNBLUTH